THE PROBLEMS WITH THE OTHER SACRAMENTS
APART FROM THE NEW MASS

OTHER WORKS
BY RAMA P. COOMARASWAMY

*The Problems with the New Mass:
A Brief Overview of the Major Theological Difficulties
Inherent in the* Novus Ordo Missae

*The Invocation of the Name of Jesus,
as Practiced by the Western Church*

*The Destruction of the Christian Tradition,
Updated and Revised*

Rama P. Coomaraswamy

THE PROBLEMS
WITH THE
OTHER SACRAMENTS
APART FROM THE NEW MASS

With 'The New Rite of Baptism'
by Rev. Father Dominic Savio Radecki, C.M.R.I

REVIVISCIMUS

SAN RAFAEL, CA

First published in the USA
by Reviviscimus Press,
an imprint of Sophia Perennis
© Peter Coomaraswamy 2010
Chapter 6, 'The New Rite of Baptism'
© Rev. Fr. Dominic S. Radecki, C.M.R.I., 2010

All rights reserved

Series editor: James R. Wetmore

No part of this book may be reproduced or transmitted,
in any form or by any means, without permission

For information, address:
Reviviscimus, P.O. Box 151011
San Rafael, CA 94915
reviviscimus.com

Library of Congress Cataloging-in-Publication Data

Coomaraswamy, Rama P.
The problems with the other sacraments, apart from
the new mass / by Rama P. Coomaraswamy.
p. cm.
ISBN 978-1-59731-461-9 (pbk.: alk. paper)
1. Sacraments—Catholic Church.
2. Catholic Church—Controversial literature.
3. Catholic Church. Ordo Missae. 4. Mass. I. Title.
BX2200.C625 2010
234'.16—dc22   2010043357

CONTENTS

Editor's Introduction 1

Preface 3

Introduction 5

The Magisterium of the Church and Related Issues 9

1. General Introduction 53
2. The Sacrament of Order 74
3. The Demise of Extreme Unction 124
4. Confirmation 137
5. What Happened to Confession? 145
6. Baptism (with 'The New Rite of Baptism' by Fr. Dominic Radecki) 161
7. Marriage 190

ADDITIONAL ESSAYS

I. Is Baptism of Desire & Blood a Catholic Teaching? 201
II. An Essay on Catholic Marriage 228
III. The Gates of Hell Shall Not Prevail 276

ACKNOWLEDGMENTS

The editors would like to acknowledge

Fr. Anthony Cekada
for his generous help as 'doctrinal consultant',

Fr. Julian Larrabee
for his correction and translation of the Latin passages,

And Eric Galati
for his invaluable diplomatic efforts.

EDITOR'S INTRODUCTION

Ever since Dr. Rama P. Coomaraswamy's *The Problems with the New Mass* was published by TAN books in 1990, readers have been awaiting the promised sequel, *The Problems with the Other Sacraments*. Although it was posted in several different versions over the intervening years on Dr. Coomaraswamy's website, and two chapters from it appeared in the author's deep and comprehensive *The Destruction of the Christian Tradition* (World Wisdom Books, 2006), the complete work is now available for the first time in book form through Sophia Perennis.

As the Novus Ordo Catholic Church continues its spiritual and now increasingly material fall, *The Problems with the Other Sacraments* remains a timely work—perhaps even more timely than when it was first written, now that the "cosmetic" traditionalism of Benedict XVI has begun to mute some of the more blatant liturgical abuses that followed in the wake of the Second Vatican Council, while doing nothing to restore the validity of the Catholic sacraments that were so deeply compromised, if not destroyed, by that "Robber Council" and its aftermath: the only thing worse than an obvious anti-Catholic revolution is a false and deceptive restoration.

And time continues to pass. In the 45 years since Vatican II, the generations who remember what Catholicism was (for all its faults) before the greater Church was dismembered have been reduced to a skeleton crew; even some sincerely traditional Catholics, who are courageously attempting to survive as a part of a Catholic remnant, are not familiar with certain points of doctrine that any Catholic school child knew in the 1950's.

And this is precisely why books like *The Problems with the Other Sacraments* are so important. Now that the worldwide pedophilia scandal has touched the Vatican itself, resulting in what some have described as the worst crisis in the Catholic Church since the Reformation—and also in view of the fact that Benedict has come out directly for One World Government in his 2009 encyclical *Caritas in Veritate*—Catholics, young and old, desperately need to get a sense of what has been lost. They should also be alerted to the fact that true Catholic alternatives exist to the crumbling shell that was once Roman Catholicism, so that, by the light of the Holy Spirit, they can see to choose their path in these darkest and most uncertain of times.

PREFACE

The essays in this book were written over many years. Some have been published in several languages, others have had great difficulty in being published at all, and have reached friends and colleagues only in xerox form. At the request of several readers I have brought them together under the title of *The Problem with the Other Sacraments*. The title has been chosen because in many ways they are a sequel to my book on *The Problems with the New Mass* published in 1990 by TAN.

The first essay ["The Magisterium of the Church and Related Issues"] is the last written. It deals with the criteria available to Catholics in these confused times for deciding what to believe and how to act. It is perhaps the most important essay because everything that follows flows from the criteria it establishes (or more precisely, resumes).

What follows is a series of chapters dealing with the changes in the Sacraments other than the Mass. After a *General Introduction* which deals with the principles of Sacramental Theology, the Post-Conciliar changes in the sacraments are discussed. How does the Church judge the validity of a Sacrament and what is the extent to which we must as Catholics demand that these criteria be fulfilled by the clergy? Have the changes in the Sacrament of Holy Orders, especially those involving the Consecration of Bishops, rendered them null and void? And if this is so, are priests ordained by such falsely consecrated "bishops" indeed priests? The chapter (originally an essay) dealing with this critical matter has been in print for well over ten years, and has been translated into French, Spanish and German. To date its contention that the rite for consecrating bishops, while highly acceptable to Protestants, is barely Catholic and is almost certainly invalid, has never been refuted.

I am grateful to Father Dominic Radecki, C.M.R.I. for his contribution on the changes in the rite of Baptism. The issue of Baptism is complex. One does not have to be a Catholic to baptize a Catholic, though of course one must use the correct form and intend to do what the Church (or Christ) intends. Many Protestant baptisms are valid, and in so far as most Protestant sects continue to baptize, the need to totally destroy this rite was not present. However, innumerable and highly significant changes were made and a multiplicity of different Baptism rites for different occasions created, each with a host of "options." Underlying these changes are significant alterations in the understanding of the purpose of the rite. This in turn may well effect the intention of the officiating minister and hence vitiate validity even though proper form and matter are used.

Each of these chapters have been read by many traditional priests both in this country and abroad. Their suggestions, comments and corrections have been incorporated. The list would be too long for me to name them all. Many of the articles are used in traditional seminaries in this country, Europe and South America. Some will find their contents offensive, but it is my sincere hope that in all that I have said, I have but faithfully reproduced the teaching of the Church of All Times. If it can be shown that I have been in error on some points, I shall be most grateful for correction.

INTRODUCTION

This book is primarily written for Catholics who are unhappy with the changes introduced by Vatican II and the Post-Conciliar Church. Hopefully, it will enable them to sort out the issues and to act appropriately as Catholics.

Some of these chapters have been published separately; they are nevertheless included within the body of this text in order that this book can be presented as an integrated entity.

It is always necessary to establish common ground with the reader. With this in view I would propose that all Catholics by definition believe in God; believe that Jesus Christ is God (and man); that Jesus Christ established a visible Church; and that this Church is what is commonly called the Roman Catholic Church.

There can be little discussion about the first two principles for no Catholic as a Catholic can deny the existence of God or the divinity of Jesus Christ. What creates confusion in these days is the nature of the visible Church that Christ established. Its character was quite obvious for some 1900 years—up to the time of Vatican II. It taught the same doctrines and used essentially the same "Apostolic" rites and sacraments since its foundation. These have generally been referred to as the "deposit of the faith" which it is the Church's duty to guard and reserve unadulterated till the end of time. This principle is incorporated in the creed where we say "One, Holy, Apostolic and Catholic" Church. However, subsequent to this Council changes were introduced in doctrine and rites which have raised a serious question: "is it the same Church?"

As there is only one God, only one Jesus Christ, and hence only one Revelation, it is clear that there can only be one Church. Now the Post-Conciliar Church claims to be that Church despite the fact that this new organization has changed the rites and doctrines which were inherited from the Apostles and which were held and/or taught up to the time of Vatican II. It is precisely this which has confused the average thinking Catholic.

Only two possibilities exist. Either the post-Vatican II (also called the "New" and "Conciliar" Church) has changed from the Church as it existed prior to the time of this most dubious "council," or the two churches are one and the same and the changes that have occurred are not of a substantial nature. If one holds that the "New Church" is significantly different from the traditional (tradition meaning "handed down") Catholic Church, one is obliged as a Catholic to adhere to that Church which Christ founded. If on the other hand one believes that the changes instituted in the wake of Vatican II are insignificant and not substantial, one is obliged as a Catholic to accept and respect them.

There is much talk today about "the Faith." Faith of course has two aspects. First of all, it is objective and as such pertains to the doctrines taught by the Church as part of Revelation. As such Faith is a "gift." But faith also has a subjective aspect which relates to our acceptance of what the Church teaches. The Faith (and not some vague feeling which passes for faith) is important for as St. Paul said, "it is impossible to please God without faith." The objective aspect of faith or the teaching of the Church is incorporated in what is called her Magisterium which is defined in the first section of this book. No Catholic can knowingly deny or reject what the Magisterium or teaching authority of the Church holds to be true without placing themselves outside the Church. We (subjectively) must give our assent to this teaching authority. To refuse to do so is to deny Christ who defines Himself as the Truth.

Many Catholics are confused by what has happened to the Church. Much of the confusion lies in the Catholic desire to be "in obedience" to the pope who is or should be Christ's vicar or representative on earth. What is forgotten is that obedience is a "moral" virtue, and as such ranks lower than the theological virtues of Faith, Hope and Charity. In other words, obedience is fine, but one must be aware of just what one is in obedience to. If one is in obedience to a false faith, one in essence apostatizes from the Catholic Faith. If one obeys a pope who himself is not in obedience to Christ, one places oneself in disobedience to our Divine Master.

Anyone who attends the Tridentine Mass or rejects the teachings of Vatican II, places him or herself in disobedience to the Post-Conciliar popes. This brings us to yet another tactic of those who would sit on the fence. They claim that the doctrinal changes introduced and promulgated by Vatican II are "pastoral" and not "doctrinal," or again, that only the "extraordinary teachings of the Magisterium" (which are given once or twice in a century) demand our intellectual assent. Now both the Ordinary and the Extra-Ordinary Magisterium are part and parcel of the "teaching authority of the Church." Both demand our intellectual assent as Catholics. What are we to say when we find that the Post-Conciliar "popes" have "magisterially" declared the documents of Vatican II to be the "highest form of the ordinary Magisterium" to which every Catholic "must give their intellectual assent"? It follows that anyone who considers himself to be in obedience to the Post-Conciliar hierarchy must accept ALL the teachings incorporated in the documents of Vatican II as well as all the Sacramental changes subsequently introduced. They must further abstain from attending the Tridentine Mass or the "Mass of All Times" as it has been so correctly labeled.

Many Catholics have rejected the changes introduced. They hold that to refuse to obey a pope who is himself no longer in obedience to Christ in no way denies the authority of the papacy. It is because of their respect for this institution and their knowing that no Catholic can be saved if he or she is in disobedience to the true Vicar of Christ, that they refuse to obey an individual whom they see as lacking all true papal authority. According to Plato a king must rule by divine law (i.e., by enforcing God's laws). Should he command or rule in his own name or by his own authority (as against God's), then he becomes a tyrant. The same is true of the individual who sits in Peter's chair.

"One, Holy, Catholic and Apostolic." These are the criteria. Is the Post-Conciliar Church one with the Church that Christ established and which has been maintained through 19 centuries? This is for the reader to decide. Is it Catholic, which is to say "universal" in time and place or is it a local phenomenon established after the close of Vatican II? Is it Apostolic in the sense that it uses the same rites and teaches the same doctrines that the Apostles did? Again, this is a decision that every Catholic must make. Finally, is it Holy? This is hard for individuals to judge. However its fruits are certainly of a dubious nature. Millions of Catholics have abandoned the faith; thousands of priests and religious have abandoned their vocations. Confessions and baptisms are down. Conversions of former Catholics to other religions abound far in excess of those entering the Church. Certainly, it has canonized an enormous number of saints under new and relaxed regulations. But at the same time it has refused to canonize such individuals as Pius IX and Merry de Val, individuals whose canonization process had been completed under the old rules. Little is it realized that the criteria for sanctity have been changed. The time-honored procedures which involved an examination of the life and writings of the candidate for canonization have been eroded by questions of political expediency; exemptions from the requirement for miracles have been granted and the "devil's advocate" is gone. But all in all, it is not for us to judge of holiness.

And so it is that Catholics must make a choice. It is hoped that these essays along with my book on *The Problems with the New Mass* will assist them in doing so.

RAMA P. COOMARASWAMY, M.D.

THE MAGISTERIUM OF THE CHURCH AND RELATED ISSUES

Before embarking on a study of the Magisterium we should pause for a moment lest the present confusion within the Catholic Church tempt us to an attitude of despair. The present confusions have their purpose, even though we with our limited outlook cannot always understand. As St. Paul explains: "To them that love God all things work together unto good" (Rom. 8:28), and St. Augustine adds: "*etiam peccata*, even sins." In the same sense, in the *Exultet*, on Holy Saturday, the Church sings: *Felix culpa, quae talem ac tantum meruit habere Redemptorem*: "O happy fault (of our fist parents), that merited so great a Redeemer." As Augustine says: "God in His wisdom has deemed it better that good should come out of evil than that evil should never have been. God has the power and wisdom to turn to His own glory the evil which He permits on earth. Angels and saints can take only joy from the divine wisdom which rules the world so wonderfully."[1]

Holy Mother Church, like the loving mother she is, has provided us with the necessary guidelines on how to think and behave in the present circumstances. These are provided for us in what is called her teaching Magisterium. The present essay is dedicated to an understanding of the nature and purpose of the Authentic Magisterium of the Catholic Church.[2]

---

1. Lines taken from Georges Panneton's *Heaven or Hell,* Newman Press, Westminster Maryland, 1965: "Consider the Jews in Egypt. They had saved the land from famine, but had subsequently been enslaved. How cruel and unjust the God of Abraham must have appeared to them. But would they have followed Moses into the wilderness in any other circumstance? One may be permitted to doubt it."

2. In discussing the layman Eusebius' attack on the heretic Nestorius, Patriarch of Constantinople, Dom Gueranger wrote: "When the shepherd turns into a wolf the first duty of the flock is to defend itself. As a general rule, doctrine comes from the bishops to the faithful, and it is not for the faithful, who are subjects in the

⊕

The Church, which is the Body of Christ, is as it were the presence of Christ in the World.[3] Now Christ combined in Himself and bestowed on His Apostles whom He sent forth the three qualities of Teacher (Prophet), Ruler and Priest—symbolized in his Vicar by the triple crown or papal tiara.

With regard to this Christ told us that He who believed in Him would know the truth which gives true liberty (John 8:31–32) but he who did not would be condemned (Matt. 10:33; Mark 16:16). He allowed Himself to be called the Master and even stressed that He was the true Master who not only taught the truth, but was the Truth (Matt. 8:19; John 3:17 and Matt. 23:8–10). Now he communicated these truths to his Apostles and sent them forth to teach in His name, telling them that "just as my Father sent me, so also I send you," telling them "He who hears you hears me, and he who rejects your words, rejects me, and he who rejects me rejects the Father who sent me" (Matt. 10:40 and Luke 10:16). And so we see that the Apostles were given the charge of continuing Christ's mission as infallible Master. Moreover Christ demanded an absolute obedience to this teaching function—for he who does not believe will be condemned. Of course, He also specified that it must be His teaching and not some other person's teaching—not even the teaching of an angel from heaven if it departed from His teaching. He further promised that "the Spirit of Truth" would always be with them, provided they accepted this Spirit; and again, He left them free to reject this Spirit or accept some other spirit if they so willed—but then of course they would no longer be participating in His charisms and would lose their infallibility. As He said, "therefore go ye into all

---

order of Faith, to pass judgment on their superiors. But every Christian by virtue of this title to the name Christian, has not only the necessary knowledge of the essentials of the treasure of Revelation, but also the duty of safeguarding them. The principle is the same, whether it is a matter of belief or conduct, that is of dogma or morals."

3. "God showed me the very great delight that He has in all men and women who accept, firmly and humbly and reverently, the preaching and teaching of Holy Church, for He is Holy Church. For He is the foundation, He is the substance, He is the teaching, He is the teacher, He is the end, He is the reward." Julian of Norwich, *Showings*, Chapter 16.

nations and teach them to safeguard all that I have taught you. And I will be with you till the end of the world." (Matt. 12:18–20).

Perhaps the most important error abroad today relates to the teaching authority of the Church; specifically to the idea that the Ordinary Magisterium of the Church is not infallible. Lest there be doubt about this, let us listen to Pope Leo XIII:

> Wherefore, as appears from what has been said, Christ instituted in the Church a living authoritative and permanent Magisterium, which by His own power He strengthened, by the Spirit of Truth He taught, and by miracles confirmed. He willed and ordered, under the gravest penalties, that its teachings should be received as if they were His own. As often therefore, as it is declared on the authority of this teaching that this or that is contained in the deposit of divine revelation, it must be believed by everyone as true. If it could in any way be false, an evident contradiction follows: for then God Himself would be the author of error in man. The Fathers of the [First] Vatican Council laid down nothing new, but followed divine revelation and the acknowledged and invariable teaching of the Church as to the very nature of faith, when they decreed as follows: "All those things are to be believed by divine and Catholic faith which are contained in the written or unwritten word of God, and which are proposed by the Church as divinely revealed, either by a solemn definition or in the exercise of the ordinary and universal Magisterium."
>
> *Satis Cognitum*

Because the Magisterium provides us with the only solid objective criteria by which we may judge what is true and false, it is important that we examine its nature in greater detail.

The Catholic Dictionary defines the Magisterium as:

> The Church's divinely appointed authority to teach the truths of religion. "Going therefore teach ye all nations . . . teaching them to observe all things whatsoever I have commanded you" (Matt. 28:19–20). This teaching, being Christ's, is infallible. . . .[4]

---

4. Donald Attwater, *Catholic Dictionary* (NY: Macmillan, 1952).

TWO DIFFERENT MODES EXIST FOR THE EXERCISE OF THIS LIVING AND INFALLIBLE MAGISTERIUM

This Magisterium or "teaching authority" of the Church exists in two different modes. It is termed SOLEMN or EXTRAORDINARY when it derives from the formal and authentic definitions of a general council, or of the Pope himself: that is to say, dogmatic definitions of the ecumenical councils, or of the Pope's teaching *ex cathedra* (see below for an explanation of this term). Such truths are *de fide divina et Catholica*, which means that every Catholic must believe them with divine and Catholic Faith.[5]

Included under the category of *solemn* are symbols or professions of the faith, such as the Apostles' Creed, the Tridentine or Pianine Profession and the Oath against Modernism required by Pius X since 1910 (and no longer required by the Post-Conciliar Church).[6] Finally included in this category are "theological censures or those statements that qualify and condemn propositions as heretical".[7]

The Magisterium is termed ORDINARY AND UNIVERSAL when it manifests itself as those truths which are expressed through the daily continuous preaching of the Church, referring to the universal practices of the Church connected with faith and morals as manifested in the "unanimous consent of the Fathers, the decisions of the Roman Congregations concerning faith and morals, in the

---

5. "Must," that is, if he wishes to call himself Catholic.
6. The Church could never require its members to take an Oath which violates the infallible truth. These specifics are drawn from Tanquerey's *Manual of Dogmatic Theology*, Desclee: NY, 1959.
7. According to Tanquerey, "The Church is infallible when it condemns a certain proposition with some doctrinal censure. A doctrinal censure is "a qualification or restriction which indicates that a proposition is opposed, in some way, to faith or morals." It is *de fide* that the Church is infallible when she specifies that a doctrine is heretical; it is certain that the Church is infallible when she states that a doctrine approaches heresy or that a doctrine errs in a matter of faith, or that it is false. All this is apparent from the consensus of theologians, and from the practice of the Church from the earliest days. The Church has always made judgments against false propositions and also imposed upon the faithful the obligation of adhering to these judgments. Many assert that in all doctrinal censures the Church is infallible." Tanquerey, op. cit.

consensus of the faithful, in the universal custom or practice associated with dogma (which certainly includes the Roman liturgy or traditional Mass), and in the various historical documents in which the faith is declared. Included in this category are Papal Encyclicals."[8] It is termed PONTIFICAL if the source is the Pope, and UNIVERSAL if it derives from the Bishops in union with him.[9] Such truths, as Vatican I teaches, are also *de fide, divina et Catholica*.[10]

---

8. Etienne Gilson, Introduction to *The Church Speaks to the Modern World* (NY: Doubleday [1954; 1961]). "These letters are the highest expression of the ordinary teaching of the Church. To the extent that they restate the infallible teachings of the Church, the pronouncements of the Encyclical letters are themselves infallible. Moreover, while explaining and developing such infallible teachings, or while using them as a sure criterion in the condemnation of errors, or even while striving to solve the social, economic and political problems of the day in the light of these infallible teachings, the popes enjoy the special assistance of the Holy Spirit." Another way to look at Encyclicals is to ask if in issuing them the Pope uses his Apostolic authority; if he is dealing with matters of faith and morals, and if he intends to define and to bind the consciences of all Catholics. "If he does, he is speaking from the Chair of Peter and exercising his *ex cathedra* authority. And [given] that the possibility of error occurs or can occur in such documents where it is a matter of some novel teaching, the magisterium can eventually correct such an error without compromising itself.... It will therefore be the eventual task of the magisterium to evaluate the objections made to the Declaration and then to explain how it is compatible with previous teaching, or to admit that it is not compatible and proceed to correct it" (*Archbishop Lefebvre and Religious Liberty*, TAN: Ill., 1980 and *The Remnant*, June 15, 1982). Suffice it to say—the matter will be discussed in detail later—that not only this Declaration, but also Michael Davies' opinion, are contrary to innumerable Magisterial statements of the traditional Church.

9. Also from Tanquerey, op. cit. Other classifications can be found, but the essential principles remain the same. Melchior Cano (or Canus), one of the principal theologians of the Council of Trent, taught that there are ten theological "loci" or places where the "teaching imparted by Christ and the Apostles could be found." They are the following: (1) The Scriptures; (2) The Divine and Apostolic Traditions; (3) The Universal Church; (4) The Councils, and above all the General (Ecumenical) Councils; (5) The Roman Church; (6) The holy fathers; (7) The scholastic theologians; (8) natural reason; (9) the philosophers and jurors [of Canon law]; and (10) human history. According to him the first seven belong to the realm of theology, while the last three relate to the other sciences. (Quoted in Rohrbacher, *Histoire Universelle de L'Eglise Catholique*, Letouzey et Ane, Editeurs, Paris, vol. x, p. 118).

10. The infallibility of Council teachings is dependent upon the Pope's approbation. The pseudo-Council of Pistoia never received this and was never recognized as a Council. Michael Davies claims that the Declaration on Religious Liberty made by

It is termed *living* because, being true, it exists and exerts its influence, not only in the past, but in the present and future. As Vatican I explains, it is infallible:

> All those things are to be believed with divine and Catholic faith, which are contained in the word of God, written or handed down, [i.e., Scripture or Tradition], and which the Church, either by a solemn judgment, or by her ordinary and universal Magisterium, proposes for belief as having been divinely revealed.
>
> Vatican I, Session III

This statement is important because there are many theologians who proclaim that the teachings of the Ordinary Magisterium are not binding. Some attempt to mitigate the authority of the ordinary Magisterium by claiming that it can at times contain error.[11] Others claim on their own authority that only those doctrines in the ordinary and universal Magisterium that have been taught everywhere and always are covered by the guarantee of infallibility. Still others attack this teaching by limiting the contents of the Ordinary Magisterium—removing from it anything not couched in absolutist or solemn terminology. Finally there are those who claim that the magisterium can change—that it can teach differently today than in the past because doctrine and truth evolve. Before dealing with these secondary errors, it is necessary to understand why the Magisterium is infallible.

THE INFALLIBILITY OF THE MAGISTERIUM

As noted in Chapter I, the Church, by God's will, is a hierarchical

---

Vatican II is "only a document of the ordinary magisterium" of the Church, and that, following Archbishop Lefebvre, that "the possibility of error occurs or can occur in such documents where it is a matter of some novel teaching. The magisterium can eventually correct such an error."

11. According to this view, the ordinary and universal Magisterium consists in some manner of the sum total of bishops in every place and throughout the course of history from the time the Church was founded down to the present day; while at the same time the community of bishops (with the Pope) at any given period during the course of history, is in no way infallible in its ordinary teaching. This is essentially the position of Archbishop Lefebvre.

institution. At its head is the Pope, the vicar of Christ, the rock on which the Church is founded. He is endowed with all the unique authority of Jesus Christ who is the Shepherd and Bishop of our souls (1 Peter 2:25), and depending upon Him, the Pope is also—but vicariously—the shepherd and bishop of the whole flock, both of the other bishops and of the ordinary faithful (John 21:15–17). He is the evident and effectual sign of the presence of Christ in the world, and it is through him that Christ who is invisible in the bosom of the Father, visibly presides over all the activities of this enormous Body and brings it under His control. As Dom Grea has said, the Pope is, with Jesus Christ—a single hierarchical person—above the episcopate, one and the same head of the episcopate, one and the same head, one and the same doctor, pontiff and legislator of the universal Church. Or more precisely, Jesus Christ Himself is the sole Head, rendered visible, speaking and acting in the Church through the instrument whom He provided for Himself. Christ proclaims Himself through His Vicar, He speaks through him, acts and governs through him. When Christ speaks, acts, and governs through the pope, the pope is endowed with infallibility, a quality which derives, not from him as a private person, but from his being a single hierarchical person with Christ.[12]

---

12. Dom Grea, *The Church and its Divine Constitution*, quoted from *Forts dans La Foi*, edited by Father Noel Barbara. The term "episcopate" refers to the body of bishops. Strictly speaking one cannot speak of a "bad pope." Being the instrument of Christ, a pope as such is necessarily "good." Such adjectives as applied to popes relate to the state of their soul and not to their function. A sinner just like anyone else, the pope, even when he functions as Christ's minister, can be as a human being in a state of grace or one of mortal sin. It is a teaching of elementary theology that the state of a minister's soul has no influence or effect on his ministry, because this effect comes totally and exclusively from Christ who is its source. Thus it is that whenever a pope is functioning in his office of pope, it is Christ who speaks, who acts, and who governs through him. There is never any justification for a member of the believing Church to disobey a valid pope when it is Christ who speaks, acts and governs through him. And just as one cannot speak of a "bad pope," so also one cannot speak of a "heretical Pope," of one who is only "materially" a pope, or of one who is only "juridically" a pope. Assuming a valid election, assuming that the individual is a member of the "believing Church," either a man is, or he is not, a pope. He can never be "half a pope.

16 THE PROBLEMS WITH THE OTHER SACRAMENTS

This conception is made clear by Pope St. Leo's third sermon on the anniversary of his own election where he paraphrases the words of Christ:

> I make known to thee thy excellence, for thou art Peter: that is, as I am the invulnerable rock, the cornerstone, who make both one, I the foundation beside which there can be laid no other; so thou too art a rock, in my strength made hard, and I share with thee the powers which are proper to me. And upon this rock I will build my Church and the gates of hell shall not prevail against it. . . .
> *Office of St. Peter's Chair at Antioch*

The pope is also a private person (an ordinary human being) and a private theologian (doctor). It is however, only when he functions as a single hierarchical person with Christ that he is endowed with infallibility (or partakes of the Church's, i.e. Christ's, infallibility). It is only then that Christ's scriptural statement "he who hears you, hears me" applies. And it follows logically that his authority is extended through those bishops who are in union with him in governing the flock. The bishops have no independent authority apart from him for the simple reason that he has no independent authority apart from Christ. Thus it is that he is called the Bishop of bishops, and that he confirms them in their doctrine—not the other way around. Thus it is that no statement of an Ecumenical Council has any authority until it receives his approbation.

The pope then has an almost limitless authority. He can however lose this authority in a variety of ways. He can lose it when he dies (physical death); if he loses his reason (madness); if he separates himself from the Church (schism); or when he loses his faith (heresy and therefore spiritual death). At such a point the pope is no longer pope because it is the very nature of this bishop's function and ministry to be the Vicar of Christ and nothing else.

The pope's authority is almost unlimited—however, it is not absolute. He has full powers within his charge, but his powers are limited by his charge. In order fully to understand this doctrinal point, let us once again recall the nature of this charge.

The ecclesiastical hierarchy was instituted by God to teach, that is to say, to transmit the deposit of the faith. At the head of this teaching Church Christ appointed a Vicar to whom He gave full powers to feed the faithful and the shepherds (John 21:1–17). Consequently, it is within the bounds of this function, the transmission of the deposit of the faith, that the Pope has full powers. He has these precisely to enable him to transmit the deposit of the faith—in its entirety—in the same meaning and the same sense (Fr. Heinrich Denzinger, *Enchiridion Symbolorum, Definitionum et Declarationum de Rebus Fidei et Morum*, §1800). For, as Vatican I clearly taught, the Holy Spirit has not been promised to Peter's successors in order that they might reveal, under His inspiration, new doctrine, but in order that, with His help, they may carefully guard and faithfully expound the revelation as it was handed down by the Apostles, that is to say, the deposit of the faith (*Pastor Aeternus*, Denzinger, *Enchiridion Symbolorum, Definitionum et Declarationum de Rebus Fidei et Morum*, §1836).

Hence it follows that the Pope can and must make all his determinations entirely within the bounds of orthodoxy, and this is true whether they concern the reformation of the Liturgy, of Canon Law, or to use the phraseology of earlier Councils, the reformation of the clergy in its head or in its members. The Pope may indeed abrogate all the decisions of his predecessors, even those deserving of special mention, but always and only within the limits of orthodoxy. As *The Catholic Encyclopedia* (1908) states: "The scope of this infallibility is to preserve the deposit of faith revealed to man by Christ and His Apostles." It goes without saying that under such circumstances, any changes introduced would affect only matters that are mutable and never the faith itself. A Pope who presumed to abrogate the smallest iota of dogma, or even attempted to change the meaning of the Church's constant teaching, would step outside the bounds of orthodoxy and outside the limits of his function of preserving the deposit of the faith. He would, in doing so, teach a new doctrine and a new gospel, and as such would be subject to the anathema pronounced by St. Paul in his Epistle to the Galatians (1:8–9).

It is then clear that the infallibility of the Magisterium or teaching authority of the Church derives from the Pope functioning as one hierarchical person with Christ. Thus the source of this infallibility is Christ, and indeed, it could be not be otherwise. For the Church to claim infallibility on any other grounds would be absurd. And just as there is only one source, so also there is only one Magisterium. When the Pope uses his infallibility—be it by solemn proclamation or within the bounds of the Ordinary Magisterium, he partakes, not of some personal infallibility, but of Christ's infallibility. As the official text puts it, "when he speaks *ex cathedra* . . . he has the same infallibility as that with which the divine Redeemer invested His Church when it is defining a doctrine concerning faith or morals; and that therefore, such definitions of the Roman Pontiff are of themselves, and not from the consent of the Church, irreformable" (Fr. Heinrich Denzinger, *Enchiridion Symbolorum, Definitionum et Declarationum de Rebus Fidei et Morum*, §1839).

THE MEANING OF *EX CATHEDRA* AND THE REASON FOR THE DEFINITION OF PAPAL INFALLIBILITY

When does a Pope use his infallibility, or to use the technical phrase, speak *ex cathedra*? In Holy Scripture *cathedra* is synonymous with the authority of a master or teacher (Psalms 1:1; Matt. 23:2; Luke 20:46). Once again the teaching of the Church is manifest and clear. He teaches *ex cathedra* when serving in the capacity of Pastor and Doctor (shepherd and teacher) of all the faithful, in virtue of his supreme Apostolic authority, when defining a doctrine with regard to faith and morals that must be held by the whole Church. Four conditions are required:

(1) The Pope must be functioning as Pastor and supreme Doctor. It is not his teaching as a private or particular Doctor that is in question.

(2) He must be dealing with matters of faith or morals, and it is only the proposed doctrine—not the adjoining considerations, the *obiter dicta*—that is guaranteed by infallibility.

(3) He must intend to define; his teaching must be given with authority and with the intent that it be believed by the entire Church.

(4) He must manifest his intention to bind all Catholics.

The Pope is not required to use any specific formulas to accomplish this. All that is required is that he clearly manifest his intention to compel the entire Church to accept his teaching as belonging to the deposit of the faith.

It is obvious that by the very nature of his function as the Vicar of Christ, this authority has always been with Peter and his valid successors. Why was it then necessary that this doctrine be defined in an extraordinary manner at the time of Vatican I? The answer to this question is highly instructive.

The Church does not ordinarily define a doctrine in an extraordinary manner unless it comes under dispute or is denied by a significant number of the faithful (as the Assumption of the Blessed Virgin). Nor does a doctrine so defined become more true than it was before.

> The Church has the duty to proceed opportunely in defining points of faith with solemn rites and decrees, when there is a need to declare them to resist more effectively the errors and the assaults of heretics or to impress upon the minds of the faithful clearer and more profound explanations of points of sacred doctrine... because the Church has defined and sanctioned truths by solemn decree of the Church at different times, and even in times near to us, are they [truths not so defined] therefore not equally certain and not equally to be believed. For has not God revealed them all?
>
> Pope Pius XI, *Mortalium Animos*

In the decades prior to Vatican I, the popes repeatedly condemned liberal Catholicism and parallel efforts aimed at bringing the Church's thinking into line with the modern world—Pope Pius IX summarized these censures in his *Syllabus of Errors*. Those who came under such strictures attempted to defend themselves by claiming that their attitudes had never been formerly condemned by the teaching Magisterium and that such documents only represented the private opinion of the Pontiffs. Such a claim placed the infallibility of the Pope in doubt. During Vatican I furious debates were waged on the subject. The liberals were perfectly aware of the fact that if they voted for the definition of infallibility they would condemn themselves, but that if they voted against it, they would be denying a doctrine of the Church. Every conceivable objection capable of preventing, or of at least postponing the definition, was put forth and strongly supported by those who labeled themselves as inopportunists.[13] One orthodox bishop, Anthony Claret—later canonized—was so distressed by these attempts that he died of a heart attack during the Conciliar debate. The cases of Popes Liberius, Honorius I, Paschal II, Sixtus V and others were brought forth in an attempt to influence the Fathers against defining something the liberals claimed was both unnecessary and insane. Needless to say, they were supported in this by the secular press, by world leaders, and even by governments. It is of interest to note that the Freemasons held a simultaneous anti-Council in Naples which proclaimed several principles as essential to the dignity of man—principles which later were incorporated into the documents of Vatican II.[14]

Unlike John XXIII, whose machinations in favor of the liberals at Vatican II will be detailed later, Pope Pius IX, aware of his responsibilities, did everything in his power to fulfill his obligations towards our divine Master. Listen to the comments of Cardinal Manning:

> The campaign against the Council failed, of course. It failed because the Pope did not weaken. He met error with condemnation and replied to the demands to modify or adapt Catholic truth to the spirit of the age by resisting it with the firmness and clarity of Trent—and despite the prophecies of her enemies that the declaration of Papal Infallibility would mark the death blow to the Church, she emerged stronger and more vigorous than ever. This of course evoked the full fury of the City of Man. The hatred of the world for the Church was made manifest, and at the same time manifested the divine nature of the Catholic Church; for the hatred of the world was designated by Christ Himself as one of the marks of His Mystical Body which must not only teach

---

13. It is never inopportune to declare the truth: Cardinal Newman was one of the leaders of this faction.
14. *Approaches* (Ayrshire, Scotland), no. 89, 1985.

Christ crucified, but will live out the mystery of His crucifixion and resurrection until He comes again in Glory.... Had Christ been prepared to enter into dialogue with his enemies, had he been prepared to adapt, to make concessions, then He would have escaped crucifixion—but of what value would the Incarnation have been? Pope Pius IX followed the example of Christ whose Vicar he was and, as the highest point attracted the storm, so the chief violence fell upon the head of the Vicar of Christ....[15]

One does not have to be an expert in theological matters to know that, if the Conciliar fathers had found themselves incapable of unequivocally refuting every one of the objections of the inopportunists, and of showing in a peremptory manner that throughout the preceding nineteen centuries not one Pope—even among those whose lives had been scandalous in the extreme—had ever erred in his function as Pope, in his teaching function as the universal Pastor and Doctor, the Church could never have solemnly promulgated this dogma. Indeed, if the issues and facts had not been made absolutely clear, the adversaries of infallibility and the enemies of the Church would certainly have published abroad all the supposedly false teachings of the previous popes and used this as a means of making the Church appear ridiculous. "No man," say the Fathers of the great Council of Nice, "ever accused the Holy See of a mistake, unless he was himself maintaining an error."[16]

When the final vote came, the adversaries of this dogma, foreseeing how things would go, left Rome in order to avoid personally participating in this decision. They, however, not wishing to be ejected from the Church, declared in advance that they accepted the decision—a decision that ultimately depended, not on the Council, but on the Pope promulgating the Council's teaching.[17]

---

15. Cardinal Henry Manning (an Anglican Convert), *Three Pastoral Letters to the Clergy of the Diocese*, several editions.

16. Rev. M. Muller, C.S.S., *Familiar Explanation of Catholic Doctrine* (New York: Benziger, 1888?).

17. The infallibility of Council teachings is dependent upon the Pope's approbation. The pseudo-Council of Pistoia never received this and was never recognized as a Council. The Post-Conciliar "popes" have declared Vatican II (all of it) to be the "highest form of the ordinary magisterium."

Unable to any longer deny this principle, the liberals in the Church rapidly shifted tactics. "The Pope is infallible," they said, "and such is certain for the church has proclaimed it as a dogma. But be careful! The Pope is not infallible every time he opens his mouth." And under the pretense of defending this dogma by sharply defining its limits, they cleverly stressed the concept that the Pope only uses this privilege on rare occasions—once or twice in a century. Today we hear the same cry from those who would defend the Post-Conciliar changes. "Nothing *de fide* has been changed," by which they mean no part of the extraordinary Magisterium. The children of this world are wiser in their generation than the children of light (Luke 16:8).[18]

Because the infallible nature of the Ordinary Magisterium is currently so much in dispute, the following pertinent quotations are appended:

> Even if he makes this submission efficaciously which is in accord with an act of divine faith . . . he should extend it to those truths which are transmitted as divinely revealed by the ordinary Magisterium of the entire Church dispersed throughout the world.
>
> Pius IX, *Tua Libenter*

Leo XIII reiterated the teaching of Vatican I to the effect that the sense of the sacred dogmas is to be faithfully kept which Holy Mother Church has once declared, and is not to be departed from under the specious pretext of a more profound understanding.

---

18. An important consequence of the declaration on infallibility at Vatican I was that the *Syllabus of Errors* of Pius IX was clearly declared to fall within the realm of the Ordinary Magisterium. Prior to this many attempts were made to examine the sources of the condemned errors in order to show that they were not worded in such a way as to make them binding. It also protected the list of errors—*Lamentabili*—associated with Pope St. Pius X's *Pascendi*. Here again the modernists tried the same tactics, forcing Pius X to declare them to be binding in his *Moto Proprio "Praestantia Scripturae"* (18, Nov. 1907). ("Anyone having the temerity to defend any proposition, opinion or reproved doctrine will *ipso facto* incur . . . excommunication *latae sententiae* simply reserved to the Roman Pontiff.") Again, the Oath against Modernism has been dropped. Despite this, anyone who cannot give his assent to this Oath, once required of every prelate at every step in his journey towards the priesthood or episcopacy, places himself outside the true Church.

He adds:

Nor is the suppression to be considered altogether free from blame, which designedly omits certain principles of Catholic doctrine and buries them, as it were in oblivion. For there is the one and the same Author and Master of all the truths that Christian teaching comprises: *the only-begotten Son who is in the bosom of the Father.* That they are adapted to all ages and nations is plainly deduced from the word which Christ addressed to His Apostles: *Go therefore teach ye all nations: teaching them to observe all things whatsoever I have commanded you: and behold I am with you all days even to the consummation of the world.* Wherefore the same Vatican Council says: "By the divine and Catholic faith those [doctrines] are to be believed which are contained in the word of God either written or handed down, and are proposed by the Church whether in solemn decision or by the ordinary universal magisterium, to be believed as having been divinely revealed." Far be it then for anyone to diminish or for any reason whatever to pass over anything of this divinely delivered doctrine; whosoever would do so, would rather wish to alienate Catholics from the Church than to bring over to the Church those who dissent from it. Let them return; indeed nothing is nearer to our heart; let all those who are wandering far from the sheepfold of Christ return; but let it not be by any other road than that which Christ has pointed out.... The history of all past ages is witness that the Apostolic See, to which not only the office of teaching but also the supreme government of the whole Church was committed, has constantly adhered *to the same doctrine in the same sense and in the same mind.*... In this all must acquiesce who wish to avoid the censure of our predecessor Pius VI, who proclaimed the 18th proposition of the Synod of Pistoia "to be injurious to the Church and to the Spirit of God which governs her, inasmuch as it subjects to scrutiny the discipline established and approved by the Church, as if the Church could establish a useless discipline or one which would be too onerous for Christian liberty to bear."

Leo XIII *Testem Benevolentiae*

24 THE PROBLEMS WITH THE OTHER SACRAMENTS

The Pope is infallible in all matters of Faith and Morals. By matters of faith and morals is meant the whole revelation of the truths of faith; or the whole way of salvation through faith; or the whole supernatural order, with all that is essential to the sanctification and salvation of man through Jesus Christ. The Pope is infallible, not only in the whole matter of revealed truths; he is also indirectly infallible in all truths which, though not revealed, are so intimately connected with revealed truths, that the deposit of faith and morals cannot be guarded, explained, and defended without an infallible discernment of such unrevealed truths. The Pope could not discharge his office as Teacher of all nations unless he were able with infallible certainty to proscribe and condemn doctrines, logical, scientific, physical, metaphysical, or political, of any kind which are at variance with the Word of God and imperil the integrity and purity of the faith, or the salvation of souls. **Whenever the Holy Father, as Chief Pastor and Teacher of all Christians, proceeds, in briefs, encyclical letters, consistorial allocutions, and other Apostolic letters, to declare certain truths, or anything that is conducive to the preservation of faith and morals, or to reprobate perverse doctrines, and condemn certain errors, such declarations of truth and condemnations of errors are infallible, or *ex Cathedra* acts of the Pope** [emphasis mine]. All acts *ex Cathedra* are binding in conscience and call for our firm interior assent, both of the intellect and the will, even though they do not express an anathema on those who disagree. To refuse such interior assent would be, for a Catholic, a mortal sin, since such a refusal would be a virtual denial of the dogma of infallibility, and we should be heretics were we conscious of such a denial (Alphonse Liguori, *Theol. Moral. lib.* I, 104). It would even be heresy to say that any such definition of truths or condemnations of perverse doctrines are inopportune.

Father Michael Muller, CSSR[19]

This Magisterium [the ordinary and universal] of the Church in regard to faith and morals, must be for every theologian the

---

19. Op. cit., note 16.

proximate and universal rule of truth, for the Lord has entrusted the Church with the entire deposit of the faith—Holy Scripture and Tradition—to be kept, to be upheld and to be explained. In the same manner, we must not think that what is proposed in the encyclicals does not require in itself our assent because the Popes did not exercise their supreme magisterial powers in them. Our Lord's words "he who listens to you listens to Me" also applies to whatever is taught by the ordinary Magisterium of the Church.

Pope Pius XII, *Humani Generis*

In a word, the whole Magisterium or doctrinal authority of the Pontiff as the supreme Doctor of all Christians, is included in this definition [at Vatican I] of his infallibility. And also all legislative or judicial acts, so far as they are inseparably connected with his doctrinal authority; as for instance, all judgments, sentences, and decisions, which contain the motives of such acts as derived from faith and morals. Under this will come the laws of discipline, canonization of the saints, approbation of Religious Orders, of devotions, and the like; all of which intrinsically contain the truths and principles of faith, morals and piety. The definition, then, does not limit the infallibility of the Pontiff to his supreme acts *ex cathedra* in faith and morals, but extends his infallibility to all acts in the fullest exercise of his supreme Magisterium or doctrinal authority.

Cardinal Manning, *The Vatican Council and its Definitions*[20]

At this point we can come to certain conclusions: (1) Christ instituted a hierarchical Church which was His own Mystical Body, and as such the prolongation of His presence in the world. (2) He revealed to this Church certain truths and entrusted these to it as a precious pearl—the deposit of the faith. (3) He established a Magisterium in order to keep intact the deposit of revealed truths for all time and to assure their availability to all mankind. (4) He instructed the Church to teach these truths. The Magisterium is a "divinely appointed authority to teach ... all nations ... all things

---

20. New York: D.J. Sadlier, 1887, pp. 95–96.

whatsoever I have commanded you." (5) This single Magisterium of the Church is entirely in the Pope, the vicar of Christ, and through him in all the bishops that are in union with him. (6) In so far as these truths are revealed to us by Christ, they are infallibly true. (7) The pope when he functions in his capacity as the Vicar of Christ, as one hierarchical person with our Lord, is to be obeyed as if he were Our Lord. (8) When the pope teaches in this capacity—*ex cathedra*—he teaches infallibly. (9) The Pope and the bishops in union with him are in no way empowered to teach anything other than what pertains to this original deposit "in the same sense and mind that they have always been understood." (10) Obviously doubts may arise as to the exact nature or meaning of some point of doctrine contained in this deposit. When such occurs, the hierarchy functions to explain and define, but not to innovate. "The Pope [and by extension, the hierarchy] is only the interpreter of this truth already revealed. He explains, he defines, but he makes no innovation."[21] (11) "The revelation made to the Apostles by Christ and by the Holy Spirit whom He sent to teach them all truth was final, definitive. To that body of revealed truth nothing has been, or ever will be added."[22] (12) There is no need for the Pope to use special formulas or attach anathemas to his *ex cathedra* teachings. (13) The Ordinary Magisterium is to be believed with the same divine and Catholic faith as is the Extraordinary Magisterium.

SUPPLEMENTARY COMMENTS ON THE MAGISTERIUM

The Magisterium is also called "living," not because it evolves in the manner that modern man erroneously ascribes to all things, but because it exists today as a viable entity within what the theologians call the "visible Church." It is living because it is vivified by the Holy Ghost. As Cardinal Manning explains:

---

21. *Exposition of Christian Doctrine*—a course of instruction written by a seminary professor of the Institute of the Brothers of the Christian Schools, McVey: Phil., 1898.
22. Op. cit., note 14.

This office of the Holy Ghost consists in the following operations: first, in the original illumination and revelation...; secondly, in the preservation of that which was revealed, or, in other words, in the prolongation of the light of truth by which the Church in the beginning was illuminated; thirdly, in assisting the Church to conceive, with greater fullness, explicitness, and clearness, the original truth in all its relations; fourthly, in defining that truth in words, and in the creation of a sacred terminology, which becomes a permanent tradition and a perpetual expression of the original revelation; and lastly, in the perpetual enunciation and proposition of the same immutable truth in every age.[23]

In giving assent to the teaching authority of the Church we should recognize the fact that we are giving assent, not to a series of dry doctrines decided upon by mere men, but rather to Christ Himself. Moreover, insofar as the Church and Christ are one, this obligation of giving assent also extends to certain matters intimately related to the faith such as the Sacraments instituted by Christ and the ecclesiastical laws by which she governs herself. As St. Catherine of Sienna says, "the Church is no other than Christ Himself, and it is she who gives us the Sacraments, and the Sacraments give us life."[24]

The Catholic Church is not a congregation of people agreeing together, it is not a School of Philosophy or a Mutual Improvement Society. It is rather the Living Voice of God and Christ's revelation to all people, through all time. It teaches only what its divine Master taught. It is in God's name that the Church makes the awesome demand she does on the faith of men—a demand that cannot be merely waved aside as being incompatible with the so-called rights of private judgment.

It will be argued that the Church has been far from pure in her worldly actions. This is to misunderstand her nature. She is by definition a perfect society, the divinely instituted Mystical Body of Christ. The human failings of individual Catholics—or groups of

---

23. Cardinal Henry Manning, *The Temporal Mission of the Holy Ghost* (London: Burns & Oates, 1909.)
24. Quoted by Jorgensen in his *Life of St. Catherine of Sienna*.

Catholics—in no way alters the Church's essentially divine character. She certainly contains sinners within her bosom, for she, like Christ, is in the world for the sake of sinners. Those who would reject the teachings of her divine Master because of her human failings, are similar to the Pharisees who rejected Christ because he ate with publicans. Despite such defects, the fundamental nature and purpose of the Church cannot change. She has never asked the world to follow other than the doctrine of Christ. The Proximate end (purpose) of the Church is to teach all men the truths of Revelation, to enforce the divine precepts, to dispense the means of grace, and thus to maintain the practice of the Christian religion. The ultimate end is to lead all men to eternal life.[25]

Man is free to examine the reasonableness and validity of the Church's claims; he is also free to accept or reject them. If he chooses the latter, which is in essence to refuse the authority of God's Revelation, he is forced, if he is rational, to seek some other basis and authority for his actions and beliefs. And this brings us to the topic of:

PRIVATE JUDGMENT

In the last analysis man must, in religious matters, rely upon some authority. Either this derives from some objective teaching authority that is independent of himself, or else it derives from an inner feeling that can be characterized as "private judgment."[26] Clearly, the prevailing basis for religious beliefs in the modern world—be they Protestant or modernist-Catholic—is private judgment, which is to say that paramount authority resides in that which at any moment commends itself to the individual or group most strongly.[27] According to Vatican II, "man's dignity is such that in religious matters he is to be guided by his own judgment."[28] Such a principle by its very nature represents a revolt against the Church

---

25. W. Wilmers, S.J., *Handbook of the Christian Religion* (NY: Benzinger, 1891). This manner in which the Church sees itself is a far cry from the teaching of Vatican II and the Post-Conciliar "popes." The Document *The Church Today* teaches "Christians are joined with the rest of men in search for truth," and Paul VI tells us that today "the Church is seeking itself. With a great and moving effort, it is seeking to define itself, to understand what it truly is. . . ."

(and Christ), for it proclaims that what the Church teaches is not morally obligatory. Vatican II seems to have forgotten that man's freedom resides, not in his being at liberty to believe anything he wants, but in his ability to accept or refuse what God teaches; that his dignity resides, not in acting like a god, but in his conforming himself to divine principles.

Private Judgment always starts out by accepting some of the teachings of the established faith and rejecting others—it is only a

---

26. Atheists and those that deny the existence of any "religious issue" also exercise private judgment—either their own or by submitting to the private judgment of others. Ultimately the only authority for private judgment is what an individual or group "feels" is true. Some claim their beliefs are based on reason, but if reason were a sufficient guide to religious truth, and if all men reasoned alike, all would believe the same "truths." The Church teaches that we are not allowed to believe anything against reason, but at the same time offers to us many mysteries or truths which, even though they cannot be proved by reason, are in themselves reasonable. Such truths are said to be "beyond reason" in the sense that they derive from Revelation. If neither Revelation nor reason is the source of our beliefs, then they must arise from our sub-conscious. Thus William James defines religion as the "feelings, acts and experiences of individual men in their solitude, so far as they apprehend themselves to stand in relation to whatever they may consider the divine" (quoted in Fulton Sheen, *God and Intelligence in Modern Philosophy* [Longmans: NY, 1925]). The idea that religion is a feeling arising in the subconscious is a condemned proposition of Modernism (Immanentism).

27. "Groups" or "ecclesiastical communities" may agree on broad issues, but never on detailed doctrine. The Protestant denominations early found it necessary to distinguish between "fundamental" and "non-fundamental" beliefs—the latter of which their followers were free to "pick and choose." Catholics are forbidden to make such distinctions. They must believe **all** that the Church teaches—even those things of which they may not be specifically aware. Yet this is the basic concept that underlies the modern ecumenical movements: as long as we are "baptized in Christ," we are free to believe anything we want. In order to get around the difficulty Vatican II teaches that "when comparing doctrines, they should remember that in Catholic teaching there exists an order or "hierarchy" of truths, since they vary in their relationship to the foundation of the Christian faith" (*De Oecumenismo*). Dr. Oscar Cullman (one of the Protestant "observers") considers this passage the "most revolutionary" to be found in the entire Council, and Dr. McAfee Brown concurs while adding that the dogmas of the Immaculate Conception and the Assumption which are "stumbling blocks in the ecumenical discussion" should clearly be well down on the scale of the "hierarchy of truths" (Michael Davies, *Pope John's Council*, Augustine: Devon, 1977).

28. *Religious Freedom*, Paragraph 11.

matter of time before the "new" suffers in turn from the same principle. Within Luther's own lifetime dozens of other Protestant sects were formed, and one might add that within the Post-Conciliar church the same thing has happened. That this is less obvious is because this Church blandly accepts the most divergent views—other than traditional orthodoxy—as legitimate. St. Thomas Aquinas said, "the way of a heretic is to restrict belief to certain aspects of Christ's doctrine selected and fashioned at pleasure" (*Summa* II–II, 1.a.1). Obviously, this "picking and choosing" is nothing other than the free reign of private judgment. And as sects give rise to other sects, it soon happens that all truth and falsehood in religion becomes a matter of private opinion and one doctrine becomes as good as another. Again, it is only a matter of time before all doctrinal issues become irrelevant (who can ever agree about them anyway?). What follows is that morality loses its objective character, and being based on "social contract," can alter in accord with prevailing social needs.[29] Man, not God, becomes the center of the universe and the criterion for truth; doing good to others becomes his highest aspiration, and progress his social goal. The idea of sin is limited to what hurts our neighbor or the state. What need is there for God, for truth, for doctrines, for authority, for the Church and for all the claptrap of the ages that has held man back from his worldly destiny? All that is asked of modern man is that he be "sincere," and that he not disturb his neighbor excessively. If in

---

29. Consider the following statement given out in June 1978 by the *Catholic Theological Society of America*: "Any form of sexual intercourse, including both homosexuality and adultery, could be considered acceptable, so long as it is 'self-liberating, other-enriching, honest, faithful, socially responsible, life-serving and joyous.'" (The traditional Church considers homosexuality a sin "crying unto heaven for vengeance on earth"—Gen. 18:20–21; Rom. 1:26–32.) It will be argued that Rome protested against this statement—however all the individuals responsible are still functioning as Catholic priests with full faculties to hear confession and some of them teach in seminaries. No recantation was ever required. Much closer to the Catholic position is the statement of the Rev. Jesse Jackson, the black activist leader: "One has to have an ethical base for a society. Where the prime force is impulse, there is the death of ethics. America used to have ethical laws based on Jerusalem. Now they are based on Sodom and Gomorrah, and civilizations rooted in Sodom and Gomorrah are destined to collapse."

this milieu he manages to retain any religious sense at all, it is considered a "private matter." Man's dignity, which traditionally was due to the fact that he was made in the image of God, is now said to derive from his independence of God. In reality, man has been so seduced by the serpent—"Ye shall be as gods"—that he has proclaimed himself his own God. (As Paul VI said on the occasion of the moon landing, "honor to man...king of earth,...and today, prince of heaven!"). He lives by his own morality and only accepts the truths that he himself has established. (It used to be said of the Protestants that every man was his own Pope.) A satanic inversion has occurred and man cries out, as did once the Angel of Light— "*Non Serviam*—I will not serve any master other than myself."[30]

Of course, all this occurs in stages. What is remarkable is the similarity of pattern seen in all "reformation" movements. What starts out as the denial of one or two revealed truths (or of truths derived from revelation), progressively ends up in the denial of them all.[31] Similar also are the various subterfuges by which this is achieved. Almost all reformers declare that they are "inspired by the Holy Spirit" (and who can argue with the Holy Spirit?) and end up by ignoring or denying His existence. All claim to be returning to "primitive Christianity," which is nothing other than Christianity as they think it should have been all along. All, or almost all, claim that they are adapting the Faith to the needs of modern man, which is nothing else than an appeal to the pride and arrogance of their

---

30. To quote Michael Davies (*Pope Paul's New Mass*, p. 140): "It was the Council as an event which gave the green light to the process of the formal deification of man." He quotes Father Gregory Baum, one of the *periti* (experts) at the Council, and currently head of the Congregation in charge of seminaries, as stating "I prefer to think that man may not submit to an authority outside of himself." Or again, John Paul II's statement: "To create culture, we must consider, down to the last consequences and entirely, Man as a particular and independent value, as the subject bearing the person's transcendence. We must affirm Man for his own sake, and not for some other motive or reason; solely for himself! Even further, we must love man because he is man, by reason of the special dignity he possesses" (Address to UNESCO, June 2, 1980).

31. A Catholic cannot deny any truth the Church teaches. He must accept them all. As Pope Leo XIII said, "To refuse to believe in any one of them is equivalent to rejecting them all" (*Sapientiae Christianae*).

followers and an attempt to make Christianity conform to their personal needs.[32] All quote Scripture, but selectively and out of context, and never those parts that disagree with their innovative ideas—thus it follows that they reject the traditional interpretation given to the sacred writings by the Church Fathers and the Saints. All mix truth with error, for error has no attractive power on its own. All attack the established rites, for they know that the *lex orandi* (the manner of prayer) reflects *lex credendi* (what is believed); once the latter is changed, the former becomes an embarrassment to them.[33] All use the traditional terms of religion: love, truth, justice and faith, but attach to them a different meaning. And what are all these subterfuges but means of introducing their own private and personal judgments on religious matters into the public domain? Finally, none of the reformers fully agree with each other except in their rejection of the fullness of the established Catholic faith, for error is legion and truth is one. As one mediaeval writer put it, "they are vultures that never meet together except to feast upon a corpse."[34]

The traditional Church has of course always eschewed the use of "private judgment" in religious matters. From a traditional point of view, man should seek to "think correctly rather than to think for himself." (What kind of mathematician would a person be who computed for himself and considered the correct answer to be a matter of "feeling" arising from his subconscious?) The Jewish fathers considered private judgment the greatest form of idolatry

---

32. Few recognize the internal contradiction between returning to primitive practice and adapting the faith to the needs of modern man. The combination attacks the faith at both ends and leaves very little in the middle.

33. Pertinent is Paul VI's statement quoted in *La Documentation Catholique* of 3 May, 1970 to the effect that his *Novus Ordo Missae* (the new mass) "has imparted greater theological value to the liturgical texts so that the *lex orandi* conformed better with the *lex credendi*." This is a frank declaration that either the liturgical texts in use for hundreds of years by the Catholic Church did not possess the degree of theological value which was desirable, or that his new "mass" reflects a change in the *lex credendi*. Jean Madiran commented on this to the effect that "the new Eucharistic prayers must conform better than the Roman Canon [did] with the true faith; this is also the opinion of the Taizé community, the Anglicans, the Lutherans, and the World Council of Churches...." (*Itineraires*, Dec. 1973).

because it made oneself rather than God the source of truth. As has been pointed out above, man's liberty lies, not in his freedom to decide for himself just what is true and false, but in his freedom to accept or reject the truth that Christ and the Church teach and offer. It is a saying of common wisdom that no man should be his own advocate or physician, lest his emotions interfere with his judgment.[35] If we are careful to obtain authoritative advice and direction in the management of our physical and economic well-being, it becomes absurd for us to relegate the health of our soul to the whims of our emotions. As Socrates said, "Being deceived by ourselves is the most dreadful of all things, for when he who deceives us never departs from us even for a moment, but is always present, is it not a most fearful thing?" (*Cratylus*, 428 D). As soon as we make ourselves, rather than God speaking through the Church, the criterion of truth, we end by making man *qua* man the center of the universe, and all truth becomes both subjective and relative. This is why Pope Saint Pius X said we must use every means and bend every effort to bring about the total disappearance of that enormous and detestable wickedness so characteristic of our time—the substitution of man for God (*E Supremo Apostolatu*).

There is of course an area in which legitimate use can, and indeed must, be made of what is sometimes—though erroneously—called

---

34. It is of interest to listen to Luther's own words on the nature of heresy, words he used prior to his open rupture with the Church, but at a time when he had already embraced and expressed certain opinions inconsistent with Apostolic teaching:

> The principal sin of heretics is their pride.... In their pride they insist on their own opinions... frequently they serve God with great fervor and they do not intend any evil; but they serve God according to their own wills.... Even when refuted, they are ashamed to retract their errors and to change their words.... They think they are guided directly by God.... The things which have been established for centuries and for which so many martyrs have suffered death, they begin to treat as doubtful questions.... They interpret the Bible according to their own heads and their own particular views and carry their own opinions into it [*Theological Lectures on the Psalms*, Dresden 1876; quoted by J. Verres in *Luther*, Burns Oates: London, 1884]. *Ex ore tuo te judico!*

35. It has also been said that a man who is his own spiritual guide has Satan for his spiritual director.

"private judgment." In that case what are being made are not judgments in the Protestant sense, which are mere opinions, but rather objectively certain judgments which are nevertheless reasonable.[36] It must never be forgotten that the intellect of a private individual is capable, in certain far from infrequent circumstances, of making judgments which are not liable to error, because—within due limits—the human intellect is infallible. As Father Hickey states in his *Summa Philosophiae Scholasticae*, "the intellect is '*per se*' infallible, although '*per accidens*' it can err." And as Dr. Orestes Brownson states, "private judgment (in the Protestant sense) is only when the matters judged lie out of the range of reason, and when its principle is not the common reason of mankind, nor a Catholic or public authority, but the fancy, the caprice, the prejudice or the idiosyncrasy of the individual forming it."[37]

---

36. Cf. Dr. Orestes Brownson: "Private judgement is only when the matters judged be out of the range of reason, and when its principle is not the common reason of mankind, nor a Catholic or public authority, but the fancy, the caprice, the prejudice or the idiosyncrasy of the individual forming it" (*Brownson's Quarterly Review*, Oct. 1851). "Here is the error of our Protestant friends. They recognize no distinction between reason and private judgment. Reason is common to all men; private judgment is the special act of an individual.... In all matters of this sort there is a criterion of certainty beyond the individual, and evidence is adducible which ought to convince the reason of every man, and which, when adduced, does convince every man of ordinary understanding, unless through his own fault. Private judgment is not so called ... because it is a judgment of an individual, but because it is a judgment rendered by virtue of a private rule or principle of judgment.... The distinction here is sufficiently obvious, and from it we may conclude that nothing is to be termed 'private judgment' which is demonstrable from reason or provable from testimony." (Ibid., Oct., 1852).

37. *Brownson's Quarterly Review*, October (1885?). Furthermore, "Catholics establish with certainty, by objective criteria, the fact that the Church is infallible and then listen in docility to her teachings and at no point does mere opinion play any part in the procedure; whereas Protestants *opine* that Holy Scripture is Divinely revealed (this cannot be proved without the Church); they *opine* that it is to be interpreted by each individual for himself; they *opine* that their opinion as to its meaning will be sufficient for their salvation; and each and every interpretation they make of its meaning (except where no conceivable doubt exists from the text) is no more than an *opinion*." John Daly, *Michael Davies—An Evaluation*, Britons Catholic Library, 1989. I am grateful to this author for his suggestions and corrections in this part of the text.

Such, for example, is the judgment a man makes use of in seeking the truth, and which makes him aware that in matters where he lacks full understanding, it is appropriate to use a guide. Again, there is the use of judgment in the application of principles to a given situation (conscience as the Catholic understands it), or in areas where the Church has never specifically spoken and where it allows for differences of legitimate theological opinion. In all these situations there is a criterion of certainty beyond the individual and evidence is adducible which ought to convince the reason of every man, and which, when adduced, does convince every man of ordinary understanding. Having stated the distinction between mere opinion and the proper individual use of judgment we can further add that such judgment can never rationally be used to abrogate principles or deny revealed truths. These same distinctions make it clear how false it is to accuse Traditional Catholics who adhere to the teachings and practices of the Church of All Times, and who reject innovations that go against the deposit of the faith, of using private judgment in a Protestant sense. To label them as "rebels" or "Protestants" because they refuse to change their beliefs is either an abuse of language or pure hypocrisy.

Private judgment in the Protestant sense is inimical to the spiritual life not only because it denies the authority of Revelation, but because it also denies intellection. God gave us an intellect by means of which we can know truth from falsehood and right from wrong. Reason is normally the "handmaid of the intellect," which means its function is that of ratiocination or discoursing from premises to conclusions. Truth does not depend on reason, but rather truth becomes explicit with the help of reason. We do not say something is true because it is logical, but rather that it is logical because it is true. Reason must then feed on some sustenance, and this it gets from above or from below; above from intellection and Revelation; below from feelings and sense perceptions. Modern man, while occasionally using his higher cognitive faculties, in the practical order refuses to grant their existence. More precisely, being Nominalist, he refuses to accept any premises from above and limits the function of reason to dealing with what comes from below, from his feelings or sense perceptions. In this schema Reason is placed at the apex of man's faculties (Rationalism). Given these truncated principles, it follows that all truth is based on feelings and sense perceptions and hence is relative.[38] Modern man lives on opinions divorced from knowledge, which in Plato's words are ugly things.[39] At the same time he makes a parallel attack on the will. While mechanists and evolutionists deny free will altogether, pseudo-theologians have obliterated it in the name of a false concept of grace. (What else is justification by faith, but the denial of good works, those acts we willfully perform? Surely grace builds on nature and will abandons us in proportion to our refusal to cooperate with it.)[40]

Those who see the futility of resolving religious issues on the basis of their (or someone else's) personal and subjective opinions, and who seek objective and external sources for the Truth, must inevitably turn to the various churches for a solution. Of all the various ecclesiastical communities that hold out the possibility of finding objective truth, only one has consistently rejected private judgment as a source. Only one proclaims that God Himself (through Christ and the Apostles) has revealed the truth, and only one claims and

---

38. Father Smarius, S.J., puts it thus: "The chief cause of this moral degeneracy may be traced to the principle of private judgment introduced by Luther and Calvin, as the highest and only authority in religion and morality. Since the time of these Reformers, religion ceased to be the mistress, and became the slave of man. He was no longer bound to obey her, but she was bound to obey him. His reason was no longer subject to her divine authority, but she became the subject of his prejudices and passions. The Scriptures, although cried up as the supreme authority, lost their objective value, and men no longer listened to the words 'Thus saith the Lord', but gave ear to the freaks and fancies of every upstart prophet and doctor, whose best reason for the faith was, 'I believe so', 'it is my impression', 'it is my opinion'. Reason itself was dethroned, and feeling became the exponent of truth. Men judged of religion as they did of their breakfasts and dinner . . . new fashions of belief became as numerous as new fashions of dress. . . . ." *Points of Controversy* (NY: O'Shea, 1873).

39. Plato, *Republic*, IV, 506c.

40. The current expression of this error is the Protestant claim to be "saved." Those who are certain of their salvation would do well to consider the words of St. Paul: "I fight, not as one beating the air: but I chastise my body, and bring it into subjection, lest perhaps when I have preached to others, I myself should become a castaway" (1 Cor. 10:1–5). The Church has always taught that as long as man has the use of his faculties, he is capable of denying God and falling from grace.

can demonstrate that it has retained this "deposit" intact from Apostolic times down to the present. This is, of course, the One, Holy Catholic and Apostolic Church. To quote St. Alphonsus Liguori:

> To reject the divine teaching of the Catholic Church is to reject the very basis of reason and revelation, for neither the principles of the one nor those of the other have any longer any solid support to rest on; they can be interpreted by everyone as he pleases; every one can deny all truths whatsoever he chooses to deny. I therefore repeat: If the divine teaching authority of the Church, and the obedience to it are rejected, every error will be endorsed and must be tolerated.[41]

THE UNITY OF THE CHURCH

One Lord, one faith, one baptism.
St. Paul (Eph. 4:4–5)

Having determined the nature of the teaching authority of the Church we can now turn to yet another quality inherent in her nature: INERRANCY. In essence, she cannot wander from the original deposit and still claim to be the One, Holy, Catholic and Apostolic Church.

It is amazing to what a degree these four qualities hang together — lose one and you lose them all. The Church is one in the doctrines she teaches. She is called holy and without spot or wrinkle in her faith; which admits of no sort of errors against the revealed word of God. She is called Catholic not only because her teachings extend across time and space in this world, but because the term means universal and the doctrines she teaches are true throughout the entire universe, in heaven, on earth and in hell. She is called Apostolic because she teaches the same doctrines which the Apostles taught, and because she retains intact the Apostolic Succession. Only the Catholic Church has these qualities, and it follows that other Churches which deny one or more of her teachings cannot be

---

41. Appendix to his work on the Council of Trent.

considered as the Church which Christ founded any more then they can claim union with her.[42]

Oneness or unity exists as a characteristic of this Church, not because the faithful agree with "the bishops in union with the Pope," but because all its members including the bishops and the Pope agree in one faith established by Christ, use the same Sacrifice and are united under one Head.[43] It is not the agreement of the faithful with **any** faith the hierarchy may wish to teach, or to use **any** rite the hierarchy may wish to establish, but rather the agreement of both the laity and the hierarchy (whom one hopes are also to be numbered among the faithful) with the doctrines and the rites that Christ and the Apostles established. Nor is the concept of unity restricted to the living, for by the very nature of things, we must be in agreement with all those Catholics who have gone before us back to the time of Christ, with those Catholics in the Church Suffering (Purgatory) and the Church Triumphant (Heaven).

It is repeatedly claimed by the present hierarchy that the Church has lost this unity and that the various divisions among Christians constitute a scandal that must be repaired. The Latin title for the Vatican II document on Ecumenism is *Unitatis Redintegratio* or "The Restoring of Unity." John XXIII established the *Secretariat for Promoting Christian Unity* and specified that **Unity** was the word, not **Reunion**. A new "unity" is to be restored by claiming all Christian bodies that accept baptism are part of the true Church. In a similar manner the Documents of Vatican II state that the Church

---

42. This paragraph is not intended to exhaust the meaning of this term in the Creed. The Church is holy, not only because she admits no errors against the revealed word of God, but also because she is holy in her Sacraments and morals; because her children, as long as they are preserved in their baptismal innocence or restored to it, are holy, and because of the communion of saints. The Apostolic Succession is the "initiatic chain" which conveys the power of confecting the Sacraments from one generation to the next. This "succession" pertains to the order of bishops who in this manner preserve the "Apostolic function" down through the ages.

43. That "Head" is Jesus Christ whose representative or "vicar" on earth is the Pope. Hence it follows that to refuse to obey a pope who commands us to do what is against the laws of God is never to "attack" the papacy, but rather to defend it.

that Christ established **subsists** in the Catholic Church rather than **is** this Church. Recently the entire body of English Post-Conciliar "bishops"—some 42 individuals in all—publicly declared in an official communiqué on the nature of the Church that the Catholic Church embodies the Church of Christ in a special way, but that such a statement is not intended to exclude the fact that other Christian bodies also belong to the Church of Christ. They further stated that the Church which Christ established also subsists in the Anglican Church. The response of an Anglican bishop is pertinent: "What has been swept aside from the ecumenical scene is the idea that the Church of Christ is identical with the Roman Catholic Church. Instead we have a picture of the Church of Christ embracing all the Christian churches, though not in the same way...."[44] If such is the position of the English [Catholic] hierarchy, it would seem clear

---

44. *The Remnant*, Feb. 15, 1984. As the Documents of Vatican II state, "all those justified by faith through baptism are incorporated with Christ. They therefore have a right to be honored with the title of Christian, and are properly regarded as brothers in the Lord by the sons of the Catholic Church.... From her very beginnings there arose in this one and only Church of God certain rifts which the Apostle strongly censures as damnable. But in subsequent centuries more widespread disagreements appeared and quite large Communities became separated from full communion with the Catholic Church—developments for which, at times, men of both sides were to blame. However, one cannot impute the sin of separation to those who at present are born into these communities and are instilled therein with Christ's faith. The Catholic Church accepts them with respect and affection as brothers. For men who believe in Christ and who have been properly baptized are brought into a certain though imperfect communion with the Catholic Church." Elsewhere the Document states "The brethren divided from us also carry out many of the sacred actions of the Christian religion. Undoubtedly, in ways that vary according to the condition of each Church or Community, these actions can truly engender a life of grace and can be rightly described as capable of providing access to the community of salvation" (*Decree on Ecumenism*). The Anglican minister James Atkinson makes the following comment on such passages: "The council Fathers made a valuable concession, the significance of which has not been sufficiently grasped, when they conceded a unity in baptism, an insight of Luther himself, and a frequent emphasis of the late Cardinal Bea when he headed the ecumenical commissariat." ("Rome and Reformation Today," *Latimer Studies*, no. 12, Oxford). He quotes Luther as saying "A Christian or baptized man cannot lose his salvation, even if he would, by sins, however numerous; unless he refuses to believe" (*The Babylonian Captivity*).

that it has apostatized to a man from unity of the faith. And what of Rome, which never reprimanded them?

As opposed to such a view, and based on what has been the constant teaching of the Church, unity exists and has always existed in the true Church. This unity exists even if the majority of the present hierarchy deviate from orthodoxy—indeed it is a matter of faith that such is the case.[45] This is witnessed by the *de fide* statement of the Holy Office on November 8, 1865:

> That the unity of the Church is absolute and indivisible, and that the Church had never lost its unity, nor for so much as a time, ever can.[46]

If the new Church is telling us it lacks unity, it is also telling us that the pope and the bishops in union with him have deviated from orthodoxy and hence lost all magisterial authority. That the greater majority of modern-day Catholics agree with such an errant hierarchy adds nothing to their authority. The personal views of the hierarchy do not make up the "deposit of the faith, but rather, it is the deposit that provides the hierarchy for their *raison d'être*. It is the office of the Church ... in fulfilling Christ's function as teacher, not to make new revelations, but to guard from error the deposit of faith, and authentically, authoritatively, to proclaim

---

Now the idea that unity of any kind rests on baptism alone, or that we are "justified through faith in Baptism," is false. These teachings violate a whole host of traditional Catholic doctrines such as "there is no salvation outside the Catholic Church." There is no such thing as being a partial Catholic; nor can the Church admit that the rites of non-Catholics are a source of grace. How different is the statement of Pius XII: "Only those are to be included as real members of the Church who have been baptized and profess the true faith and have not been so unfortunate as to separate themselves from the unity of the body or been excluded from it by legitimate authority for serious faults." St. Fulgentius teaches: "For neither baptism, nor liberal alms, nor death itself for the profession of Christ, can avail a man anything in order to salvation if he does not hold the unity of the Catholic Church" (*Ad Petrum Diaconum*, C. 39).

45. If not, the "gates of hell" would have prevailed. Actually, if only one true Catholic were to be left alive on earth, unity would reside in him.

46. Quoted in *The Reunion of Christendo: A Pastoral Letter to the Clergy*, Archbishop Henry Manning (NY: Appleton, 1866).

and interpret the Gospel of Jesus Christ."[47] As the Holy Office states, "the Primacy of the Visible Head is of divine institution, and was ordained to generate and to preserve the unity both of faith and of communion...."[48] Authority exists to protect the faith and not the other way around. In the face of the Post-Conciliar attitude, it is of interest to recall the statement of the Anglican convert Henry Manning:

> We believe union to be a very precious gift, and only less precious than truth.... We are ready to purchase the reunion of our separated brethren at any cost less than the sacrifice of one jot or tittle of the supernatural order of unity and faith.... We can offer unity only on the condition on which we hold it—unconditional submission to the living and perpetual voice of the Church of God... it is contrary to charity to put a straw across the path of those who profess to desire union. But there is something more divine than union, that is the Faith.
>
> There is no unity possible except by the way of truth. Truth first, unity afterwards; truth the cause, unity the effect. To invert this order is to overthrow the Divine procedure. The unity of Babel ended in confusion.... To unite the Anglican, the Greek and the Catholic Church in any conceivable way could only end in a Babel of tongues, intellects, and wills. Union is not unity.... Truth alone generates unity. The unity of truth generates its universality. The faith is Catholic, not only because it is spread through the world, but because throughout the world it is one and the same. The unity of the faith signifies that it is the same in every place [and time].[49]

As the English Bishop John Milner said of the Anglo-Catholic Ecumenical movement in the 19th Century: "If we should unite ourselves with it, the Universal Church would disunite itself from us."

If we are then to speak of believing in the One, Holy Catholic and

---

47. Canon George Smith, *The Teaching of the Catholic Church* (NY: Macmillan, 1949).
48. Op. cit., note 39.
49. Op. cit., note 39.

Apostolic Church we must understand the phrase in the same sense and mind that the Church has always understood it.[50]

> There is only one true Church which remounts to Apostolic time by means of its traditions.... For us, we recognize only one ancient and Catholic Church, which is one by its nature, by its principles, by its origin, by its excellence, which reunites all its children in the unity of one same faith....
>
> St. Clement of Alexandria

> Such is the faith, which the Church received; and although she is spread throughout the universe, she guards with care this precious treasure, as if she inhabited but one house; she professes each of these articles of faith with a perfect conformity, as if she had only one soul and one heart. Behold what it is she teaches, what it is she preaches, what it is she transmits by tradition, as if she had only one mouth and only one tongue....
>
> St. Irenaeus

> What they [the Church Fathers] believe, I believe; what they held, I hold; what they taught, I teach; what they preached, I preach....
>
> St. Augustine[51]

It is with these principles in mind that we shall, in *Chapter I*, investigate the sources of the Church's teaching and practices.

---

50. Lutherans and Anglicans also use the Nicene Creed in which this phrase is found. They of course hold that Catholics teach a false religion, and that as such they have no right to use the phrase. John Paul II did not hesitate to repeat the Nicene Creed with the Lutherans when he joined them in their service in Rome in 1983. One wonders whether he understood the phrase in the Lutheran or the Catholic sense.

51. Quotations in this section are respectively from *Stromta*, *lib*. vii (St. Clement of Alexandria); *Adversus Haereses*. lib. 1.10; and lib.1 (St. Irenaeus); and *Contra Julianum*. cap. 3 (St. Augustine). The quote from Augustine is given in Cardinal Joannes Franzelin's *Tractatus de Divina Traditione et Scriptura, De Prop. Fide: Rome,* 1870.

THE PRESENT SITUATION

Few would deny but that the present situation in the Church is one of massive confusion. No two priests or bishops teach the same doctrine and every possible aberration is allowed in liturgical functions. How is a Catholic seeking to live the faith able to sort out the issues? The answer is the Magisterium. It is amazing to what degree this organ provides us with answers as to how to react and function, the limits of obedience to a false hierarchy, and even with regard to the authority of a pope who officially promulgates heresy under the cover of magisterial authority.

We can of course debate as to what is part of the ordinary Magisterium and what is not, but the criteria provided by Vatican I are all we really need to determine this. What we cannot do is deny the *de fide* teaching that the ordinary Magisterium is just as infallible as the extra-ordinary Magisterium.[52]

The greatest error possible is to deny the total authority of the Magisterium (remembering that there is only one Magisterium that expresses itself in a variety of ways). To do so is to cut oneself off from truth and to turn oneself into a Protestant.[53] We have spoken of the possibility of holding theological opinions, but when one examines the Magisterium, there is almost nothing significant left about which to have theological opinions.[54] Those who would tell

---

52. An excellent summary with documentation from over 50 recognized theologians appears in *The Infallibility of the Ordinary and Universal Magisterium of the Church* by Father Bernard Lucien.

53. Father Noel Barbara has stated, "As soon as we accept the magisterium as the proximate rule of faith, we should make a firm determination to never in any way depart from her official teaching, and this not only with regard to matters of faith, but also with regard to matters of discipline. With regard to the authentic teachings we should forbid ourselves to make any distinctions between those things which we like while rejecting those we find difficult to accept. When I speak of the magisterium it should be clear that I am thinking of the authentic magisterium of the Church and not that of the popes of Vatican II. The teaching of the infallible magisterium and her disciplinary decisions are to be found in the authentic documents which are available for us to consult." (letter)

There can be no doubt but that the Post-Conciliar "popes" have rejected the authority of the Magisterium and would lead us to do the same. They thus have lost their authority because it cannot be said of them that he who hears them is hearing

us that the ordinary Magisterium can contain error are wolves in sheep's clothing. If such is the case we must all become super theologians so as to pick and choose what is true and false among some 95% of the Church's teaching. Such an attitude allows one to reject anything one doesn't personally approve of while at the same time allowing for the introduction of every possible error. It is a satanic proposition.

And all this highlights the present situation in the Church with clarity. It is clear that Vatican II teaches a host of doctrines under the cover of magisterial infallibility that directly contradict what the Church has taught through the ages as true. If one accepts the teaching of Vatican II and the definition of the Mass that is promulgated in the General Instruction on the *Novus Ordo Missae*[55]—which all must do who accept the authority of the Post-Conciliar "popes"— one is forced to deny previously taught truths, which is to apostatize from the faith.[56] Putting this in different terms, the Catholic today is forced to choose between two different Magisteria. That such is the case is glossed over by claiming that the living character of the Magisterium allows for development, progress or evolution of doctrine, another concept embraced by Vatican II. Now certain principles are clear. We can develop or deepen our understanding of the Magisterium, but the Magisterium itself cannot change under the euphemism of development. The reason for this is that Truth cannot change. Another principle involved is that once something is declared to be magisterial teaching, it takes priority over any change. Two contraries cannot be simultaneously true. It follows that one cannot remove what is magisterial from the Magisterium.

Once again this is affirmed by the Magisterium:

Hence, also, that understanding of its sacred dogmas must be perpetually retained, which Holy Mother Church has once

---

Christ. This is not a matter of "theological opinion." However, when it comes to describing or designating what these "popes" should be called, or to explaining how this has happened, (*materialiter/formaliter, sede vacante*, etc.), we are forced by circumstance into the realm of theological opinion.

55. There are those that argue that this document is not part of the magisterium. Once again we are being encouraged to become Protestants.

declared; and there must never be recession from that meaning under the specious name of a deeper understanding [Can.3]. Therefore. ... let the understanding, the knowledge, and wisdom of individuals as of all, of one man as of the whole Church, grow and progress strongly with the passage of the ages and the centuries; but let it be solely in its own genus, namely in the same dogma, with the same sense and the same understanding.

> Fr. Heinrich Denzinger, *Enchiridion Symbolorum, Definitionum et Declarationum de Rebus Fidei et Morum*, §1800

We have then the Magisterium as it existed up to the death of Pope Pius XII which can be called authentic, and that which, having its roots in an attempt to bring the Church into line with the

---

56. Despite disclaimers that Vatican II is a "pastoral council," it should be clear that John XXIII claimed it was guided by the Holy Spirit. Paul VI in closing the Council stated that "the teaching authority of the Church, even though not wishing to issue extraordinary dogmatic pronouncements, has made thoroughly known its authoritative teaching." Still later he stated that the Council "avoided proclaiming in an extraordinary manner dogmas endowed with the note of infallibility," and added that it conferred on its teachings "the value of the supreme ordinary magisterium" (Speech of Jan 12, 1966), and that "it had as much authority and far greater importance than the Council of Nicaea." Elsewhere he has called it "the greatest of Councils" and "even greater than the Council of Trent." Perhaps the most clear cut statement is to be found in a letter to Archbishop Lefebvre demanding his submission to the Post-Conciliar Church:

> You have no right any more to bring out the distinction between the doctrinal and pastoral that you use to support your acceptance of certain texts of Vatican Council II and your rejection of others. It is true that the matters decided in any Council do not all call for an assent of the same quality; only what the Council affirms in its "definitions" as a truth of faith or as bound up with faith requires the assent of faith. Nevertheless, the rest also form a part of the solemn magisterium of the Church to be trustingly accepted and sincerely put into practice by every Catholic.

John Paul II has expressed his full agreement with Paul VI who he considers as his "spiritual father," and has further stated that the Council was "inspired by the Holy Spirit" and that "obedience to the Council is obedience to the Holy Spirit." Still elsewhere he has stated that the Council is "the authentic teaching of the Church" [Sources given in my *The Destruction of the Christian Tradition*].

modern world, was established during the reign of John XXIII. Apart from Roncalli's prior Freemasonic connections, we have, as his first act on assuming the papal role, to delete the phrases referring to and praying for the conversion of the perfidious Jews from the Good Friday services. (Obviously, there were perfidious and non-perfidious Jews, just as there are perfidious and non-perfidious Catholics. Who would say Nicodemus or Simeon were perfidious? Who would not say Simon Magus was not perfidious?) This seemingly simple act, disguised under the cover of a false charity, was a declaration on his part of the principle of *non serviam*. It was like a first step in establishing the new Post-Conciliar Church. It was followed with a host of other doctrinal changes.[57]

Catholics are often confused about the term Faith. Faith has, as St. Thomas explains, two aspects. There is the objective side of The Faith—which is incorporated or expressed by the Magisterium (and this is a gift), and there is the subjective side of Faith which is the assent we give to the Revelation as taught by the Magisterium. Thus to claim to have the Catholic Faith requires that we give our whole-hearted assent to the Magisterium including those parts that we may not be fully aware of. The same is true of those who follow the Post-Conciliar pseudo-Magisterium. Those of us who believe in a Revelation that is true and who strive to be able to able to say with St. Paul, "I live, yet not I, but Christ within me," must be sure to adhere to the authentic Magisterium given us by Him who is the Way, the Light and the Truth. People who hide behind the present confusions, the shibboleths of doctrine development, obedience to the popes etc., are in essence refusing to make the choice and run the risk of being included among the lukewarm. (The degree of responsibility varies greatly with circumstance but clearly falls more on the hierarchy responsible for preserving and teaching the deposit of the Faith.) The reason why Catholics who adhere to the authentic Magisterium

---

57. Documented in the *Canon Law Digest*, vol. v, p. 20, by T. Lincoln Bouscaren, S.J., and James I. O'Connor, S.J. (Milwaukee: Bruce, 1963). As to his Freemasonic connections, these are documented by the Surite of Police in Paris when he was papal nuncio there (cf. *L'Abomination de la Desolation* by Professeur Gabriel Chabot and Commandant Rouchette, available from the latter at B.P. 151, 16105 Cognac, Cedex, France).

call themselves "traditional" is because tradition is what is "handed down." Those adhering to the Post-Conciliar pseudo-Magisterium have no right to use this term.

One can in fact define the objective side of faith as being equivalent to the authentic Magisterium. St. Thomas Aquinas teaches that faith (i.e., the authentic Magisterium) holds the first rank in the spiritual life because it is by faith alone that the soul is bound to God and that which gives life to the soul is that which binds it to God, namely faith. "God has opened to us no other way to eternal happiness than that of faith . . . he who has been raised to contemplation looks not upon faith as inferior to this extraordinary gift." The clearer and more comprehensive one's vision, the stronger does one's faith become. As St. Catherine of Sienna said, "the gift of prophecy can be recognized as true only by the light of the faith."[58]

This brings us to the issue of *orthodoxy*, which is defined as true doctrine and sound faith. It is only in light of the above need to be one with Christ and His Magisterium that heresy has meaning—and clearly also *risk*. This is why the Magisterial condemnation of error always demands our assent. It is pertinent that the Post-Conciliar Church has dropped the use of the Index and declares itself unwilling to condemn the grossest of errors. Pope John Paul I publicly stated that in the Old Church only the Truth had rights, but now we know that even error has rights. Once again, however, we must be careful. The True Church distinguishes between the possibility that we may be mistaken about some Magisterial point and therefore speaks of "material heresy" (some "matter" about which we are mistaken) as opposed to formal heresy. She requests that "competent authority" point out a material error to the individual involved and allow him six months to study the issue and correct him or herself. If after six months this correction is not made, the Church considers the individual to have added an attitude of obstinacy to the error and normally deprives the individual of at least his teaching function. In

---

58. What characterizes modern "faith," be it Catholic or Protestant-fundamentalist, is its lack of objectivity. As one professor put it, before the 60's Catholics would respond that they believe in what the Church teaches. After the 60's they said "I believe, while rejecting significant aspects of the Church's teaching."

this she is not practicing "thought control," but simply insisting that responsible people think correctly: "Brethren, let this mind be in you, which was also in Jesus Christ" (Phil. 2:5).

All this highlights the dilemma of the Catholic in the Post-Conciliar era, and there is no rational way around this. Catholics who do not wish to drift are forced to choose. In order to get a perspective on the need to take a stand, one has only to ask how many Catholics would run their stock portfolio without investigations and choices. Despite all the supposed confusions fostered by the world, the flesh and the devil, Holy Mother Church has provided us with all the criteria needed to make the right choices. The grounds for such choices are further delineated in parts of my *The Destruction of the Christian Tradition*, which is a text based on magisterial teachings.[59]

One further point. Those who insert their own opinions between the Magisterium and the faithful in essence create a cult in the pejorative sense of the word. Thus it is that both the Post-Conciliar Church and such organizations as the Society of Pius X (who advocate disobeying a Pope whose authority they recognize) are from this point of view cults and not Catholic.[60]

All this raises the issue of obedience. Now obedience is a moral virtue; Faith, Hope, and Charity are theological virtues. Obedience without the theological virtues is an absurdity because it is always possible to give obedience to a wrong authority, even to Satan himself. Faith, Hope, and Charity are the proper objects of obedience—normally they are mediated through the Church hierarchy, but they reside ultimately in Him who is the Truth, The Way and the Light. Now this Truth, Way and Light resides above all in what He taught and teaches, which is incorporated in the Magisterium—once again, both the Ordinary and Extraordinary. Hence it follows that we must

---

59. Bloomington, Indiana: World Wisdom Books, 2006

60. This issue is complex. One must remember that "the grace of God floweth where it will." Cults have to be looked at objectively in terms of the degree to which they limit the flow of grace—do they for instance retain sacramental validity and to what extent do they enforce deviation? They must also be evaluated subjectively in the sense that the person participating may be able to ignore the deviation or bypass it. But once again it is the authentic Magisterium which makes possible to proper use of judgment.

give our obedience (or what the Church calls our intellectual assent) to the entire Magisterium. Only by so doing can we think with Christ. And if we are to be Baptized with Christ, Buried with Christ and Resurrected with Christ, we must then also think with Christ.[61]

SACRAMENTAL CONSEQUENCES

One of the most important functions of the Authentic Magisterium is to protect Sacramental integrity. The Faithful have an absolute right to the Sacraments as they were given to us by God as a vehicle for the transmission of Grace. Now the Post-Conciliar establishment has violated the Magisterial structures aimed at protecting these Sacraments in every possible way. Consider the traditional Mass. This rite was protected by the Papal Bull *Quo Primum* which states that no priest can be forbidden to say this Mass, and that the faithful shall always have access to it. This Papal Bull was moreover re-affirmed by every Pope from Saint Pius V (who promulgated it) to the time of John XXIII. This is now a forbidden Mass. Many attempts to disguise this fact, such as by using the name "abrogated," or by allowing for the so-called "indult" Mass—the Novus Ordo "mass" in Latin, plus chant—now prevail. Groups petitioning for the return of the traditional Mass are asked not to refer to the Bull *Quo Primum*, which is absurd. In addition, organizations of seemingly traditional priests such as the Society of St. Peter are organized, but provided with Post-Conciliar bishops who almost certainly do not have the power to pass on Holy Orders. The fact remains that the Mass of All Times is forbidden and if someone doubts this statement, let him simply go and ask a Post-Conciliar bishop for permission to attend it. And this rite is not only forbidden; it has been replaced by a false mass in which the Words of Consecration (no longer called such) given us by Christ Himself have been changed. Remembering that we are dealing, as Scripture says, with powers and principalities, this action of the Post-Conciliar establishment must be labeled diabolical. [Cf. Rama P. Coomaraswamy, M.D., *The Problems with the New*

---

61. St. Catherine of Sienna once told the pope that if he acted in a certain way he would go to hell, and those that obeyed him would go to hell with him (*Letters*).

Mass (Rockford, IL: TAN, 1990). See also 'A History of the Traditional or Tridentine Mass', *Sophia*, vol. 1 no. 2 and vol. 2 no. 1, 1995–6 Foundation for Traditional Studies, P.O. Box 370, Oakton, VA 22124.] In a similar manner all the Sacraments that depend upon the priesthood, and particularly that of Episcopal Consecration have been rendered at least doubtful if not totally destroyed.

An excellent example illustrating many of these issues is provided by E. Sylvester Berry. According to Protestant teaching, all men are free to "worship God according to the dictates of their own conscience"; the doctrine is widely proclaimed today as "freedom of conscience" or "freedom of worship." It simply means that every man is free, not only to believe according to his own interpretation of the Scriptures, but also to worship God in his own way. This either denies that Our Lord established any definite form of worship in the New Law, or maintains that we cannot know with certainty what it is, for surely no Christian could believe that he is free to worship as he pleases, if he admits that Christ has established a definite form of worship to be used by His followers.[62]

A WORD ON THE USE OF ONE'S CONSCIENCE

Many hold that their decision as to how to behave in the present circumstances is one of following their conscience. Catholics should understand just what this means, and again the Magisterium makes it quite clear. One's Catholic conscience is not a still small voice such as Newman and the Protestants believe in. There is a theological and metaphysical teaching that *Synderesis* (the divine spark within us) cannot err, but conscience can. Our consciences are far too easily influenced by our emotions and passions, by the milieu in which we live, and this is to say nothing of the effects of Original Sin. For a Catholic, the conscience is a faculty used to apply God's laws (knowable from the Magisterium) to a given circumstance where the Church has not provided clear guidance. One cannot perform an abortion because one's conscience allows one to do so. Nor can one

---

62. *The Church of Christ*, E. Sylvester Berry, D.D. (London: Herder Book Co., 1927).

use one's conscience to choose the lesser of two evils, when both are against God's laws. One of course is responsible for a well-formed conscience, which is to say, for knowing the laws of God (as they pertain to one's station in life), as promulgated by the Church, and how they apply. But it would be impossible for the Church to formulate specifics for every possible situation nuanced or otherwise. Hence it is that Our Lord provides us with a conscience that allows us to apply the laws we know to some specific circumstance.[63] Where there is doubt as to such application, the Church recommends consulting a competent (and orthodox) confessor.

It should be abundantly clear on the basis of what has been said that a Catholic cannot reject the authentic Magisterium of the Church on the grounds of conscience. The Magisterium, the "proximate rule of faith," is in fact God's law for man. It is the Truth, and one obviously cannot deny the truth on the grounds of conscience.

The idea that God's love will protect us from the consequences of our rebellion is fraught with danger. Love is a reciprocal affair and as St. Francis de Sales instructs us in his *Treatise on the Love of God*, it has three aspects: love of delight in the divine perfections; love of benevolence, by which we will to praise the Lord, to serve him and work for His glory; and love of conformity, by which we accept all that God wills or expects of us, a love which has its consummation in the total donation of ourselves to God.

In the final analysis the Church has not left us orphans. She has provided all that we need to be Catholic in the present circumstances. Those who would argue that rejecting the heterodox teachings of the Post-Conciliar popes leads to denying the indefectability of the Church are simply not rational. It is precisely the opposite. If one accepts them one proclaims that the Post-Conciliar Church has in fact defected, for it has changed its teachings and practices which

---

63. "By following a right conscience I not only do not incur sin, but am also immune from sin, whatever superiors may say to the contrary. For conscience obliges in virtue of divine command whether written down or in a code or instilled by natural law. To weigh conscience in the scales against obedience to legal authority is to compare the weight of divine and human decrees. The first obliges more than the second and sometimes against the second." St. Thomas Aquinas, *Disputations Concerning Truth*, 17, 5.

is the essence of defection. The same can be said about rebellion. It is those who have changed Christ's teaching (and those who knowingly accept the changes) who are in rebellion. As opposed to such, it is those who have loyally adhered to the traditions, and who have refused to change their beliefs, who have proven that the Church, like the Truth she represents, has never and never can defect. The gates of hell cannot prevail against the truth.

There is a way back. The paradigm is found in the parallel of the Prodigal Son. Having demanded our inheritance and left our home, many of us have ended up eating the swill of modernism fit only for pigs. When we come to our senses we must return home to the embracing bosom of Our Father. Then it is that the "fatted lamb" who is slain and is yet alive can be returned to us—the lamb which is none other than Christ Himself. Those of us who, for whatever reason, have left our traditional home in Holy Mother Church must make the choice.

In the last analysis, we must all choose between Barabbas and Christ!

1

GENERAL INTRODUCTION

TO THE PROBLEMS WITH THE OTHER SACRAMENTS DEPENDENT ON THE PRIESTHOOD, APART FROM THE NEW MASS

It is well known that the Post-Conciliar Church has, in accord with the "Spirit of Vatican II," and with the desire of "updating" her rites, made changes in her manner of administering all the sacraments. Few would deny that the intention behind the changes was to make the Sacraments more acceptable to modern man and especially to the so-called "separated brethren."

Catholics have reacted to the changes in a variety of ways. Most have accepted them without serious consideration—after all, they emanated from a Rome they always trusted. Others consider them "doubtful," or have completely denied their efficacy; and as a result refuse to participate in them. Much of the controversy has centered around the new Mass, or *Novus Ordo Missae*, with the result that the other Sacraments—especially those which depend on a valid priesthood—have been ignored.[1] The present book will discuss the changes made in Holy Orders, along with those made in the various Sacraments dependent upon the priesthood. We shall initiate our study with a restatement of traditional Catholic theological principles relative to all the Sacraments.

According to the teaching of the Church, a Sacrament is a sensible sign, instituted by Our Lord Jesus Christ, to signify and to produce

---

1. Cf. the author's *The Problems with the New Mass* (Rockford, Ill: TAN, 1990).

grace. There are seven Sacraments: Baptism, Marriage, Holy Orders, Eucharist, Absolution (Penance or Confession), Confirmation and Extreme Unction. I have listed them in this order because Baptism and Marriage do not, strictly speaking, require a priest.[2] Holy Orders are administered by a Bishop and the remaining Sacraments require priestly "powers" to be confected or administered.

Sacramental theology by definition dates back to Christ and the Apostles.[3] It has "developed" over the centuries, which to paraphrase St. Albert the Great, does not mean it has "evolved," but rather that our understanding of it has become clearer as various aspects were denied by heretics and the correct doctrine affirmed and clarified by definitive decisions of the Church. The end result can be called the traditional teaching of the Church on the Sacraments.

The rise of Modernism gave rise to a different and Modernist view of Sacramental Theology, one which holds that the Sacraments are not so much fixed rites handed down through the ages, as "symbols" that reflect the faith of the faithful—a faith which is itself a product of the collective subconscious of those brought up in a Catholic milieu.[4] The traditional Sacraments, according to this view, reflected the views of the early Christians. As modern man has progressed and matured, it is only normal that his rites should also change. It is for the reader to decide how much such opinions have affected the changes instituted in the Sacraments in the wake of Vatican II.

THE SOURCE OF THE SACRAMENTS

'Who but the Lord," St. Ambrose asks, "is the author of the Sacraments?" St. Augustine tells us, "It is divine Wisdom incarnate that

---

2. As will be explained, Baptism can be administered by even a non-believer, providing he uses the correct words and intends to do what the Church or Christ intends. With regard to Marriage, the priest acts as a witness on the part of the Church. In Marriage the "matter" is the parties to the "contract," and the "form" is the giving of consent.

3. "If anyone shall say that the sacraments of the New Law were not all instituted by Jesus Christ our Lord...let him be anathema" (Fr. Heinrich *Denzinger, Enchiridion Symbolorum, Definitionum et Declarationum de Rebus Fidei et Morum*, §844).

established the sacraments as means of salvation," and St. Thomas Aquinas states that "As the grace of the sacraments comes from God alone, it is to Him alone that the institution of the sacrament belongs." Thus it is that the Apostles did not regard themselves as authors of the Sacraments, but rather as "dispensers of the mysteries of Christ" (1 Cor. 4:1).There is some debate as to whether Confirmation and Extreme Unction were established by Christ directly or through the medium of the Apostles. The issue is of no importance, for Revelation comes to us from both Christ and the Apostles. The latter, needless to say, would hardly go about creating sacraments without divine authority.

A BRIEF HISTORICAL PERSPECTIVE

The early Church Fathers, mostly concerned with defining doctrine, expended little effort on defining or explaining the sacraments. One should not however assume that they lacked understanding. Consider Justin Martyr (AD 114–165) who made it clear that the effect of Baptism was "illumination" or grace. And again St. Irenaeus (†AD 190) who, in discussing the "mystery" of the Eucharist, noted that "When the mingled cup [i.e., wine mixed with water] and the manufactured bread receives the Word of God, and the Eucharist

---

4. It is unfortunate that the Modernists used the term "symbol" to specify the reflection in doctrine of the beliefs of the faithful—beliefs which they held arose in the collective or individual subconscious—beliefs which were subject to change as man "evolved" and "matured." They misused this term because the early creeds were called "symbols." If one accepts their interpretation, it is obvious that "symbols" would have to change as beliefs changed. (The Modernist confuses the meaning of symbols and signs; signs can be arbitrary and can legitimately be used to indicate different meanings.) This idea and misuse of the term "symbolism" was rightly condemned by Saint Pius X in his Encyclical *Pascendi*, a situation which has given the term a bad connotation. True symbols are material (verbal, visual) representatives of realities that never change which is the sense in which the Church applied the term to the creeds in post-Apostolic times. Just as natural laws are the manifest reflection of God's will, so all natural phenomena are in one way or another symbolic of higher realities. Nature, as St. Bernard said, is a book of scripture, or to quote the psalms, "*Caeli enarrant gloriam Dei*—the heavens declare the glory of God."

becomes the body of Christ...." In these two Fathers we see the essential theology of the sacrament—the joining of "form" and "matter," (though other terms were used) and the conveyance of grace.

The earliest Church Fathers placed the Sacraments among the "mysteries" (from the Greek *mysterion*)[5] without clearly specifying the number. It was Tertullian (circa AD 150–250) who first translated this term into Latin as "sacramentum," though once again, not in an exclusive sense.[6] It is of interest to quote him in order to show that he was familiar with the essential features of sacramental theology: "All waters, therefore ... do, after invocation of God, attain the sacramental power of sanctification; for the Spirit immediately supervenes from the heavens, and rests over the waters, sanctifying them from Himself, and being thus sanctified, they imbibe at the same time the power of sanctifying.... It is not to be doubted that God has made the material substance, which He has disposed throughout all His products and works, obeying Him also in His own peculiar sacraments; that the material substance which governs terrestrial life acts as agent likewise in the celestial."[7]

From this point on the term "sacrament" was increasingly used—often interchangeably with "mystery." St. Ambrose (AD 333–397) clearly provides us with the first treatise dedicated exclusively to the subject of what he calls sacraments, specifically to those of Baptism,

---

5. The Greek Orthodox still use this word to describe the Sacraments. The primordial sense of the term is found among the classic Greek writers, and especially as used with reference to the Mysteries of Eleusis. In vesting with the stole before Mass, the priest says, "*Quamvis indignus accedo ad tuum sacrum Mysterium....*" ["Even though I come as an unworthy man to Thy holy Mystery...."], meaning of course the Mystery of the Mass.

6. The Latin word *sacramentum* had several meanings: (1) the sum which two parties to a legal suit deposited—so called perhaps because it was deposited in a sacred place. Its meaning was often extended to include a civil suit or process. (2) It was used to describe the military oath of allegiance and by extension, any sacred obligation. (3) Tertullian used the word to describe the neophyte's promises on entering the Church at the time of baptism; he also used it with regard to "mysterious communications" on the part of what we would now call a religious sister who "conversed with the angels." (4) Finally, he used it with regard to Baptism and the Eucharist.

7. Quoted from Elizabeth Frances Rogers, *Peter Lombard and the Sacramental System*, New York, 1917 (presently available from Ithaca: Cornell University Library, 2009)

Confirmation and the Eucharist. He made no attempt at a universal definition, but clearly understood the principles involved as is shown by his statement that "the sacrament which you receive is made what it is by the word of Christ." It is with St. Augustine (AD 354–430) that the first attempt is made to define clearly the term as "a sign," or "signs," which, "when they pertain to divine things, are called Sacraments." Elsewhere he states that they are called Sacraments because in them one thing is seen, and another is understood. He still uses the word as virtually equivalent to Mysteries and speaks of Easter as well as the allegory of sacred numbers which he sees in the twenty-first chapter of John's Gospel as sacraments. Marriage, Ordination, Circumcision, Noah's Ark and, the Sabbath and other observances are also so labeled. Perhaps his most important contribution to sacramental theology was the distinction he drew between the Sacrament as an outer sign and the grace that this sign conveyed. The former without the latter, as he indicated, was useless.[8]

The next person to discuss the Sacraments was Isidore of Seville (AD 560–636) who functioned in this area as an encyclopaedist rather than as an individual who provided us with further clarification. His discussion is limited to Baptism, Chrism, and the Body and Blood of the Lord. Next was Gratian (1095–1150) who made the first attempt to bring all the canon laws of the Church together. In his *Concordia Discordantium Canonum* he quotes the various definitions we have reviewed, and lists as examples the sacraments of Baptism, Chrism (Holy Orders) and the Eucharist. This collection became a standard source and Roland Bandinelli, who later became Pope Alexander III, (pope, 1159–1181) wrote a commentary on this text in which he lists the Sacraments as Baptism, Confirmation, the Sacrament of the Body and Blood (in which he treats of the Consecration of Priests), Penance, Unction and Matrimony. This commentary itself became a standard text and a pattern for Peter Lombard's *Commentary on the Sentences*.[9]

---

8. Such would occur if, for example, a layman or a priest not properly ordained were to attempt to say Mass.
9. Those seeking a more detailed review are referred to The *Dictionnaire de la Théologie Catholique*, Paris: Letouzey, 1939. Scriptural usage followed much the

Finally, it is Hugh of St. Victor (1096–1141) who reviewed the subject and provided us with a definition which most closely resembles that officially accepted today. In his text *De Sacramentis Christianae Fidei*, he defines a Sacrament as "a corporeal or material element sensibly presented from without, representing from its likeness, signifying from its institution, and containing from sanctification some invisible and spiritual grace." He also states, "add the word of sanctification to the element and there results a sacrament." He further distinguishes between those Sacraments essential for salvation, those "serviceable for salvation because by them more abundant grace is received, and those which are instituted that through them the other sacraments might be administered [i.e., Holy Orders]."

We shall conclude this historical discussion with three definitive decisions of the Church which are *de fide*, that is, "of faith."

> A Sacrament is an outward sign of inward grace, instituted by Christ for our sanctification.
>
> *Catechism of the Council of Trent*

> If anyone shall say that the sacraments of the New Law were not all instituted by Jesus Christ our Lord, or that there are more or less than seven, namely Baptism, Confirmation, Eucharist, Penance, Extreme Unction, Order, and Matrimony, or even that any one of these seven is not truly and strictly speaking a Sacrament: let him be anathema (*Canon of the Council of Trent*, Fr. Heinrich Denzinger, *Enchiridion Symbolorum, Definitionum et Declarationum de Rebus Fidei et Morum*, §844). If anyone say that the Sacraments of the New Law do not contain the grace which they signify, or that they do not confer grace on those who place no obstacle to the same, let him be anathema.
>
> *Canon of the Council of Trent*

---

same pattern. The Greek *Mysterion* was translated as *Sacramentum* and as such the term is found 45 times—some 20 times in the writings of St. Paul alone. According to Father F. Prat, it is used in three contexts: (1) secrets of God relative to the salvation of man by Christ, that is, secrets the meaning of which became clear with the New Covenant; (2) the hidden sense of an institution; and (3) hidden action, as in the mystery of the Resurrection to come.

MATTER AND FORM

The concept of "Form" and "Matter"—the words used and the material over which they are said (as for example the Words of Consecration said over wine mixed with water in the Mass) were borrowed from the hylomorphic theory of Aristotle, and introduced into Catholic theology by either William of Auxerre or St. Albert the Great. The terminology was new but the doctrine old. For example, St. Augustine used such phrases as "mystic symbols," and "the sign and the thing invisible," "the word and the element."[10]

Thus it is that, while the proper words and the material vehicle of the Sacraments date back to Christ, debates as to proper form and matter only occur after the 13th century. It should be clear that these concepts help to clarify, but in no way change, the principles enunciated by the earliest Church Fathers. The manner in which they clarify will become clear when we consider the individual sacraments.

With regard to validity, the Church clearly teaches that "A Sacramental form must signify the grace which it is meant to effect, and effect the grace which it is meant to signify."

DOES MAN NEED THE SACRAMENTS TO BE SAVED?

Not absolutely, but "relatively absolutely." The present study cannot discuss in detail the Catholic principle that "*Extra Ecclesiam nulla Salus*"—that is "outside the Church there is no salvation."[11] Suffice it to say that the Church understands by this that, apart from the invincibly ignorant, salvation is normally dependent upon being in the Catholic Church; and that the normal means of entering this Church is Baptism.[12] The other Sacraments are not absolutely necessary, but are required in so far as one is a member of the Church

---

10. *The Catholic Encyclopedia*, 1908.

11. An excellent discussion of this topic is available in Father Barbara's *Fortes in Fide*, no. 9, (1991 series).

12. To avoid any possibility of misunderstanding, it should be clear that one must live a life in accord with the teachings of the Church—Baptism, which wipes away the stain of original sin, in no way guarantees that the individual will not fall

and in so far as they are the normal means of grace instituted by Christ. Thus one must confess and receive the Eucharist at least once a year—providing a priest is available.[13] Now clearly Christ who established the Church, also established the other Sacraments as normal means of grace. Not to avail ourselves of them when they are available is as absurd as not seeking medical assistance when one is ill.

HOW THE SACRAMENTS WORK

Many so-called "conservative Catholics" are convinced of the validity of the Post-Conciliar rites because of the manifold graces they believe they receive from them. Even if we grant that they are not subject to self-deception in this area, such an argument is useless in defending validity, for it is a constant teaching of the Church that in the reception of the Sacraments, grace enters the soul in two ways. The first is *ex opere operato*, or by virtue of the work performed. The second is called *ex opere operantis*, which is to say, by virtue of the disposition of the recipient. Thus, one who participates in good faith in false sacraments can indeed receive grace—but only that grace that comes from his own good disposition, and never that much more ineffable grace which derives from the Sacrament itself.

It has also been argued that, providing the disposition of the recipient is proper, the deficiencies of a sacrament are "supplied" by the Church. Such an argument is patently false, for it implies that no matter what the minister does, the Church automatically makes up for the defect. (It would also declare all the Protestant rites as being of equal validity to those of the Church.) It is possible that Christ Himself may make up for the defect in the case of those who are "invincibly ignorant," but the Church can in no way make up such a

---

from the "state of grace" produced by this Sacrament. The issue of Baptism of Desire is discussed in an article by the present author in an 1992 issue of *The Reign of Mary*, (8500 N. St. Michael's Road. Spokane, WA 99217); http://www.cmri.org [See also the essay "Is Baptism of Desire a Catholic Teaching?" below—ED].

13. One could say that the Sacraments depending on Orders are not necessary in an absolute sense, but that, given the condition of fallen man, they are indispensable by a necessity of convenience or expedience.

defect. As A.S. Barnes, the admitted authority on Anglican Orders, says: "God, we must always remember, is not bound by the Sacraments which He Himself has instituted—but we are."

The phrase *ex opere operato* was used for the first time by Peter of Poitiers (d. 1205). It was subsequently adopted by Pope Innocent III as well as St. Thomas Aquinas to express the constant teaching of the Church to the effect that the efficacy of the action of the Sacraments does not depend on anything human, but solely on the will of God as expressed by Christ's institution and promise. The meaning of the phrase should be clear. The Sacraments are effective regardless of the worthiness of the minister or of the recipient. What this means is that the Sacraments are effective, even if the priest is himself in a state of mortal sin (it would be sacrilegious for him to administer them in a state of mortal sin—should a priest not be able to get to confession before confecting a Sacrament, he should at least make an act of contrition), and even if the recipient's disposition is not perfect (he also commits sacrilege if he receives them in a state of mortal sin—apart from Penance of course). This is because the priest is acting on the part of Our Divine Master, Jesus Christ, and the Sacraments have their efficacy from their divine institution and through the merits of Christ. The Sacraments and the priests who administer them function as vehicles or instruments of grace and are not their principle cause.[14] It is Christ who, through the priest, forgives sins or confects the Eucharist, etc., etc.

Unworthy ministers, validly conferring the sacraments, cannot impede the efficacy of signs ordained by Christ to produce grace *ex opere operato*. But what of *ex opere operantis*? Obviously, there must be no deliberate obstacle to grace on the part of the recipient. These principles follow from the nature of Grace. Grace is God's free gift to us (whether in or outside the channels which He established), but man always remains free to refuse or to place obstacles in the way of God's grace. The recipient's disposition need not be perfect—indeed, only God is perfect. It must, as is discussed in greater detail below, be appropriate.

---

14. Brother Andre of Quebec likened the priest to a seller of clothes. The salesman's personal morals had no effect on the clothes he sold.

A further principle follows: the priest and the Church must follow the pattern which Christ established in instituting a special vehicle of grace. As St. Ambrose said:

> He is unworthy who celebrates the mystery (Sacrament) otherwise than as Christ delivered it.

And as the Council of Trent states,

> If anyone saith that the received and approved rites of the Catholic church, wont to be used in the solemn administration of the Sacraments, may be contemned, or without sin be omitted by the ministers, or be changed by every pastor of the churches into other new ones; let him be anathema.

The Church, of course, has a certain latitude with regard to the manner in which the Sacraments are administered, and, as we shall see below, can change the manner of their administration and the ceremonies that surround them. However, she cannot make a Sacrament be other than what Christ intended, and she cannot create new Sacraments. The acceptance of the traditional Sacraments in their traditional form is part of that obedience that the faithful Catholic (which obviously should include members of the hierarchy[15]) owes to Christ through tradition. As evidence to this anti-innovative attitude consider the following letter of Pope Innocent I (pope, 401–417) addressed to the Bishop of Gubbio:

> If the Priests of the Lord wish to preserve in their entirety the ecclesiastical institutions, as they were handed down by the blessed Apostles, let there be no diversity, no variety in Orders and Consecrations.... Who cannot know, who would not notice that what was handed down to the Roman Church by Peter, the Prince of the Apostles, is preserved even until now and ought to be observed by all, and that nothing ought to be changed or introduced without this authority....

As St. Bernard says, "It suffices for us not to wish to be better than our fathers."

---

15. This principle is well expressed by the phrase that "members of the teaching Church (the hierarchy) must first of all be members of the believing Church."

OTHER REQUIREMENTS FOR VALIDITY

All that has been said so far being granted, it behooves us to ask just what is required for a sacrament to be valid. The Church's answer is usually given under several headings. There must be a proper minister—and where the minister is a priest, he must be validly ordained; the minister must have the proper intention; there must be proper "form" and "matter'; the recipient must be capable of receiving the sacrament. If any one of these are faulty or absent, the Sacrament is not effective. Each of these requirements will be considered sequentially.

THE MINISTER: For administering Baptism validly no special ordination is required. Anyone, even a pagan, can baptize, providing that he use the proper matter and pronounce the words of the essential form with the intention of doing what the Church does or what Christ intended. However, only a Bishop, Priest, or in some cases a Deacon, can administer Baptism in a solemn manner.[16] In marriage the contracting parties are the ministers of the Sacrament, because they make the contract and the Sacrament is the contract raised by Christ to the dignity of a Sacrament.[17]

All the other Sacraments require a duly ordained minister by which term Catholics understand a priest.

INTENTION: The Minister must have the proper intention. That is, he must intend to do what the Church intends, or what Christ intends (which is in fact the same thing). Intention is usually seen as having both an external and internal aspect. The external intention is provided to the minister by the rite he uses and it is assumed that he intends what the rite intends. His internal intention is another matter and can never be known with certainty unless he exposes it or makes it known. The minister can, by withholding his internal

---

16. In hospitals, nurses often baptize infants in danger of death. However, to baptize outside the case of necessity is to usurp a priestly function.

17. Strictly speaking, the priest is the witness on the part of the Church to this contractual Sacrament. This is further confirmed by the fact that in countries or locations where a priest is not available for long periods of time, a couple can marry, and when the priest arrives, the marriage is "solemnized." Again, a valid Protestant marriage is not repeated when the parties become Catholic.

intention, or having an internal intention that contradicts that of the rite, obviate or prevent the effect of a Sacrament. The Church, recognizing that it can never know the internal intention of the minister, assumes it is the same as his external intention, (the intention which the traditional rite provides by its very wording) unless he himself informs the Church otherwise.[18]

PROPER FORM AND MATTER: It is well known that the manner of administering the Sacraments was confided by Christ to His Church.

We know that Christ specified certain sacraments in a precise manner—*in specie* to use the theological term. Such is the case with both Baptism and the Eucharist. With regard to the other sacraments, it is generally held that He only specified their matter and form *in genere*—in a general way, leaving to the Apostles the care and power of determining them more precisely.

> Christ determined what special graces were to be conferred by means of external rites: for some Sacraments (e.g., Baptism, the Eucharist) He determined minutely (*in specie*) the matter and form: for others He determined only in a general way (*in genere*) that there should be an external ceremony, by which special graces were to be conferred, leaving to the Apostles or to the Church the power to determine whatever He had not determined—e.g., to prescribe the matter and form of the Sacraments of Confirmation and of Holy Orders.[19]

Now the Church has been around for a long time, and has long since determined the essential components of the Sacraments—almost certainly within the lifetime of the Apostles. These essentials are part of tradition and cannot be changed at will—not by any

---

18. There was a bishop in South America who was strongly prejudiced against ordaining "native" clergy. On his deathbed he confessed that when it came to native clergy he had always withheld his intention. The priest who heard his confession refused him absolution unless he gave permission for this fact to be exposed to the proper authorities. This permission was granted. All the native clergy involved were re-ordained. Such episodes are extremely rare in the history of the Church, and for obvious reasons not normally made public.

19. See *The Catholic Encyclopedia*, v. 13, p. 299.

individual, not by a council, and not even by a pope. This principle was made clear by Leo XIII in his Bull *Apostolicae Curae*:

> The Church is forbidden to change, or even touch, the matter or form of any Sacrament. She may indeed change or abolish or introduce something in the non-essential rites or "ceremonial" parts to be used in the administration of the Sacraments, such as the processions, prayers or hymns, before or after the actual words of the form are recited....
>
> It is well known that to the Church there belongs no right whatsoever to innovate anything on the substance of the Sacraments.
>
> Pius X, *Ex Quo Nono*

> It [the Council of Trent] declares furthermore that this power has always been in the Church, that in the administration of the sacraments, *without violating their substance*, she may determine or change whatever she may judge to be more expedient for the benefit of those who receive them....
>
> Session, XXI, Chapter 2, Council of Trent

The crux of the debate about "substance" revolves around the issue of "meaning." Thus, as we shall see, in some of the Sacraments, the form used varied over the centuries, and in the different (traditionally recognized) Churches. But providing the "meaning" of the form was not changed, the words used substantially carried the same import that Christ intended. This is clearly the teaching of St. Thomas:

> It is clear, if any substantial part of the sacramental form is suppressed, that the essential sense of the words is destroyed, and consequently the Sacrament is invalid.
> *Summa* III, Q. 60, Art. 8

Sacramental terminology can be confusing. "The substance of the form" refers to the words that convey its meaning. "The essential words of the form" are those words on which the substance depends. Theologians will argue about what the essential words are, but all agree on the need to maintain the integrity (i.e. the completeness) of the received forms.[20] Again, a form may contain the "essential words" but be invalidated by the addition of other words that change its meaning. As the *Missale Romanum* states, "if words are added which do not alter the meaning, then the Sacrament is valid, but the celebrant commits a mortal sin in making such an addition" (*De Defectibus*).

THE RECIPIENT: The previous reception of Baptism (by water) is an essential condition for the valid reception of any other sacrament. In adults, the valid reception of any Sacrament apart from the Eucharist requires that they have the intention of receiving it. The Sacraments impose obligations and confer grace, and Christ does not wish to impose those obligations or confer grace without the consent of man. There are certain obvious impediments to reception of the Sacraments, such as the rule that women cannot be ordained. Finally, according to ecclesiastical law, a married person cannot receive ordination (in the Western Church), and a priest who has not been laicized cannot enter the state of Matrimony.[21] There are various impediments to priestly ordination for men such as age or blindness. Obviously, someone who is blind cannot say Mass without risk of spilling the consecrated species.

The reason the Sacrament of the Eucharist is excepted from this rule is that the Eucharist is always, and always remains, the Body of Christ, regardless of the state of the recipient.

In general, attention on the part of the recipient is not essential. Obviously inattention is disrespectful of the sacred and an intentional indulgence in "distractions" would involve a proportional sin.

---

20. An illustration of this is the phrase "*Hoc est enim corpus meum*" ("For this is my body") from the traditional Mass. The elimination of the word "for" (*enim*) would not change the meaning of the phrase. Hence it would not lead to a substantial change. It follows that "for" is not an "essential" word. The "integrity" of the form however requires that it be used, and the priest sins gravely if he intentionally fails to use it.

21. A widower can of course receive Holy Orders. Married individuals who have fulfilled their obligations to the state of marriage, may, with their wife's permission, by special dispensation, (and taking the vow of celibacy) receive Holy Orders. Similarly, older couples may, by mutual consent, both enter the religious state. The Eastern Church allows for married (non-celibate) priests. Eleven of the Twelve Apostles were married (cf. St. Paul's Epistle to Timothy, chap. III, 1–7).

In Penance however, because the acts of the penitent—contrition, confession, and willingness to accept a penance in satisfaction are necessary to the efficacy of the rite, a sufficient degree of attention to allow for these is necessary.

Obviously, the recipient of a Sacrament would sin gravely if he received the sacrament (Penance apart) when not in a state of grace, or sin proportionally if he received them in a manner not approved by the Church.

Having enumerated these principles, we shall discuss some of the other Sacraments, with the obvious exception of the Holy Sacrifice of the Mass and the Eucharist which has been covered in a previous book [*The Problems with the New Mass*].

WHAT TO DO WHEN THERE IS DOUBT ABOUT A SACRAMENT

The Church, being a loving mother, desires, and indeed requires, that the faithful never be in doubt about the validity of the sacraments. For a priest to offer doubtful Sacraments is clearly sacrilegious and where this doubt is shared by the faithful, they also are guilty of sacrilege. As Father Brey states in his introduction to Patrick Henry Omlor's book *Questioning the Validity of the Masses Using the New All-English Canon*:

> *In practice*, the very raising of questions or doubts about the validity of a given manner of confecting a sacrament—if this question is based on an apparent defect of matter or form—would necessitate the strict abstention from use of that doubtful manner of performing the sacramental act, *until the doubts are resolved*. In confecting the Sacraments, all priests *are obliged* to follow the *medium certum*—that is, "the safer course."[22]

Similarly, Father Henry Davis, S.J.:

> In conferring the Sacraments, as also in the consecration in Mass, it is never allowed to adopt a probable course of action as to valid-

---

22. Patrick Henry Omlor, *Questioning the Validity of the Masses Using the New, All-English Canon* (Reno, NV: Athanasius, 1969).

ity and to abandon the safer course. The contrary was explicitly condemned by Pope Innocent XI [1670–1676]. To do so would be a grievous sin against religion, namely an act of irreverence towards what Christ Our Lord has instituted. It would be a grievous sin against charity, as the recipient would probably be deprived of the graces and effects of the sacrament. It would be a grievous sin against justice, as the recipient has a right to valid sacraments.[23]

POST-CONCILIAR CHANGES IN THE SACRAMENTS

It is well known that the Post-Conciliar Church changed all the Sacraments. While the changes in the Mass were discussed in my previous book,[24] they will be briefly reviewed before proceeding to consider the changes in the other Sacraments that either affect the priesthood or depend upon the priesthood for their confection.

THE MASS

The *Novus Ordo Missae* or new mass was promulgated on April 3, 1969, the Feast of the Jewish Passover. The traditional rite had been divided into two parts, "the Mass of the Catechumens" and "the Mass of the Faithful." The new rite was also divided into two parts, "the Liturgy of the Word," and "the Liturgy of the Eucharist." This change was in itself significant, for the term "Word," which was traditionally applied to the Sacred Species—the "Word made flesh," was now tied to the reading from Scripture. In similar fashion, the second part of the new rite stressed "Eucharist" which means thanksgiving—for indeed the new rite was merely a "sacrifice of praise and thanksgiving." All references to it being an immolative sacrifice "for the living and the dead" or the "unbloody representation of the sacrifice of the cross" have been deleted. The net result is a service which is in no way offensive to Protestants—and indeed, the Superior Consistory of the Church of the Augsburg Confession

---

23. Fr. Henry Davis, S.J., *Moral and Pastoral Theology* (London: Sheed and Ward, 1936) v. 2, p. 27.
24. Rama Coomaraswamy, M.D., *The Problems with the New Mass*, TAN, 1990.

of Alsace and Lorraine, a major Lutheran authority, have publicly acknowledged their willingness to take part in the "Catholic eucharistic celebration" because it allows them "to use these new eucharistic prayers with which they felt at home." And why did they feel at home with them? Because they had "the advantage of giving a different interpretation to the theology of the Sacrifice."[25]

The net result then is a rite which is, at best, dubiously Catholic. Closer examination tends to support the suspicion that it is indeed Protestant in outlook. Consider the definition initially given to the rite by Paul VI who is responsible for promulgating it with seemingly Apostolic authority:

> The Lord's Supper or Mass is the sacred assembly or congregation of the people of God gathered together, with a priest presiding, in order to celebrate the memorial of the Lord. For this reason Christ's promise applies supremely to such a local gathering together of the Church: "Where two or three are gathered in my name, there am I in their midst" (Matt. 1:20).
>
> *Documents on the Liturgy*, No. 1397[26]

The definition is extraordinary because it declares that Christ is no more present when the *Novus Ordo Missae* is said than He is when I gather my children for evening prayers. Moreover, whereas in the traditional rite it is clearly the priest alone who celebrates, the above definition clearly implies that the function of the priest is only to "preside," and that the supposed confection of the sacrament is effected not by the priest, but by "the people of God." One has only to leave out the prepositional phrase "with a priest presiding" to see that the action is performed by the "assembly or congregation of the people of God gathered together."

---

25. In similar manner, many other Protestant and Anglican groups either use the *Novus Ordo Missae* or have brought their own rites into concordance with it.

26. *Documents on the Liturgy*, 1963–1979, published by The Liturgical Press, Collegeville, MN, 1982. This text provides official translations of the innumerable Post-Conciliar documents related to liturgical matters. This definition is to be found in paragraph 7 of the *General Instruction* that accompanies the *Novus Ordo Missae*, an instruction which explains its meaning and the rubrics attached to it.

So offensive was this definition that Paul VI found it necessary to revise it shortly after its promulgation. Its new form reads:

> At Mass or the Lord's Supper, the people of God are called together, with a priest presiding and acting in the person of Christ, to celebrate the memorial of the Lord or eucharistic sacrifice. For this reason Christ's promise applies supremely to such a local gathering together of the Church: "Where two or three are gathered in my name, there am I in their midst" (Matt. 17:20).

In changing the definition Paul VI was careful to point out that no doctrinal differences existed between this and the former definition, and that "the amendments were only a matter of style." The stylistic change is that the presiding priest is now acting in the person of Christ. However, his function is still that of "presiding"; it is still the "people of God" who are called together to celebrate the memorial of the Lord; and the parallel with evening family prayers is retained. True, we find the traditional phrase of the priest "acting in the person of Christ." But it should be remembered that a priest can act in the person of Christ in a variety of ways other than as a sacrificing priest (which is the essential and traditional understanding of the nature of the priesthood), as for example, when he teaches, exhorts, counsels or exorcises in the name of the Lord.[27] Does the priest in saying the *Novus Ordo* provide or perform any sacrifice other than that of "praise and thanksgiving" such as Protestants believe is appropriate to Sunday services? Nowhere in the *General Instruction* (or in the rite itself) is it made clear that such occurs.

---

27. A further addition was made in the definition given in paragraph 7 of the new *General Instruction*. After the quotation from *Matthew* it added:

> For the celebration of Mass, which perpetuates the sacrifice of the cross, Christ is really present to the assembly gathered in his name; he is present in the person of the minister, in his own word, and indeed substantially and permanently present under the eucharistic elements.

Once again, there is nothing in these ambiguous phrases that would really offend a Protestant. Nowhere are we informed that the celebration involved is other than a memorial—and the very word "memorial," like the phrase "the Lord's Supper," is another 16th century Protestant Reformation term used to distinguish a Protestant service from the Catholic Mass. There is a very striking similarity between

And indeed, as we shall see, all reference to the priest performing any sacrificial function (apart from praise and thanksgiving) has also been deleted from the new rites of ordination.[28]

Consideration of the other aspects of the new rite—the *Novus Ordo Missae*—tend to confirm its Protestant and non-sacrificial orientation. Consider the fact that the Words of Consecration are no longer called the "Words of Consecration," but only the "Words of Our Lord." While the point may seem minor, it raises the question of whether any consecration in fact occurs. Moreover these words are part of the "Narration of the Institution," (an entirely new phrase to Catholic theology). Nowhere is the priest instructed to say the words of Consecration "in the person of Christ." If one follows the rubrics of the *General Instruction* (such as obedience presumably requires), they are simply said as part of the history of what occurred at the Last Supper. Now, the traditional Church has always taught that when the words are read as part of a narrative—as occurs when one reads the Gospel—no Consecration occurs. The priest must say the words *in persona Christi*, as something happening "here and now,"

---

this new phraseology and the condemned declaration of the Jansenist Pseudo-Synod of Pistoia which stated:

> After the consecration Christ is truly, really and substantially present beneath the appearances (of bread and wine), and the whole substance of the bread and wine has ceased to exist, leaving only the appearances.

This proposition was condemned by the Bull *Auctorum Fidei* as "pernicious, derogatory to the exposition of Catholic Truth about the dogma of transubstantiation, and favoring heretics." (Fr. Heinrich Denzinger, *Enchiridion Symbolorum, Definitionum et Declarationum de Rebus Fidei et Morum*, §1529). The reason it was condemned is that "it entirely omits to make any mention of *transubstantiation* or the *conversion* of the entire substance of bread into the Body, and of the whole substance of wine into the Blood which the Council of Trent defined as an article of faith."

And finally, this addition states that Christ is "really" present, as much in the assembly as in the priest and in His (Christ's) words. There is nothing within the "new" *General Instruction* to suggest to us that He is any more present in any other parties or "elements" then He is in the assembly of the people.

28. Michael Davies assures us that we can ignore the *General Introduction* and be secure with the validity of the New Mass. This is just another example of his picking and choosing which magisterial documents he likes. What priest would ever ignore *De Defectibus* which discusses the rubrics of the traditional Mass?

or the Sacred Species are not confected. Truly the new mass has changed the "immolative sacrifice" into a mere "memorial."

And what of the supposed "Words of Our Lord"? I say "supposed" because these words were also significantly changed by Paul VI. The words used by Our Lord at the Last Supper are well known—they have been handed down to us by Tradition since time immemorial. These words are not exactly the same as those found in the Gospel renditions and there was absolutely no justification for changing them to bring them into line with Scripture. (And even less for bringing them into line with the Lutheran service.) It should be remembered that the true Mass existed years before the first Scriptures were written down (and long before Luther came on the scene); one can assume that the Apostles took great care to use the exact words specified by our Lord at the "Last Supper" for the Consecration. (The twelve Apostles said Mass in slightly different ways, but always preserved these words with great care—and to this day in the 80 or more different traditional rites which have been in use in various parts of the world, preserve these words exactly.) But not only did Paul VI change the words of our Lord traditionally used in the Consecration formulas, he also altered them so that they no longer even conform to those found in Scripture. The Church has throughout the ages taught that Christ's Sacrifice on the Cross was sufficient to save all men, but that on our part it does not effectually save all, but only those that cooperate with grace. Thus it is that the traditional formula for Consecrations says "for you and for many."[29] However, the new rite insistently translates this phrase as "for you and for all," thus attacking the theological (and logical) principle that distinguishes sufficiency from efficiency, and leading one to assume that as a result of the historical Sacrifice of the Cross, all men are saved. Such a change of meaning in the Consecratory formula attacks the "substance" of the rite and even taken in isolation—apart from the numerous other defects indicated—certainly renders it of dubious validity.

---

29. While the Latin *multis* is preserved, in almost all the translations—the approval of which specifically rested with Paul VI—the word *multis* has been translated by "all."

Such then are but two or three of the ways in which the Mass inherited from the Apostles has been altered. Space does not allow for a fuller discussion and the reader is referred to the author's *The Problems with the New Mass* for a more detailed consideration. The primary intent of the present book is not to discuss the Mass, but rather the other Sacraments—principally Holy Orders and the Sacraments dependent upon it.

2

THE SACRAMENT OF ORDER

We shall consider Holy Orders first because it is that Sacrament by means of which priests are ordained, that is, given the power to say Mass and administer the other Sacraments pertinent to their function. It is said to imprint a "sacramental character" on the recipients that provides them with the special graces necessary for them to fulfill their high calling and to act "*in persona Christi.*" Priests are ordained by bishops who are consecrated by other bishops going back in an "initiatic chain" to the Apostles, and hence it is through the episcopacy that the Apostolic Succession is passed on.[1] It follows that, if the ordination rite for bishops were in some way to be nullified and rendered invalid, priests ordained by them would not be priests, and all the other sacraments dependent upon this high estate would be rendered null and void.[2] In order to place the subject under consideration in a proper perspective it will be necessary to define the "Sacrament of Order," to determine whether the rite of episcopal consecration is a true Sacrament, to specify what is required for validity, and then to examine the new rite and see whether it "signifies the grace" which it is meant to effect, and "effects the grace" which it is meant to signify.

Considerable perplexity arises from the fact that while the Sacrament of Order is one, it is conferred in stages. In the Western

---

1. Apostolic Succession is to be distinguished from "Apostolicity." The Bishops are the spiritual descendents of the Apostles, and hence the Apostolic Succession is passed on through them. Apostolicity however is one of the qualities of the true Church, not only because it preserves the Apostolic Succession, but also because it teaches the same doctrines and uses the same rites that the Apostles did.

2. The phrase "null and void" was used with regard to Anglican Orders by Pope Leo XIII.

Church these are divided into seven steps—the "Minor Orders" of acolyte, exorcist, lector and doorkeeper (porter); and the "Major Orders" of the subdeaconate, deaconate and priesthood. Almost at once confusion enters the picture, for some of the ancient texts list six, others eight and nine. In the Greek Church, the rites of which are considered unquestionably valid, subdeacons are listed in the "minor" category. In all the Churches that recognize Orders as a Sacrament (the Protestants—which category includes Anglicans—do not) we find both Deacons and Priests are "ordained" and that the Episcopate or rank of Bishop is included under the heading of Priests; it is in fact called the *summum sacerdotium* or the "fullness of the priesthood." Higher ranks in the Church such as Archbishop, Cardinal or Pope, are considered administrative and not Sacramental. Thus once a Pope is elected he is installed with appropriate ceremonies, but not with a sacramental rite.[3]

For the sake of completeness it should be noted that an ordinand (an individual about to be ordained) to any order automatically receives the graces pertaining to a lesser order. (This principle is called *per saltum*, or "by jumping"). Thus if an individual were consecrated to the priesthood without receiving the lesser orders, he would automatically receive all the power and graces that relate to the lesser orders such as, for example, exorcism. The Post-Conciliar Church has abolished many of the minor orders, but if this Church validly ordains priests, then these priests automatically receive the powers that pertain to these lower and "abolished" orders. However, when it comes to Bishops, almost all theologians hold that they must already be ordained priests, lacking which the Episcopal rite conveys nothing. The Church has never infallibly pronounced on this issue and contrary opinion—namely that the Episcopal rite automatically confers on the recipient the character of priestly orders—exists.[4] So critical is the Apostolic Succession that it is the

---

3. Sacramentally speaking there is no higher rank than that of Bishop. Such a statement in no way denies or repudiates the teaching of the Church on the Primacy of Peter.

4. Cardinal Gasparri in *De Sacra Ordinatione*, and Lennertz in his *De Sacramento Ordinis* both hold that the recipient of Episcopal Orders automatically receives—if he does not already have it—the powers of the priesthood. It is difficult

customary practice of the Church to ordain a bishop with three other bishops. The rule is not absolute, for validity only requires one, and innumerable examples of where this custom has been bypassed can be given.

It is of interest that many traditional theologians have questioned whether the elevation of a Priest to the rank of Bishop is a sacramental or juridical act. The point is important because (1) it implies that an ordinary priest has the ability (not the right) to ordain (make other priests), and because (2), if the episcopal rite involves no "imprinting of a sacramental character," the question of validity can hardly arise. However, in so far as the ordination of Bishops has a "form" and a "matter," the greater majority hold that it is in fact a Sacrament—or rather that it is the completion of the Sacrament of Orders and confers upon the ordinand the "fullness of priestly powers" and functions. Leo XIII clearly taught that such was the case. To quote him directly: "The episcopate, by Christ's institution, belongs most truly to the Sacrament of Order and is the priesthood in the highest degree; it is what the holy Fathers and our own liturgical usage call the high priesthood, the summit of the sacred ministry" (*Apostolicae Curae*).

DISTINCTIONS BETWEEN THE PRIEST AND THE BISHOP

In the traditional ordination rite of the priest, the Bishop instructs him that his function is "to offer sacrifice, to bless, to guide, to preach and to baptize." (In the Post-Conciliar rite this instruction has been deleted and the priest is consecrated to "celebrate" the liturgy which of course means the *Novus Ordo Missae*.)[5] Such an instruction is not all-inclusive, for it mentions nothing of the power

---

to see why this should not be the case since he receives the *Summum Sacerdotium* or fullness of the priesthood. The issue is discussed in *Anglican Orders and Defect of Intention* by Francis Clark, S.J. (subsequently laicized) (London: Longmans, Green, 1956)

5. Those who would question this statement would do well to read the Vatican Instruction entitled *Doctrina et Exemplo* on The Liturgical Formation of Future Priests (*Documents on the Liturgy*, no. 332, The Liturgical Press, Collegeville, MN). They will find no recommendation that seminarians be taught anything about the Sacrificial nature of their function or about the Real Presence.

of absolution—its intent being to specify the principal functions of the priest. The power to absolve is however clearly specified in other parts of the traditional rite. (Again, the Post-Conciliar rite has abolished the prayer that specifies this power.)

Bishops however have certain powers over and beyond those of priests. According to the Council of Trent, "Bishops, who have succeeded to the position of the Apostles, belong especially to the hierarchical order; they are set up, as the same Apostle [St. Paul] says, by the Holy Ghost to rule the Church of God; they are superior to priests, and can confer the Sacrament of Confirmation, ordain ministers of the Church, and do several other functions which the rest who are of an inferior order have no power to perform" (Fr. Heinrich Denzinger, *Enchiridion Symbolorum, Definitionum et Declarationum de Rebus Fidei et Morum*, §960). Again, the seventh canon on the Sacrament of Orders states: "If anyone says the bishops are not superior to priests, or have not the power of confirming and ordaining, or have that power but hold it in common with priests... let him be anathema" (ibid., 967).

However, as Father Bligh states in his study on the history of Ordination: "From the practice of the Church it is quite certain that a simple priest can in certain circumstances (now not at all rare) administer Confirmation validly, and it is almost certain that with Papal authorization he can validly ordain even to the deaconate and priesthood. The Decree for the Armenians drawn up by the Council of Florence in 1439 says that the Bishop is the **ordinary** minister of Confirmation and the **ordinary** minister of Ordination—which would seem to imply that in extraordinary circumstances the minister of either Sacrament can be a priest. Since the decree *Spiritus Sancti Munera* of 14 September 1946, it has been the common law in the Latin Church that all parish priests may confer the sacrament of Confirmation on their subjects in danger of death. And there exist four Papal Bulls of the fifteenth century which empowered Abbots, who were not Bishops, but simple priests, to ordain their subjects to Sacred Orders; two of them explicitly give powers to ordain "even to the priesthood."[6] Some have held that such ordinations were invalid

---

6. John Bligh, S.J., *Ordination to the Priesthood* (NY: Sheed and Ward, 1956).

because the popes were acting "under duress," but the fact remains that, at least with regard to the Deaconate, these powers were exercised for centuries without papal objection. In the Greek and other "Eastern Churches," the priest is the ordinary minister of Confirmation and the Bishop is the Ordinary minister of Ordination.[7]

Canon Law (1917) states that "the ordinary minister of sacred ordination is a consecrated bishop; the extraordinary minister is one, who, though without episcopal character, has received either by law or by a special indult from the Holy See power to confer some orders" (CIC 782 and 951). Now the term "extraordinary minister" is important, for it is commonly used with regard to the priest who administers the Sacrament of Confirmation; in the Post-Conciliar Church it is used to describe lay-persons who distribute the bread and wine. And so it seems necessary to conclude that a simple priest can, by Apostolic indult, be given certain powers, or, since no additional ceremony is involved, the right to exercise certain powers that normally are not considered appropriate to his status. One could draw a parallel with the Sacrament of Baptism which is normally administered by a priest, but which under certain circumstances can be administered by any Catholic [or even any pagan, if the form, matter and intention are valid—ED].

How are we to resolve these seeming conflicts? One solution is to consider the right of conferring Orders as juridical. When Pope Pius XII gave permission for parish priests to become extraordinary ministers of Confirmation, he did not confer this power by means of a sacramental rite, but through a mandate. Thus, one could hold that by his ordination every priest receives the power to confirm and ordain, but cannot utilize these powers without papal authorization. As Father Bligh says, "by his ordination to the priesthood a man receives no power whatever to confirm or ordain…" He, however, is stamped with an indelible character so that "he is a fit person to whom episcopal or Papal authority can communicate power when it seems good."

---

7. It is of interest that during the present century 12 priests of the Russian Orthodox Church, not wishing to be under state approved (KGB) Bishops, gathered together and ordained a priest.

On the assumption that the matter is jurisdictional, several questions can be raised. Did Christ Our Lord Himself lay down the rule that in normal—or perhaps all—circumstances, only bishops should confirm and ordain? Was this rule laid down by the Apostles in virtue of the authority they received from Christ? Is the rule sub-Apostolic, which would make it part of ecclesiastical law rather than revelation? Further, the necessity for the papal indult can be conceived of as arising either from an ecclesiastical law restricting the priest's valid use of his power, or from a divine law requiring that a priest who exercises these powers must receive a special authority or some kind of jurisdiction from the Pope. The Council of Trent deliberately left the answer to these questions open and undecided. In its sixth Canon on the Sacrament of Order it simply states:

> If anyone says that in the Catholic Church there is not a hierarchy, instituted by divine ordination and consisting of bishops, priests and deacons, let him be anathema.

Before adopting the phrase "by divine ordination" the Council considered the phrases "by divine institution" and "by a special divine ordination," but rejected them because it did not wish to decide the question.

Reference to the practice of the early Church suggests that normally all the Sacraments were administered either by the Bishop or by priests explicitly delegated by the Bishops. Bligh quotes De Puniet as saying that priests in Apostolic times administered the churches under the direction of the Apostles and almost certainly enjoyed the fullness of sacerdotal powers which included the power of ordination. St. Jerome taught that the priest at his ordination received the power to ordain, which power was immediately restricted ecclesiastically. Even in mediaeval times, after the bishops ordained a priest, the other clergy present would place their hands on the head of the ordinands (the "matter" of the rite) and repeat the consecratory prayer—thus acting as "concelebrants." In current traditional practice the priests bless the ordinands by placing their hands on their heads, but they no longer repeat the consecratory form. The point is important for under such circumstances it is clearly only the bishop who ordains. The Post-Conciliar Church retains this practice.

IS THE BISHOP ORDAINED OR CONSECRATED?

The question as posed is illegitimate, for Pius XII uses both terms interchangeably in his *Sacramentum Ordinis*.[8] The real issue is whether or not the raising of a priest to the rank of Bishop involves a sacramental act or an administrative decision. According to *The Catholic Encyclopedia* (1908) "most of the older scholastics were of the opinion that the episcopate is not a Sacrament; this opinion finds able defenders even now (e.g., Billot's *De Sacramentis*), though the majority of theologians hold it as certain that the Bishop's ordination is a Sacrament."[9] Whatever the answer, two points are clear: 1) the Council of Trent defines that Bishops belong to a divinely instituted hierarchy, that they are superior to priests, and that they have the power of Confirming and Ordaining which is proper to them (Sess. XXIII, c. iv, can. 6 & 7), and 2). Leo XIII, as already noted, clearly teaches that the episcopate "belongs most truly to the Sacrament of Order," and Pius XII, in defining both the matter and form to be used in the rite, implicitly teaches that it is, indeed, a sacramental act. The position taken in this chapter is that, while the issue as to whether a simple priest receives the power (not the right) to ordain remains open, the Episcopate remains part of the Sacrament of Order. Despite the fact that the power to ordain is a lesser power than that of offering the propitiatory Sacrifice for the living and the dead (i.e, the Holy Mass), and despite the fact that the priest may indeed already have this power, one can certainly hold that special graces are required of a Bishop to properly perform his functions, and that these graces are transferred to him by means of a sacramental act. It is thus that the Bishop receives within this Sacrament what is called the "*summum sacerdotium*" or the "*fullness of the priesthood.*" Again, it should be stressed that in the ordination of priests, regardless of earlier practice, both in the traditional and the Post-Conciliar practice, it is only the Bishop who repeats both the matter and the form. Consequently, when a Bishop ordains, the

---

8. Pius XII, *Sacramentum Ordinis, Acta Apostolicae Sedis*, January 28, 1948.
9. Section on "Orders," *The Catholic Encyclopedia* (NY: Appelton, 1911 (vol. xi).

"validity" of his own orders and of his sacramental act remains not only essential, but critical.

A BRIEF HISTORY OF THE SACRAMENTAL RITE OF ORDINATION

The rites used for Ordination are to be found in the *Pontifical*, a book that contains all the rites and ceremonies that are normally reserved to Bishops. Such was not always the case, for the first time we find reference to Pontificals as such is around the year AD 950.

Prior to that time, however, ordination rites existed and were to be found in various collections under a variety of different titles. One of the earliest of such collections still extant is that compiled in Rome by the schismatic anti-Pope Hippolytus—about the year 217— and it is essentially from this source that Paul VI derived the new Post-Conciliar rite of episcopal ordination.[10] Next in time are the three famous "sacramentaries" of the Roman Church, called the *Leonine* (Pope St. Leo, died in 461), the *Gelasian* (Pope St. Gelasius, died in 496) and the *Gregorian* (Pope St. Gregory the Great, died in 604). These collections of ceremonies include ordination rites. The last was revised and introduced into the Carolingian Empire during the eighth century; it was subsequently further revised and eventually became the *Pontifical*, a title that as such dates from 954. In the thirteenth century the celebrated canonist Guillaume Durand once again revised the text and this in turn was the basis of the first printed Pontifical which was issued in 1485. With the advent of printing, greater uniformity throughout Christendom became possible and Pope Innocent VII formally recommended the use of this text to all the churches in communion with Rome. Now, presumably St. Leo did not himself create the ordination rite found in his sacramentary, but rather wrote down the practice of the Church as

---

10. Hippolytus was a schismatic bishop at the time that he compiled this text. Subsequently he was reconciled and died a martyr. His situation and the nature of this text is discussed in greater detail below. The reader is reminded that prior to the later part of the fourth century, the Church was under persecution. Documentation during this era is, as a result, sparse.

he received it. No significant change in the rites of the western Church occurred between the time of St. Leo (461) and 1968.

THE ESSENTIAL ASPECTS OF THE ORDINATION RITES

In the sixth chapter of the Acts, the disciples, at the bidding of the Apostles, chose seven deacons. "These were set before the Apostles; and they praying, imposed hands upon them." The two elements discernible in this unique description of the Apostolic rite, that is, the outward gesture of imposing hands and the recitation of a prayer, form the substance of the rite of ordination.[11]

Prior to the twelfth century liturgical and theological writers did not concern themselves with determining the precise moment of ordination or the exact words required for validity. They were inspired with the principle of retaining intact all that had been handed down to them, though they did not hesitate at times to elaborate the rites further with appropriate additions. They were doubtless satisfied with the knowledge that the whole rite properly performed conferred the priesthood. However, when one reads their explanations of the symbolism involved in the rites, one can conclude that they had opinions about what was essential as opposed to what was ceremonial—thus some thought that the sacrament was conferred by the imposition of hands on the ordinand's head, while others considered that it occurred when the bishop anointed the hands or gave the newly ordained priest the paten and chalice—the so-called "tradition of instruments."[12]

As noted above, it was William of Auxerre or St. Albert the Great who introduced the Aristotelian terminology of "matter" and "form" into the discussion, a pattern followed by St. Thomas Aquinas, St. Bonaventura and all subsequent writers. Yet these individuals had differing opinions as to just what constituted proper matter and form. Once again, however, it should be stressed that

---

11. Walter B. Clancy, *The Rites and Ceremonies of Sacred Ordination: A Historical Conspectus and a Canonical Commentary* (Washington, DC: The Catholic University of America, 1962).

12. "Tradition" in this context means "passing on" or "handing over."

they accepted without question the traditional rites of the Church handed down from time immemorial. They also recognized that these rites, like the Mass itself, had undergone certain changes in the way of appropriate additions (but not deletions) over the centuries. Thus for example, the tapping of the shoulder of the Deacon with the Scriptures could not have occurred prior to the Scriptures having been written, and this occurred years to decades after the death of our Lord. Again, the "tradition of instruments" was added to the rite some time after the fourth century and is not even mentioned in any ritual composed before AD 900. One must logically assume that the essential form and matter remained unchanged from the time of the Apostles who ordained the first Deacons and Priests. Appropriate additions, unlike deletions, do not affect validity.

DETERMINING THE "SUBSTANCE" OF THE SACRAMENTAL FORM

As noted above, the form and matter of Holy Orders were not among those given *in specie*, or precise detail, by Our Lord. These being established by the Apostles, the Church was free to change the words of the form, providing she retained their "substantial" nature as specified by Christ or the Apostles.

The first "semi-official" pronouncement by the Church on the issue of the necessary "form" is to be found in the Decree for the Armenians promulgated in 1439:

> The sixth Sacrament is that of Order; its matter is that by giving of which the Order is conferred: thus the priesthood is conferred by giving the chalice with wine and of a paten with bread.... The form of the priesthood is as follows: "Receive power to offer sacrifice in the Church for the living and the dead, in the name of the Father and the Son and the Holy Ghost."

This statement reflected the opinion of St. Thomas Aquinas and the shared common practice of the Roman and Armenian churches. It was however never considered as definitive. For one thing, the Greeks, the validity of whose Orders has never been questioned, do not practice the "tradition of instruments." For another, historical studies demonstrate that this practice was introduced sometime after the fourth century. Thus it is that the Fathers at the Council of Trent left the issue open and deliberately avoided defining either the matter or form of this sacrament.[13]

EVENTS DURING THE REFORMATION

Luther and those that followed after him clearly denied that the Mass was an immolative Sacrifice, and among other things, propitiatory for the living and the dead. If such is the case, it follows that there is no need for a priesthood. Hence it is that Protestants deny that Holy Orders and the rites that flow from Orders are in fact sacraments at all. (They only accept Baptism and Marriage as such.) However the reformers faced a serious problem. The laity were unwilling to accept as religious leaders individuals who were not in some way consecrated, and in whom they did not see the character of their familiar priests.[14] As a result, the reformers devised new rites aimed at incorporating their new and heterodox theology, but

---

13. As Pope Pius XII pointed out in his *Sacramentum Ordinis*, the Church at the Council of Florence did not demand that the Greek Church adopt the tradition of the instruments. Hence it followed that the Decree to the Armenians was not meant to define the tradition of the instruments as being substantial to the rite for ordaining priests. St. Alphonsus and Pope Benedict XIV were of the opinion that Eugene IV did not intend to determine the essential matter of the sacrament but desired simply to present a practical instruction to the Armenian Church concerning the use of the delivery of the instruments, and in no way sought to settle the question. (Clancy, op. cit., #32) Father P. Pourrat comments: "The *Decretum ad Armenos* is the official document of the Church that treats of the binary composition of the sacramental rite. It was, as we know, added to the decrees of the Council of Florence; yet it has not the value of a conciliar *definition* (Father Pourrat's italics). It is "merely a practical instruction" intended for the United Armenians, and not for the whole Church. Hence, although the decree is worthy of great regard, still it does not impose itself on our faith." (*Theology of the Sacraments* [St. Louis: B. Herder, 1914, p. 51]; also cf. section on "Orders" in *The Catholic Encyclopedia*, op. cit.)

14. It is never the common people—the laity—who desire changes. On the contrary, the majority of people prefer the security of stability, especially in religious matters. And in fact, it is virtually impossible for the laity to have wished for changes in the Sacrament of Orders insofar as their use was restricted to those in religion.

clothed them in the outward forms familiar to the people. In essence they did this by changing the form of the Sacrament, and by deleting any statements in the accompanying rites (what theologians call *significatio ex adjunctis*) that specified special powers and graces such as were pertinent to the priesthood or episcopacy.

In England, Cranmer (strongly influenced by both Luther and Calvin) was the individual who master-minded the changes during the reigns of Henry VIII and Edward VI—changes incorporated into the Anglican Ordinal.[15] During this period innumerable "presbyters" and "bishops" were "ordained" with rites aimed at voiding the Catholic understanding of their function.[16] Shortly after this first apostasy of the English realm the true faith was restored under Catholic Queen Mary. Almost at once the problem of the validity of these Cranmerian ordinations came into question.

In June of 1555 Pope Paul IV issued the Bull *Praeclara Carissimi*, in which he stated that anyone ordained a Bishop who was not *rite et recte ordinatus* (properly and correctly ordained) was to be ordained again. He further clarified this statement in another Brief entitled *Regimini Universalis* (issued October 1555) in which he stated *eos tantum episcopos et archiepiscopos qui non in forma ecclesiae ordinati et consecrati fuerunt, rite et recte ordinatos dici non posse* ("Anyone ordained to the rank of bishop or archbishop by rites other than those used by the Church are not properly and correctly ordained"). To be properly and correctly ordained it was necessary to use the "customary form of the Church." In accord with the traditional practice of the Church, the fact that rites were performed by

---

15. The Episcopalians use this ordinal. Prior to the American Revolution they were American Anglicans. However, the Anglican Church recognizes the King or Queen of England as the head of their church and such would have been inappropriate in America after 1776. Doctrinally however they are virtually the same ecclesiastical body. Thus for example, Episcopalians adhere to the same "39 articles" which among other things deny that the Mass is an immolative Sacrifice, or that the priesthood is a sacrament.

16. The Reformers "loved" the term *presbyter* which literally translated from the Latin meant "elder." This allowed them to use a Latin word meaning "priest" in an altered sense in English. (The early Church avoided using the term *sacerdos* or priest because of the confusion with the pagan priesthood that might result.)

schismatics did not invalidate them. Where doubt existed conditional re-ordination was required.

This practice of the Church did nothing to solve the issue of what was correct form and matter, and what has to be understood is that the theologians of that period were not concerned with determining the matter and the form, but with assuring themselves that the entire rite of the Church be used with the proper intention on the part of the officiating consecrator. But it was also a period when the number of Protestant sects was growing by leaps and bounds, and with them the number of rites containing major and minor changes. As in the Mass, minor changes did not necessarily invalidate the rite or even make it depart from what was considered customary form.

To make matters worse, affairs in the Anglican Church later took a conservative turn. After the reign of Queen Elizabeth the Puritans with their anti-sacramentarian attitudes gained increasing control. But in 1662 under Archbishop Laud, there was a reaction in the opposite direction which resulted in the creation of a "High Anglican" party that Romanized much of the Anglican liturgy while firmly retaining her reformist principles. Words were added to the consecratory forms of Orders to bring them closer to Catholic practice—specifically the term "priest" and "bishop" were introduced into their formulas and the claim put forth that the Anglican body was, like the Greek Church, separate but "orthodox." The "branch theory" was born and they claimed the status of a "sister Church." Regardless of the words used however, the adherence to Protestant theology (Anglicans still had to adhere to the "39 Articles") left these rites with at least a defect of intention.[17] And so the debates went on as to what was proper form and matter, and what

---

17. For the sake of completeness the form in the *Edwardine Ordinal* for the Anglican Priesthood is: "Receive the holy ghost: whose synnes thou doest forgeue, they are forgeuen: and whose synnes thou doest retayne, they are retayned: and bee thou a faithful dispensor of the word of God, and of his holy Sacraments. In the name of the father and the sonne and the holy ghost. Amen." This was changed in 1662 to: "Receive the Holy Ghost for the office and work of a Priest in the Church of God, now committed unto thee by the imposition of hands. Whose sins thou dost forgive," etc.

constituted the essential words required to confer the priestly and/or Episcopal character on ordinands.

A Sacrament must by definition be an "outward sign of inward grace instituted by Christ for our sanctification" (*Catechism of the Council of Trent.*) As Leo XIII stated in his *Apostolicae Curae*, "all know that the Sacraments of the New Law, as sensible and efficient signs of invisible grace, ought both to signify the grace which they effect, and effect the grace which they signify. Although the signification ought to be found in the essential rite, that is to say, in the 'matter and form', it still pertains chiefly to the 'form' since the 'matter' is the part which is not determined by itself but which is determined by the 'form.'" (One can illustrate this with Baptism where the matter is water and the form is "I baptize you in the Name of the Father and of the Son and of the Holy Ghost.") The "form" is then of paramount importance and it is primarily this which we will concern ourselves in what follows.

THE WORK OF FATHER JEAN MORAN

By the middle of the 17th century, both as a result of printing and the increase in international travel, scholars became familiar with the ordination rites in use throughout the world. In 1665, Jean Moran, a French Roman Catholic theologian, published a work in which he set out a large collection of ordination rites of both the Eastern and Western Churches. Following the principle that the matter and form must be things that are held in common by all these valid rites, he concluded that for matter what was required was

---

And for the Episcopate: "Take the Holy Goste, and remember that thou stirre up the grace of God, which is in thee, by imposicion of hands: for God hath not geuen us the spirite of feare, but of power and loue and of sobernesse." This was altered in 1662 to: "Receive the Holy Ghost for the office and work of a Bishop in the Church of God, now committed unto thee by the imposition of hands; In the name of the Father, and the Son, and the Holy Ghost. And remember that thou stir up" etc. Several theologians have stated their opinion that the 1662 forms would be valid "if used in a Catholic setting or in orthodox circumstances." (*Why are Anglican (Episcopalian) Orders Invalid?* by Ref. M.D. Forrest, M.S.C. (St. Paul, MN: Fathers Rumble and Carty's Radio Replies Press).

the imposition of hands,[18] and that all the forms agreed in requiring that the office conferred must be specified. To quote him directly:

> Let Protestants search all Catholic rituals not only of the West, but of the East; they will not find any one form of consecrating Bishops (or priests), that hath not the word Bishop (or priest) in it, or some others expressing the particular authority, the power of a Bishop (or priest) distinct from all other degrees of holy orders.

This of course was a private opinion and theologians continued to debate as to whether it was sufficient that the office conferred be mentioned in the other parts of the rite—the so-called principle of *significatio ex adjunctis*. Further, as already mentioned, Protestant sects who had in earlier times avoided the word "priest" like the plague, began to re-introduce the word "priest" within the context of their rites—understanding by the term "priest," not a "sacrificing priest," but an individual elected by the community to preach the Word of God. In a similar manner they re-introduced the term "Bishop"—but understood in a purely juridical or administrative sense and often translated as "overseer." This particular issue—namely, the need to mention the office of the ordinand within the "form"—was seemingly settled by Leo XIII's *Apostolicae Curae* which criticized the Anglican form prior to 1662 for lacking this specification, and criticized the Anglican form after 1662 for using the terms "priest" and "bishop" in other than the Catholic sense.

THE DEFINITION OF PIUS XII

As a result of the work of Jean Moran, Catholic theologians shifted the grounds of their objection to Protestant ordination rites. Two things became clear: (1) the fact that they had no "tradition of the instruments" could no longer be said to invalidate them, and (2) **the prayer "Accept the Holy Ghost" which the Anglicans used in their**

---

18. Because the matter has become a contentious issue in recent times, it should be noted that while usual practice involves the extension of both hands, it suffices if only one is extended over the head of the ordinand. (cf. discussion in *Dictionnaire de la Théologie Catholique*, Paris: Letouzey)

episcopal ordinations and which they claimed transferred the sacramental power, was not universally used, and hence could not be said to constitute an essential part of the rite. Debate on the issue of the "form" continued until 1947 when Pius XII determined for all future times just what the matter and the form for the Sacrament of Order was.

His definition is to be found in the Decree *Sacramentum Ordinis*,[19] which document has, according to such renowned theologians as J. M. Hervé and Felix Capello, all the characteristics of an infallible definition.[20] According to Father Bligh, "its purpose was not speculative... but practical." The rite itself was in no way changed, and indeed, Pius XII insisted that it should not be. His aim was "to put an end to scruples about the validity of Orders received by priests who felt that some possibly essential part of the long and complicated rite had not been properly performed in their cases." For the future it intended "to remove all disputes and controversy: the character, graces and powers of the sacrament are all conferred simultaneously by the imposition of hands and the words *Da quaesumus*... the other ceremonies—the vesting, anointing, tradition of instruments and second imposition of hands—do not effect

---

19. Pius XII, *Sacramentum Ordinis*, *Acta Apostolicae Sedis*, January 28, 1948.

20. Hervé, J.M., *Manuale Theologiae Dogmaticae*, Tom. iv, ed nova A Orentino Larnicol C.S. Sp. Recognita, 1962: "*Atque Pius XII, in Const. Apostl. 'Sacramentum Ordinis', ut omnino videtur, loquitur ut Pastor et Doctor Supremus, et vere definit doctrinam de fide vel moribus (doctrinam de essentia sacramenti Ordinis, quae intime connectitur cum aliis veritatibus revelatis), ab universa Ecclesia tenendum*" ["And Pius XII, in the Apostolic Constitution *Sacramentum Ordinis*, as is absolutely clear, speaks as the supreme shepherd and teacher, and truly defines a doctrine of faith or morals (the doctrine of the essence of the sacrament of Holy Orders, which is intimately connected with other revealed truths), which must be held by the whole Church"]. Similarly, Mgr. G.D. Smith argues that when the Church defines what is and what is not sufficient to confer a Sacrament, such decisions involve an implied infallibility. ("The Church and her Sacraments" in *Clergy Review*, April 1950, and referred to by Father Francis Clark in his *Anglican Orders and Defect in Intention*, op. cit., above). Father Clancy (op. cit., #32) gives many other authorities that concur in this opinion. To quote Francisco Miranda Vincente, Auxiliary Bishop of Toledo: "This Apostolic Constitution is a true and solemn dogmatic declaration, and at the same time, as the terms used in the fourth and fifth point indicate, it is a doctrinal and disciplinary decree."

what they signify; they signify in detail what has already been effected by the matter and the form."

FORM AND ESSENTIAL WORDS FOR ORDAINING PRIESTS (PIUS XII)

Pius XII stated that "the form consists of the words of the 'Preface', of which these are essential and required for validity":

*Da, **quaesumus**, omnipotens Pater, in hunc famulum tuum Presbyterii dignitatem; innova in visceribus eius **spiritum** sanctitatis, ut acceptum a Te, Deus, secundi meriti munus obtineat; censuramque morum exemplo suae conversationis insinuet.* ("Grant, we beseech Thee, Almighty Father, to this Thy servant, the dignity of the priesthood; renew the spirit of holiness within him so that he may obtain the office of the second rank received from Thee, O God, and may, by the example of his life, inculcate the pattern of holy living.")

Similarly, in the ordination of bishops, the same infallible document states that "the form consists of the words of the Preface of which the following are essential and therefore necessary for validity":

Comple in sacerdote tuo ministerii tui summum, et ornamentis totius glorificationis instructum coelestis unguenti rore sanctifica. ("Fill up in Thy priest the perfection [*summum* can also be translated "fullness"] of Thy ministry and sanctify him with the dew of Thy heavenly ointment, this thy servant decked out with the ornaments of all beauty").

It should be stressed that Pius XII in no way changed the rite—indeed, he stressed that the rite was to remain intact. At the end of the document he states:

We teach, declare, and determine this, all persons notwithstanding, no matter what special dignity they may have, and consequently we wish and order such in the Roman Pontifical.... No one therefore is allowed to infringe upon this Constitution given by us, nor should anyone dare to have the audacity to contradict it.

THE PROBLEM OF *SIGNIFICATIO EX ADJUNCTIS*

According to the majority of theologians, "Catholic theology teaches that if a properly constituted minister of a Sacrament uses due matter and form, with at least the minimum personal intention necessary, his sacrament is valid, even if he adheres to a sect which is openly heretical."[21] Now if this is the case, it would seem that the remainder of the rite—the so-called "ceremonial" part—is not essential for validity. (As has been pointed out elsewhere, a priest who uses these criteria within a non-Catholic rite is guilty of sacrilege, but sacrilege as such does not invalidate the Sacrament.)

Despite this principle, Pope Leo XIII taught that the revised 1662 form of Anglican Orders is invalid (among other reasons) because the terms "priest" and "bishop" mean vastly different things to Anglicans than they do to Catholics. This, he said, is made clear from the other parts of the Anglican rite which deliberately delete every reference to the sacrificial nature of these exalted states. To quote him directly:

> In the whole [Anglican] ordinal not only is there no clear mention of the sacrifice, of consecration, of the priesthood (*sacerdotium*), and of the power of consecrating and offering sacrifice, but, as We have just stated, every trace of these things which had been in such prayers of the Catholic rite as they had not only entirely rejected, was deliberately removed and struck out. . . .
>
> *Apostolicae Curae*

In the traditional Catholic rite innumerable references make it clear that the primary function of the priest is to offer the Sacrifice; his other functions are also delineated (so also with the Bishop). The fact that other parts of the rite make the meaning of the form quite clear is termed *significatio ex adjunctis*. It would seem that while a positive *significatio ex adjunctis* may not be essential for

---

21. Francis Clark, S.J., "*Les ordinations anglicaines, problème oecumenique*," *Gregorianum*, vol. 45, 1964. In essence, his address to the Fathers at Vatican II on this topic. See also his review of Michael Davies' *The Order of Melchisedech*.

validity, a negative one—as for example when every reference to the sacrificial nature of the priesthood is deliberately omitted—may invalidate the form.[22]

THE POST-CONCILIAR RITE FOR ORDAINING PRIESTS

The issue of *significatio ex adjunctis* becomes critical in evaluating the validity of the Post-Conciliar rite for ordaining priests. Like its Anglican prototype, the new Latin "form" contains the word "priest"; furthermore, the remainder of the new rite fails to specify the sacrificial nature of the priesthood.

It is interesting to consider Michael Davies' assessment of the new rite.[23] He points out that, while the "form" used in the new rite is not

---

22. The importance of *significatio ex adjunctis* is a confusing issue insofar as the Church teaches that "form, matter, valid orders and intention are all that are required for validity of the sacraments" (Council of Florence). Clearly, for a priest to fulfill these criteria in an inappropriate setting (as for example, a Satanic Mass), however sacrilegious, is possible. With regard to Anglican Orders, Leo XIII discussed the importance of the defects of the rite surrounding the form, but left the issue confused. As Francis Clark, S.J. points out, theologians have given seven different interpretations to his words (*Anglican Orders and Defect of Intention*). Francis Clark defines *significatio ex adjunctis* in the following terms: "The sacramental signification of an ordination rite is not necessarily limited to one phrase or formula, but can be clearly conveyed from many parts of the rite. These other parts could thus contribute, either individually or in combination, to determining the sacramental meaning of the operative formula in an unambiguous sense. Thus the wording of an ordination form, even if not specifically determinate in itself, can be given the required determination from its setting (*ex adjunctis*), that is, from the other prayers and actions of the rite, or even from the connotation of the ceremony as a whole in the religious context of the age" (*The Catholic Church and Anglican Orders*, CTS, 1962, quoted by Michael Davies in his *Order of Melchisedech*). The term "negative" *significatio ex adjunctis* is not hallowed by theological usage and is a phrase of convenience. Francis Clark lays great stress on this concept without using the term—cf. his *Anglican Orders and Defect of Intention*, op. cit. A clearer way of demonstrating negative *significatio ex adjunctis* is the following: a priest saying the proper words of Consecration in the Mass follows them with a statement or intention that negates the meaning of those words. The deliberate removal of all references to the sacrificial nature of the priesthood (or of ordaining for bishops) in the Anglican ordinal is equivalent to denying the purpose for which a man is ordained.

23. Taken from his *Order of Melchisedech* which strongly defends the validity and legitimacy of the new rite.

greatly different from that specified by Pius XII, it nevertheless contains nothing "to which any Protestant could take exception," and nothing that is "in the least incompatible with Protestant teaching." Now, if the form is "indeterminate," and if the remainder of the rite fails to specify that it intends to ordain sacrificing priests, then the new rite suffers from exactly the same defects as its Anglican prototype. The fact that Leo XIII irreformably condemned the Anglican rite on precisely these grounds obviously justifies raising questions about the validity of the Post-Conciliar result.

Paul VI promulgated the new ordination rites for deacon, priest and bishop with his Apostolic Constitution *Pontificalis Romani Recognitio* of 18 June 1968. Where the rite for ordaining a priest is concerned, the first point to make is that the matter and essential form designated by Pius XII in *Sacramentum Ordinis* remain unchanged. [This is not entirely true as the next section points out.—ED] This is a point in favor of the new rite. It is the only point in its favor. The traditional rite of ordination has been remodeled "in the most drastic manner," and following Cranmer's example, this has been achieved principally by the subtraction of "prayers and ceremonies in previous use," prayers and ceremonies which gave explicit sacerdotal signification to the indeterminate formula specified by Pius XII as the essential form. This formula does indeed state that the candidates for ordination are to be elevated to the priesthood—but so does the Anglican. Within the context of the traditional Roman Pontifical there was not the least suspicion of ambiguity—within the new rite there most certainly is. While the new rite in no way suggests that it is not intended to ordain sacrificing priests, where (and if) it does refer to the sacrifice of the Mass it does so in muted tones, and considerable stress is laid on the ministry of the Word—a change in emphasis well calculated to please the Protestants. Cranmer's reform has been followed not simply in the composition of the new Ordinal, denuded of almost every mandatory reference to the sacrifice of the Mass—the very term "Sacrifice of the Mass" does not occur in either the Latin or vernacular.

So much is this the case that Michael Davies believes that the strongest—and perhaps only—argument in favor of its validity is that it was promulgated by a valid Pope (Paul VI). While the principle that a valid pope cannot promulgate an invalid sacrament is correct, Michael Davies seems oblivious to the possibility that his argument can be inverted. If the rite is shown to be invalid, or for that matter, even doubtful, one is forced to question the legitimacy of the pope.[24]

Michael Davies is of course mistaken when he states that the Post-Conciliar "form" for ordaining priests is unchanged. Consider once again the words specified by Pius XII:

> *Da, **quaesumus**, omnipotens Pater, in hunc famulum tuum Presbyterii dignitatem; innova in visceribus eius **spiritum** sanctitatis, ut acceptum a Te, Deus, secundi meriti munus obtineat; censuramque morum exemplo suae conversationis insinuet.* ("Grant, we beseech Thee, Almighty Father, to this Thy servant, the dignity of the priesthood; renew the spirit of holiness within him so that he may obtain the office of the second rank received from Thee, O God, and may, by the example of his life, inculcate the pattern of holy living").

The sacrosanct character of the substance of a sacramental form has already been discussed. Pope Pius XII specified that for validity the Sacrament of Order must clearly specify the sacramental effects involved. These are, in the rite under consideration (*Sacramentum Ordinis*), the power of Order and the Grace of the Holy Ghost.

If we examine this new formula we see that the first part expresses the power of the priestly order, but not the grace of the Holy Ghost. The word "priesthood," however, has lost its specifically Catholic meaning during the past few centuries, so that the second sentence

---

24. It should be noted that Sacramental rites have never been considered valid because they were instituted by a Pontiff, but because they were instituted by Christ. A Pontiff may, when doubt arises, specify what it was that Christ intended. A pope cannot create a new Sacrament. Hence it is important to know whether the claim that the Post-Conciliar Sacraments are substantially the same as the traditional ones becomes important. If they are, then why the changes? If they are not, then are they Sacraments? In the second edition of *The Order of Melchisedech* Michael Davies considers it a "fundamental doctrine" that "any sacramental rite approved by the Pope must certainly be valid...." In essence, this means that should the pope say "'green apples' is a valid sacramental form," we must accept it.

fulfills two functions: it specifies that the priesthood is an "office of the second rank," and further specifies that the "grace of the Holy Ghost" accompanies the Sacrament.

When we come to the Post-Conciliar form, confusion reigns. In the Latin, the form specified in Paul VI's official promulgation (found in the *Pontificalis Romani Recognitio*) uses the phrase "*in hos famulos tuos* (similar to the traditional form and that of Pius XII), while the *Acta Apostolica*—equally official—uses the phrase "*his famulis tuis*." Further, regardless of which Post-Conciliar form is considered "official," both delete the word "*ut*."

What do these changes signify? The deletion of the word "*ut*" (meaning "so that") removes the causal relationship between the two sentences. No longer is it made clear that the ordinand receives the "office of the second rank" as a *result* of the "renewal of the Spirit of Holiness." Whether or not this invalidates the rite is open to question and much depends on the reason why *ut* was deleted.

By changing *in hos famulos tuos* (on these Thy servants) to *his famulis tuis*, not only are the words of Pius XII further altered, but their sense is changed. *In hos famulos tuos* implies giving something to the ordinand in such a manner that it enters into him and becomes interior to him. To specify *his famulis tuis* has the sense of giving something to someone merely as an external possession—without the idea of it entering into him and becoming part of him. The significance of this difference should hit home, as Father Jenkins points out, when we remember that we are speaking here of the order of priesthood which involves the indelible character imprinted upon the very soul of the recipient. This idea is clearly conveyed in the traditional expression, but not in the new form created by Paul VI.[25] Rather, the new formula communicates the idea that the priesthood is an external office (such as the "Presidency"), and such

---

25. Father William Jenkins has discussed this issue in great detail in *The Roman Catholic*, vol. III, No. 8 and 11 (1981) Oyster Bay Cove, NY, 11771. Still further confusion results from consulting *The Documents on the Liturgy, 1963–1979* (Collegeville, MN: Liturgical Press). Document 324 tells us that the Latin taken from *Acta Apostolicae Sedis* is *in hos famulos tuos*, but the current official English translation is "Grant to these servants of yours" rather than "confer on these Thy servants."

as Reformers believed in; therefore such a change in meaning is clearly "substantial."

Things are made even more confusing when the vernacular is used. The "provisional" ICEL (English) translation used between June 1968 and June 1970 asked the Ordinand be given "the dignity" of the "presbyterate." Now the term "presbyter" has been used throughout history by the Reformers to designate their non-Sacrificing and non-ordained "ministers." As I have clearly shown elsewhere, the term in English can in no way be considered as equivalent to "priest"—indeed, it signifies just the opposite, and even the High Anglicans reject its use.[26] This casts still further doubt on validity—as is recognized by the fact that after 1970 the ICEL translation no longer used it, but reverted to "priesthood." However, the innovators seem determined to maintain the doubtful status of the rite. Even though in 1970 they changed "presbyter" back to "priesthood," they also changed the meaning of the second part of the formula by mistranslating and changing "the office of the second rank" (the importance of which was demonstrated above) to "co-workers with the Order of bishops." Needless to say, this latter phrase is completely indeterminate and can mean almost anything except "office of the second rank."

Highly significant in the Post-Conciliar presidential "ordination" is the omission, or rather deletion, of the phrase which states that a priest is ordained according to the Order of Melchisedech, for Melchisedech, who is both king and priest, is a figure of the Messias who offers a sacrifice of bread and wine.[27]

Consider some of the other deletions. In the traditional rite the

---

26. Rama P. Coomaraswamy, M.D. *Once a Presbyter, Always a Presbyter*, The Roman Catholic, vol. V, no. 7, August 1983.

27. The significance of this omission is clarified when we read in Psalm 109 that "the Lord swore and will not repent: thou art a priest for ever after the Order of Melchizedek." St. Paul refers to this in Hebrews 7:21 when he says "For those [Jewish] priests were made without an oath by Him who said 'unto Him the Lord swore...,' by so much was Jesus made the surety of a better priesthood." It further distinguished the priesthood of Christ in which the Catholic priest shares, from the Aaronic priesthood which terminated with the Crucifixion. Cf. Rev. J.M. Neal and R.F. Littledak, *Commentary on the Psalms*, vol. III, p. 450 (London: Masters, 1874).

Bishop addresses those to be ordained stating "it is a priest's duty to offer the sacrifice, to bless, to lead, to preach and to baptize." This admonition has been abolished in the new ceremony. In the traditional rite, while the men to be ordained lie prostrate on the floor, the litany of saints is sung: "That thou wouldst recall all who have wandered from the unity of the Church, and lead all unbelievers to the light of the Gospel." This unecumenical petition is excluded. Again, in the traditional rite, after the newly ordained priests are vested with stole and chasuble, the Bishop recites a long prayer including the words "Theirs be the task to change with blessing undefiled, for the service of Thy people, bread and wine into the body and blood of Thy Son." This prayer has been abolished.

In the traditional rite, after the anointing and consecrating of the hands which are then bound together, the bishop extends to each priest the Chalice containing wine and water, with a paten and host upon it for the priest to touch, while he says to each: "Receive the power to offer sacrifice to God, and to celebrate Mass, both for the living and the dead in the name of the Lord." This has also been abolished. Again, just before the postcommunion, each new priest kneels before the Bishop who lays both hands upon his head and says: "Receive the Holy Ghost, Whose sins you shall forgive, they are forgiven them; and whose sins you shall retain, they are retained." Again, this has been abolished. The final blessing of the Bishop: "The blessing of God Almighty come down upon you and make you blessed in the priestly order, enabling you to offer propitiatory sacrifices for sins of the people to Almighty God" has been abolished. So much for the *significatio ex adjunctis* of the new rite.

But if all this is not enough to cast doubt on the validity of Post-Conciliar ordinations, there is yet more. Obviously, one of the requirements for valid ordination of a priest is a validly ordained Bishop. No matter how correct the rites used for the priesthood are, the absence of a validly ordained bishop would make the rite a farce.[28] Let us then look at what has been done for the Episcopate.

---

28. It is pertinent that the "bishops" selected for ordaining the priests of the Society of St. Peter ("The Pope's own Traditional Order") are Ratzinger and Meyer.

98 THE PROBLEMS WITH THE OTHER SACRAMENTS

COMPARING THE TRADITIONAL WITH THE POST-CONCILIAR MATTER AND FORM FOR ORDAINING BISHOPS

As noted above, Pope Pius XII, **while in no way changing the rite used since time immemorial**,[29] determined in a presumably infallible manner that:

> In the Ordination or Consecration of Bishops the matter is the imposition of hands which is done by the consecrating Bishop. The form consists of the words in the Preface of which the following are essential and therefore necessary for validity: *Comple in sacerdote tuo ministerii tui summam, et ornamentis totius glorificationis instructum coelestis unguenti rore sanctifica.* ("Fill up in Thy priest the perfection [*summam* can also be translated 'fullness'] of Thy ministry and sanctify him with the dew of Thy heavenly ointment, this thy servant decked out with the ornaments of all beauty.")

Later in the same document he states:

> We teach, declare, and determine this, all persons notwithstanding, no matter what special dignity they may have, and consequently we wish and order such in the *Roman Pontifical*.... No one therefore is allowed to infringe upon this Constitution given by us, nor should anyone dare to have the audacity to contradict it....

One would have thought that this statement by Pius XII had set-

---

Both of these received their episcopal "consecration" by the new rites to be discussed in the body of this text. If they are in fact not bishops, all the priests they ordain—even if they use the traditional rites as they state they intend to do—are no more priests than any layman.

29. As Pius XII stated in his *Apostolic Constitution*: "Those things which we have above declared and established regarding the matter and the form are not to be understood in such a way as to make it allowable for the other rites as prescribed in the *Roman Pontifical* to be neglected or passed over even in the slightest detail; nay, rather we order that all the prescriptions contained in the *Roman Pontifical* itself be faithfully observed and performed."

THE SACRAMENT OF ORDER   99

tled the issue once and for all. Not so! Only 20 years later we find Paul VI issuing his Apostolic Constitution entitled *Pontificalis Romani* (June 23, 1968) in which he retains the matter—the laying on of hands—but in which he specifies that the form for ordaining bishops is to be:

> *Et nunc effunde super hunc electum eam virtutem, quae a te est. Spiritum principalem, quem dedisti dilecto filio tuo Jesu Christo, quem ipse donavit sanctis apostolis, qui constituerunt Ecclesiam per singula loca, ut sanctuarium tuum, in gloriam et laudem indeficientem nominis tui.* ("So now pour forth upon this chosen one that power which is from You, the governing Spirit whom You gave to your beloved Son, Jesus Christ, the Spirit given by him to the holy apostles, who founded the Church in every place to be your temple for the unceasing glory and praise of your name.")[30]

We have then two forms, or more precisely two groups of "essential" words wherein the substance of the form is to be found, and both of which are stated to be required for validity. How are we to explain this apparent disparity? We know that the Church has the right to change the wording of the form for Holy Orders, but only in so far as she doesn't change their "substance" or meaning. The problem to be resolved then, is whether both forms mean the same thing. Several approaches are possible:

(1) We can compare the wording of the two forms and find those words or phrases held in common. Doing this however yields the following common element: the single word "*et*" which means "and." Now, **obviously "and" cannot represent the substantial aspect of these two forms and such an approach must be rejected as absurd.**

---

30. Pius XII said that the words in his form were "essential" and required for validity. Paul VI states that the words that constitute his form "belong to the nature of the rite and are consequently required for validity." He further states in the same document that "it is our will that these our decrees and prescriptions be firm and effective now and in the future, notwithstanding to the extent necessary, the apostolic constitutions and ordinances issued by our predecessors and other prescriptions, even those requiring particular mention and derogation." (*Pontificalis Romani, Acta Apostolicae Sedis,* July 29, 1968.)

(2) Another way to determine the substance of the form is to consider the various consecratory prayers in use throughout the universal Church (Eastern and Western). This was indeed done by Jean Moran, and still later, by the English bishops in their *A Vindication of the Bull Apostolicae Curae*.[31]

In each of the rites which the Catholic Church has recognized, the "essential form" is contained in a "consecrating prayer" to accompany the imposition of hands, and these prayers are in all cases of the same type, defining in some way or other the Order to which the candidate is being promoted, and beseeching God to bestow upon him the graces of his new state.[32]

They then proceed to give a list of these prayers which includes the ancient *Leonine Sacramentary* "still preserved in the modern Pontifical," the Greek, the Syro-Maronite (which is also the Syro-Jacobite), the Nestorian, the Armenian, the Coptic (or Alexandro-Jacobite) and the Abyssinian, together with the ancient Gallican, the rite in the Apostolic constitutions, and the "Canons of St. Hippolytus." They proceed to list the significant words respectively in each— the "High Priesthood" (*summi sacerdotii*), the "Pontifical dignity," the term "Bishop," the "perfect (or complete) priest," and the "Episcopate." This specification is to be found in all the known used forms (i.e., in the essential words of the various Western Catholic and Orthodox Churches).[33] It is even found in the Canons of Hip-

---

31. *A Vindication of the Bull Apostlicae Curae, A Letter on Anglican Orders by the Cardinal Archbishop and Bishops of the Province of Westminster in reply to the Letter Addressed to them by the Anglican Archbishops of Canterbury and York* (NY: Longmans, Green and Co., 1898); Also to be found in Bishop Peter Richard Kendrick's *The Validity of Anglican Ordinations* (Philadelphia: Cummiskey, 1848).

32. "It is not essential to express the word, 'deacon', 'priest', or 'bishop', but the form must at least express some clear equivalent. Thus 'the order of the Blessed Stephen' is a clear equivalent of the order of Deacon. It is not essential to express the main power of the priest or the bishop in the form, but if this main power were expressed, it too would be an equivalent. However, it is essential to express *either* the order *or* its main power, and if the main power is not only left out, but positively excluded, then the right name, though kept, is not the right name in reality but only a shadow. Now, the main power of a true priest is to offer a true sacrifice, and at least one of the main powers of a bishop is to make priests." Semple, H.C., S.J., *Anglican Ordinations* (NY: Benzinger Brothers, 1906).

THE SACRAMENT OF ORDER 101

polytus. **The form of Paul VI does not fulfill these requirements.** Present in the words specified by Pius XII, **this specification is conspicuous by its absence in the Post-Conciliar form. Neither the rank, nor the power, nor a clear equivalent is mentioned.** And as Leo XIII made clear in his *Apostolicae Curae*, the mentioning of the Holy Ghost—if "Governing Spirit" is in fact the Holy Ghost—is insufficient.

(3) Another way to determine what is substantial is to consider the opinions of the theologians during the post-Reformation period. They are reviewed in some detail by Paul Bradshaw in his history of the Anglican Ordinal. One such individual was the Benedictine Wilfrid Raynal who stated that a valid form must express the distinctive character of the order being conferred in one of three ways: (a) An allusion to the type found in the ancient Testament of

---

33. Taken from Semple's book (op. cit.) the following are the various presumed consecratory forms for bishop (presumed, as the Church never so specified prior to Pius XII):

Ancient Roman and Ancient Gallican: ".... and therefore to these Thy servants whom Thou has chosen to the ministry of the HIGH PRIESTHOOD."

Greek: "Do Thou O Lord of all, strengthen and confirm this Thy servant, that by the hand of me, a sinner, and of the assisting minsters and fellow-Bishops, and by the coming, the strength, and grace of the Holy Ghost ... he may obtain the EPISCOPAL DIGNITY."

Maronite: "Thou who canst do all things, adorn with all virtues ... this Thy servant whom Thou hast made worthy to receive from Thee the sublime ORDER OF BISHOPS."

Nestorian: "We offer before Thy Majesty ... this Thy servant whom Thou hast chosen and set apart that he may be a BISHOP."

Coptic: "O Lord, God, Almighty Ruler ... bestow, therefore, this same grace upon Thy servant N., whom thou has chosen as BISHOP."

Armenian: "The Divine Grace calleth this N. from the Priesthood to the EPISCOPATE. I impose hands. Pray that he may become worthy of the rank of BISHOP."

Liturgy on the Constitutions of the Apostles: "Give O God ... to this Thy servant whom Thou hast chosen to the EPISCOPATE to feed Thy people and discharge the Office of PONTIFF."

Canons of Hippolytus: "O God the Father of our Lord Jesus Christ ... look down upon Thy servant N., granting him Thy strength and power, the spirit which Thou didst give to the holy Apostles, through our Lord Jesus Christ. Give to him, O Lord, the EPISCOPATE."

the order conferred; (b) The mention of some spiritual power which is the distinctive privilege of the order to which the candidate is raised; or (c) The actual mention made of the office under the name which from earliest times has become attached to it, viz. *summus sacerdos* for Bishop or *sacerdos secundi ordinis* for Priest. He further added that the actual mention of the words "Bishop" and "Priest" must really and truly bear the meaning attached to them by the Universal Church. A formal denial of the distinctive character of these two sacred offices must vitiate the Intention, and would render the ordination null and void. Now, as Bradshaw points out, "all the Western and Eastern forms fulfilled these requirements." **The new rite of Paul VI does not.**

All debate is resolved by the statement of Pius XII in his *Sacramentum Ordinis*. As the renowned theologian J.M. Hervé, who considers this definition infallible, states: *Forma vero, quae et una est, sunt verba, quibus significatur effectum sacramentale, scilicet potestas Ordinis et gratia Spiritus Sancti*—"Now, the form which is also one (i.e., the substance of the form), is the words by which the sacramental effect is signified, namely the power of Orders and the grace of the Holy Spirit."[34]

Consider once again the form specified by Paul VI:

> So now pour forth upon this chosen one that power which is from You, the governing Spirit whom You gave to your beloved Son, Jesus Christ, the Spirit given by him to the holy apostles, who founded the Church in every place to be your temple for the unceasing glory and praise of your name.

It is perfectly clear that in no place is it specified that the rank or dignity of a Bishop has been conferred. The request that God give the "governing Spirit" (*Spiritum principalem*—whatever that is) "whom you gave to your beloved Son, Jesus Christ, the Spirit given by him to the holy Apostles" may imply that he is raised to the rank of the Apostles, but it doesn't clearly so state. The sacramental effect is not clearly specified and at best we are left with another Post-Conciliar ambiguity. Again, in the former, the grace of the Holy Spirit is

---

34. Hervé, J.M., op. cit.

clearly indicated by the time honored phrase *Coelestis unguenti rore* while in the latter we are left with a phrase entirely new to sacramental theology—*spiritum principalem*. Insofar as some will argue that this phrase (or the phrase *eam virtutem quae a te est, Spiritum Principalem*) suffices for the substance of the form, and indeed, in so far as it is the only phrase in the new form for which such a claim could be made, it behooves us to examine it in detail.

SPIRITUM PRINCIPALEM — WHAT IS IT?

Apart from the concoction ascribed to Hippolytus (discussed below) the phrase *spiritum principalem* is not to be found in any known ordination rite, as can be seen by referring to either *A Vindication of the Bull Apostolic Curae*, or Bishop Kenrick's book *The Validity of Anglican Ordinations Examined*, both of which list all the known episcopal rites. The phrase is found in only one place in Scripture—Psalm 50:14—*redde mihi laetitiam salutaris tui et spiritu principali confirma me*—"restore unto me the joy of thy salvation and strengthen me with a governing (or upright) spirit." The context is that of David asking God's forgiveness for his adulterous relationship with Bathsheba and the strength to control his passions, and thus can be applied to any individual.[35]

---

35. *Concordantiae Bibliorum Sacrorum quas digessit Bonifatius Fischer, O.S.B.*, published by Friedrich Fromman Verlag Gunther Holzborg, Stutgard-Bad, Germany, 1977. The translation into English is from the Douay version. The Psalm in question is the penitential song of David in response to the Prophet Nathan's chiding of him for his adultery with Bathsheba. According to Father Boylan's commentary, *Spiritu Principali* is, apparently, parallel to the *spiritus rectus* of verse 12. *Principalis* represents the Greek *Hegemonikos* meaning princely, leading, or ruling. The Hebrew is *n'dibhah*, a spirit of "readiness," of "willingness" to learn, to do the right and good (cf. Matt. 26:41); "the spirit indeed is willing" [= ready]. St. Augustine understands the verse in the following sense: "An upright spirit renew in my inner parts, which are bowed and distorted by sinning" (*Commentary on Psalm* 51). Cornelius Lapide follows Bellarmine in translating the phrase as "I ask that you stabilize and confirm me in the good by means of the governing spirit." Father Joseph Pohle, the well known professor of dogmatics, specifically denies that "spiritum principalis" is the Third Person of the Holy Trinity. (*The Divine Trinity*, p. 97— translation of Arthur Preuss, familiarly known as Pohle-Preuss).

104 THE PROBLEMS WITH THE OTHER SACRAMENTS

What does the word *Principalem* mean? Cassell's New Latin Dictionary translates it as (1) first in time, original; first in rank, chief; (2) of a prince; (3) of the chief place in a Roman camp. *Harper's Latin Dictionary* also translates it by the term "overseer." Now this latter term is of great interest because it the one used by the Reformers to distort the true nature of a Bishop. As *A Vindication of the Bull Apostolicae Curae* points out:

> The fact that the Anglicans added the term Bishop to their form did not make it valid because doctrinally they hold the bishop to have no higher state than that of the priest—indeed, he is seen as an "overseer" rather than as one having the "fullness of the priesthood."

It is pertinent that Post-Conciliar theologians have recognized the difficulty of adequately translating this phrase into the vernacular. Prior to 1977 it was rendered in English as "Perfect Spirit," but since then Rome has officially insisted on the phrase "governing" or "ruling" Spirit, and in French, "the Spirit of Authority."[36] Father B. Botte, O.S.B., the individual (apart from Montini) primarily responsible for the creation of this new rite for ordaining Bishops, tells us in the semi-official journal *Notitiae* that the meaning of the phrase need not necessarily be drawn from its Scriptural use. Indeed, he states that in the third century it probably had a meaning quite different from that used during the time of David and that in Hippolytus' document it almost certainly meant Holy Spirit. He explains that meaning in the following words:

> The expression has, for the Christian of the Third Century (the time of Hippolytus) a theological meaning which has nothing in

---

36. *Notitiae* states that the proper translation of the word *principalis* is "governing", and the same issue of this semi-official journal carries the "Declaration on the Translation of Sacramental Formulas" promulgated by Paul VI on January 25, 1974, a document which states that "difficulties can arise when trying to express the concepts of the original Latin formula in translation. It sometimes happens that one is obliged to use paraphrases and circumlocutions.... The Holy See approves a formula because it considers that it expresses the sense understood by the Church in the Latin text."

common with the thought of the king of Judah [David] twelve centuries earlier. Even assuming that "principalis" is a mistranslation, it is not important here. The only problem is to know what meaning the author of the prayer (Hippolytus) wanted to give the expression.

The statement as applied to a Sacramental form is a quite extraordinary new force. It admits that not only are we unsure of the meaning of *principalis* but that the word itself may be a mistranslation. It further admits that this critical word is not derived from either Christic or Apostolic sources. But even more, Father Botte, with exquisite historical insight (some seventeen centuries after the fact), proceeds to tell us just what Hippolytus did mean!

The solution must be sought in two directions: the context of the prayer and the use of *hegemonikos* (Greek for *principalis*) in the Christian language of the third century. It is clear that "spirit" means the person of the Holy Ghost. The whole context so indicates: everyone keeps silent because of the descent of the "Spirit." The real question is why among other relevant adjectives, has *principalis* been chosen? The research must be widened here.

Father Botte then proceeds to give us a truly innovative theological interpretation of the primary function of the different members of the hierarchy in orders, and moreover one which the new rite incorporates:

> The three hierarchies have the gift of the Spirit, but it is not the same for each of them. For the bishop it is the *Spiritus Principalis*; for the priests who are the counselors of the bishops, it is *Spiritus Consilii*; for the deacons who are the right hand of the bishop it the *Spiritus Zeli et Sollicitudinis*. It is evident that these distinctions are made in accord with the functions of each rank of minister. It is clear then that *principalis* must be understood in relation to the specific function of the bishop. One only has to reread the prayer to be convinced of this. . . . God has never left his people without a chief, nor his sanctuary without ministers. . . . The bishop is the chief of the Church. Hence the choice of the term *hegemonikos* is self-explanatory. It is the gift of the Spirit that

pertains to the chief. The best translation would seem to be "the Spirit of Authority."[37]

Those unfamiliar with Catholic teaching will perhaps not be shocked by this statement made by the person who was the principle architect of the new rite of Holy Orders. Suffice it to say that the primary function of the Bishop is to ordain priests; the primary function of the priest is to offer the immolative sacrifice. Without this power, the power to forgive sins cannot be received. It is a common saying among Catholic theologians that the priest must receive first the power over the real Body of Christ, and only afterward over the mystical body of Christ or over the Christian people whose sins he forgives or retains. Nowhere in the new rite for ordaining priests is it made clear that he is given the power to offer sacrifice, and nowhere in that of bishops that he is given the power to ordain!

The new form also asks that this "Governing Spirit" that is given to the ordinand be the same that was given to the Holy Apostles. It should be clear that such a request in no way states that the ordinands are themselves raised to the rank of the Apostles. (It would after all be legitimate to ask God to give any Catholic layman the same Holy Spirit that was given to the Apostles.) Now, Leo XIII makes note of the fact that the Anglican rite has the phrase "Receive the Holy Ghost" but that this "cannot be considered apt or sufficient for the Sacrament which omits what it ought essentially to signify." And so, even if we grant that this governing Spirit could be the Holy Spirit, the form lacks sufficient "power" to function in a sacramental manner. What is more, its use thrusts the sacramental form into a

---

37. Luther defined the priesthood in these terms: "The function of the priest is to preach; if he does not preach, he is no more a priest than a picture of a man is a man. Nor does it make a man a bishop if he ordains this kind of clapper-tongued priest, or consecrates church bells, or confirms children. Never! These are things that any deacon or layman might do. What makes a priest or bishop is the ministry of the word." Elsewhere he says "Everyone who knows that he is a Christian would be fully assured that all of us alike are priests, and that we all have the same authority in regard to the word and the sacraments, although no one has the right to administer them without the consent of the members of his Church, or by call of the majority." Quoted by Father W. Jenkins, "The New Ordination Rite: An Indelible Question Mark," *The Roman Catholic*, vol. III, no. 8, Sept. 1981.

totally Protestant setting. [Origen in his *Homilies on Jeremiah* used the term "Governing Spirit," in an exegesis of Psalm 50, to designate the Father, while the Puritan preacher and theologian Richard Sibbes applied it to the Holy Spirit. In later times it became associated by various writers on ritual magic with the angels governing the seven planets, and finally passed into contemporary occultism and New Age angelology. It was also invoked by Cuban Communist revolutionary Che Guevara, who wrote: "I knew that the moment the great governing spirit strikes the blow to divide all humanity into just two opposing factions, I would be on the side of the common people" (quoted in *Becoming Che: Guevara's Second and Final Trip through Latin America* by Carlos "Calica" Ferrer, 2005, translated by Sarah L. Smith, 2006, p. 170).—ED]

THE PROTESTANT UNDERSTANDING OF THE EPISCOPAL RANK

Many Protestant sects retain the title of "bishop" among their clergy. This is true for the Lutherans in Germany, but not in America. It is also true of the Anglicans, the Episcopalians, and certain Baptist sects. Yet all of these denominations deny that either the priesthood or the episcopacy involves any imprinting of a sacramental character. In what sense then do they understand the function of their bishops?

Their primary function is jurisdictional. While it is true that Anglican bishops "ordain" and "confirm," both are in their view non-Sacramental acts. In England they are appointed by the reigning King or Queen who is the current "head" of their Church. Among other Protestant sects they are "elected" from among the people. And thus, in all these situations they are seen as "overseers." The inclusion of the term "bishop" and "high priest" in a Protestant rite in no way confers on such a rite validity in the Catholic sense, especially when all reference to Catholic understanding of their function is deliberately removed from the content of the sacramental form and from the remainder of the rite. Moreover, Leo XIII instructs us in his *Apostolicae Curae* that such terms when used in ambiguous situations must be understood in their Protestant sense.

108 THE PROBLEMS WITH THE OTHER SACRAMENTS

Thus the use of "governing spirit" is not only inoffensive to Protestants; it also functions to make the new rite highly acceptable to them. This is not to deny that Catholic bishops have such a function; what is offensive in a supposedly Catholic rite is the implication, if not the ecumenically inspired surrender, that this is their primary—or even their only—function.

In determining Anglican orders to be "null and void" Leo XIII discussed the "negative" effect of the remainder of the rite—its *significatio ex adjunctis*—upon an indeterminate sacramental form. The deliberate deletion from the rite of all reference to a Catholic understanding of Orders made it quite clear that the Sacramental form was meaningless. If the new Post-Conciliar rite follows the Anglican prototype in this, then clearly it is subject to the same condemnation that was leveled against Cranmer's creation. Before discussing this aspect of the problem however, we must examine with greater care the source from which Paul VI drew his new sacramental form.

THE SOURCE OF PAUL VI'S ORDINATION RITE

When Paul VI approved the new rite for ordaining bishops in June of 1968 he stated that "it was necessary to add, delete, or change certain things, either to restore texts to their earlier integrity, to make the expressions clearer, or to describe the sacramental effects better ... it appeared appropriate to take from ancient sources the consecratory prayer which is found in the document called *The Apostolic Tradition of Hippolytus of Rome*, written in the beginning of the third century, and which is still used in large parts in the ordination rites of the Coptic and Western Syrian liturgies."

Needless to say, he does not tell us why it was necessary "to add, delete or change certain things" which had presumably been adequate for some 2000 years. As to whether the result expresses things more "clearly" or "describes the sacramental effects better," this the reader will have to see for himself. But Paul VI is up to his old tricks again. While he is correct in pointing to *The Apostolic Tradition of Hippolytus* as the source of his new rite, he stretches the truth to the limit in stating that this highly questionable document is "still used in large part in the ordination rites of the Coptic and Western Syrian liturgies." In fact the Hippolytus text has almost nothing in common with the eastern rites, and the crucial words—especially the critical phrase of "governing spirit"—is nowhere to be found within these eastern rites.

Let us then compare these still used rites with the new rite. The first paragraph below is translated from pages 204–5 of the *Pontifical of the Antiochian Syrians*, Part II, printed in 1952, Sharfe, Lebanon, and carries the *Imprimatur* of Ignatius Gabriel Cardinal Tappuni, Syrian Patriarch of Antioch. This is the rite used by the Coptic and West Syrian Liturgies. The second paragraph is the consecratory prayer promulgated by Paul VI—supposedly taken from the first. It is taken from the new rite in English as used in the United States.

THE ANTIOCHIAN PONTIFICAL

O **God**, Thou hast created everything by Thy power and established the universe by the will of Thine only Son. Thou hast freely given us the grasp of truth and made known to us Thy holy and excellent love. Thou hast given Thy beloved and only-begotten Son, the Word, Jesus Christ, the Lord of Glory, as pastor and physician of our souls. By His Precious Blood Thou hast founded Thy Church and ordained in it all grades pertaining to the priesthood. Thou hast given guidance that we may please Thee in that the knowledge of the name of Thine Anointed has increased and spread in the whole world. Send on this Thy servant Thy Holy and Spiritual Breath so that he may tend and oversee the flock entrusted to him, namely—to anoint priests, to ordain deacons, to dedicate altars and churches, to bless houses, to make appointments, to heal, to judge, to save, to deliver, to loose and bind, to invest and divest, as well as to excommunicate. Grant him all the power of Thy saints—the same power Thou gavest to the Apostles of Thine only begotten Son—that he may become a glorious **high priest** with the honor of Moses, the dignity of the venerable Jacob, in the throne of the Patriarchs. Let Thy people and the flock of Thine inheritance be well established through this Thy servant. Give him wisdom and prudence and let him understand Thy will, O Lord so that he can discern sinful things, know the sublimities of justice and judgment. Grant him this power to solve difficult problems and all bonds of iniquity.

PAUL VI'S CONSECRATORY PRAYER

God the Father of our Lord Jesus Christ, Father of mercies and God of all consolation, you dwell in heaven, yet look with compassion on all that is humble. You know all things before they come to be; by your gracious word you have established the plan of your Church. From the beginning you chose the descendants of Abraham to be your holy nation. You established rulers and priests and did not leave your sanctuary without ministers to serve you. From the creation of the world you have been pleased to be glorified by those whom you have chosen [all consecrating bishops]. *So now, pour out upon this chosen one that power which is from you, the governing spirit whom you gave to your beloved son Jesus Christ, the Spirit given by him to the Holy Apostles, who founded the Church in every place to be your temple for the unceasing glory and praise of your name.* (The essential words of Paul VI's form are in italics, but are not to be found in the Antiochian Pontifical.) [Principal consecrator alone:] Father, you know all hearts. You have chosen your servant for the office of bishop. May he be a shepherd to your holy flock, and a **high priest** blameless in your sight, ministering to you night and day; may he always gain the blessing of your favor and offer gifts of holy Church. Through the Spirit who gives the grace of high priesthood grant him the power to forgive sins as you have commanded, to assign ministries as you have decreed, to loose every bond by the authority which you gave to your Apostles. May he be pleasing to you by his gentleness and purity of heart, presenting a fragrant offering to you, through Jesus Christ, your Son, through whom glory and power and honor are yours with the holy spirit in your holy Church now and forever. [All:] Amen.

The essential "form" as specified by Paul VI is italicized. The two words printed in bold script represent the only two significant words that the prayers have in common. In the Antiochian rite, while the essential words are not specified (the theological terms "form" and "matter" are not used in the eastern Churches), the bishop's hands—the matter of the sacrament—are placed on the ordinand's head for the entire prayer, while in the new Roman rite, only during the repetition of the essential form. As pointed out in the Introduction, form and matter must be united to effect the sacrament.

Clearly the prayer taken from the Antiochian Pontifical is intended to consecrate a Catholic bishop and fulfills several times over all the requirements we have discussed in the section on the history of sacramental rites. The latter has barely a dozen words in common with the former and is suitable for use in the most liberal Protestant communions. It is hardly just to say that one is derived from the other.

Obviously deleted from the eastern liturgical prayer are such phrases as "anointing priests"—there is a vast difference between "ordaining priests" and "assigning ministries." Also deleted are references to his function of protecting the Church against heresy. The Post-Conciliar "bishop" is to "loose every bond" but not "to loose and bind, to invest and divest, as well as to excommunicate." Retained however are two important words—that of "bishop" and "high priest," but they are placed outside the "essential" form. Moreover, one can seriously question whether the terms "bishop" and "high priest" can be understood in the Catholic sense of the words. In view of any proper indication in the *significatio ex adjunctis*, one may be permitted to doubt it.

Where then does the new "form" of Paul VI come from? The answer is the "Apostolic Tradition" of Hippolytus.[38]

THE "APOSTOLIC TRADITION" OF HIPPOLYTUS

The real source of Paul VI's new consecratory prayer is the so-called *"Apostolic Tradition"* of Hippolytus—a composite document of dubious origins for which there is no evidence whatsoever that it was ever actually used to consecrate a bishop. We shall consider two

---

38. Father Clancy, quoting Johannes Quasten's *Patrology*, tells us in his historical study of the Rite of Ordination that "The Apostolic Tradition had no appreciable effect on the development of the rite of ordination in the west."

aspects of the problem raised by the use of this source: Who was Hippolytus and what do we really know about the form he used?

Hippolytus was a highly enigmatic person who lived in the third century. He was born about 160 and is thought to have been a disciple of St. Irenaeus. He became a priest under Pope Zephyrinus about the year 198 and won great respect for his learning and eloquence. Because of doctrinal differences with the Pope, Hippolytus left Rome, found a bishop to consecrate him, and established a schismatic Church, as a result of which he was formally excommunicated. He drew up his *Apostolic Tradition* while he was outside the Church, presumably to establish a "pontifical" for his schismatic sect. Subsequently, after Maximus became emperor and instituted a new persecution against the Christians, both Hippolytus and the reigning Pontiff (Pontianus) were arrested and sent to the mines in Sardinia. It was here, just prior to his death, that he became reconciled to the Church. Both he and the Pope were martyred together and later canonized. The Hippolytic schism ended with this event.

The text written by Hippolytus as a "pontifical" for his schismatic sect was named by him *The Apostolic Tradition.* (He was not the last to lend authority to his acts by referring them back to "earlier authority"!) Insofar as Hippolytus was extremely conservative—he objected to the legitimate relaxation of the Church's laws, especially those related to forgiving and readmitting to communion those Christians who in times of persecution had sacrificed to the Roman gods—it has been assumed that he preserved the rites then in use; but this is by no means certain.

Now Hippolytus wrote in Greek, and once the Roman Church adopted the almost exclusive use of Latin, his works were for all practical purposes forgotten in the West. The particular work in question, *The Apostolic Tradition*, was rediscovered by Job Ludolf in Ethiopia in 1691. In 1848 another version came to light through the study of Coptic documents. Still later a Sahidic version was found, and then, around 1900, a Latin translation from the Greek in the sixth century came to light. None of these versions were complete and scholars therefore were forced to "reconstruct" the various segments in order to produce a relatively cohesive document. According to Professor Burton Scott Easton of Cambridge University, we can summarize what we know of this document in the following words:

> The original Greek of the Apostolic tradition has not been recovered, except in small fragments. The Latin is generally trustworthy, but is incomplete. The only other primary version, the Sahidic, is likewise incomplete, and the results of the moderate abilities of its translator have been further confused in later transmission. The Arabic is a secondary text, offering little that the Sahidic does not contain. The only practically complete version, the Ethiopic, is tertiary and is otherwise unreliable. All four of these versions presuppose a common Greek original, in which two different endings have been conflated. The other sources, the Constitutions, the Testament and the Canons are frank revisions, in which the original is often edited out of recognition or even flatly contradicted. Under these conditions the restoration of a really accurate text is manifestly impossible.[39]

With this in mind, and with absolutely no idea of what Hippolytus considered to be the "form" or essential words involved, let us consider his consecratory prayer as scholars have reconstructed it:

> God the Father of our Lord Jesus Christ, Father of mercies and God of all comfort, who dwellest on high, yet hast respect to the lowly, who knowest all things before they come to pass. Thou hast appointed the borders of Thy Church by the words of Thy grace, predestinating from the beginning the righteous race of Abraham. And making them princes and priests, and leaving not thy sanctuary without a ministry, Thou has glorified among those [or possibly, "in those places"] whom Thou hast chosen. Pour forth now the power which is Thine, of Thy governing spirit which [Greek version].... Thou gavest to Thy beloved Servant [Greek but not Latin] Jesus Christ which he bestowed on his holy apostles [Latin] ... who established the Church in every place,

---

39. Burton Scott Easton, *The Apostolic Tradition of Hippolytus*, translated into English with an introduction and notes (Cambridge: Cambridge Univ. Press, 1934); republished by Arenon Books, England, 1962.

the Church which Thou hast sanctified unto unceasing glory and praise of Thy name. Thou who knowest the hearts of all, grant to this thy servant whom Thou hast chosen to be bishop, ["to feed Thy holy flock," in some versions] and to serve as Thy high priest without blame, ministering night and day, to propitiate Thy countenance without ceasing and to offer Thee the gifts of the holy Church, and by the Spirit of high-priesthood to have authority to remit sins according to Thy commandment, to assign the lots according to Thy precept, to loose every bond according to the authority which Thou givest Thy apostles, and to please Thee in meekness and purity of heart, offering to thee an odor of sweet savor. Through Thy Servant Jesus Christ our Lord, through whom be to Thee glory, might, honor, and with the Holy Spirit in the holy Church both now and always world without end. Amen [Greek].[40]

Such then is the true nature and source of the Post-Conciliar sacramental prayer for ordaining bishops. Clearly we have no exact knowledge of the form that Hippolytus used, and just as clearly, there is no evidence that the form adopted by Paul VI was ever used to ordain anybody. What are we to say when the Church teaches:

> Matter and form must be certainly valid. Hence one may not follow a probable opinion and use either doubtful matter or form. Acting otherwise, one commits a sacrilege.[41]

---

40. According to Father (subsequently Cardinal) J. Tixeront (*Holy Orders and Ordination* [St. Louis: Herder, 1928]), the Consecrating Bishop held his hands over the ordinand's head throughout the entire prayer. According to Father Semple, S.J. (op. cit.), after asking God to give the ordinand that spirit which "Thou didst give to the holy Apostles," Hippolytus continued: "Give to him, O Lord, the Episcopate." He adds the following note: "But if a priest is ordained, all is done with him in like manner as with a Bishop, except that he shall not sit in the chair. The same prayer shall be prayed in its entirety over him as over the Bishop, with the sole exception of the name of EPISCOPATE. A Bishop is in all things equal to a Priest except in the name of the chair, and in Ordination, which power of ordaining is not given to the latter.")

41. Quoted from Father Brey's introduction to Patrick Henry Omlor's book, *Questioning the Validity of Masses using the New All-English Canon* (Reno, Nevada: Athanasius Press, 1969). This is the common teaching of moral theologians.

THE COUP DE GRACE

In the traditional rite, **prior** to the superimposition of hands—the matter of the rite—the Consecrator took the open book of the Gospels, and, saying nothing, laid it upon the neck and the shoulders of the Bishop-elect, so that the printed page touched the neck. One of the chaplains knelt behind, supporting the book until it was given into the hands of the Bishop-elect. After this the consecrator superimposed his hands on the head of the ordinand, saying "Receive the Holy Ghost," and then proceeded with a short prayer and the preface which contained the words of the form. There was a moral continuity of action so that the form was not really separated from the matter.

In the new rite the principal consecrator lays his hands upon the bishop-elect in silence. Following this the principal consecrator places the open Book of the Gospels upon the head of the bishop-elect; two deacons, standing at either side of the bishop-elect, hold the Book of the Gospels above his head until the prayer of consecration is completed. Here the continuity of action is broken, which is to say that the matter and the form are separated by the imposition of the Gospels over the head of the bishop-elect.

Whatever we may think of the new "form," tradition makes it clear that the form must be added to the matter in order for the sacrament to be effected. In Holy Orders, it is the superimposition of the hands which is the matter (as confirmed by Leo XIII in his *Apostolicae Curae*).

As Augustine said with regard to Baptism: "What is the Baptism of Christ? A washing in water by the word. Take away the water and you have no Baptism; take away the word, and you have no Baptism." And again: "And in water the word cleanses. Take away the word and what is water but water? The word comes to the element and a sacrament results."[42]

Now the matter and form must be united or concurrent. "The matter and form must be united—so far as union is possible—to

---

42. Bernard Leeming, S.J., *Principles of Sacramental Theology* (London: Longmans Green, 1955).

produce the one external rite, and so to produce a valid Sacrament...." However, in Holy Orders, "moral simultaneity is sufficient, that is, these Sacraments are valid though the proximate matter is employed immediately before or after the use of the word. What interval would suffice to render the Sacrament invalid cannot be determined; the interval of the recital of the "Our Father" appeared sufficient to St. Alphonsus, but in such matters we should not rely on probabilities, we should make sure the matter and form are as united as we can make them."[43]

In the new rite, the placing of the Gospels on the head of the bishop-elect comes after the superimposition of hands and thus breaks the "moral simultaneity" between the matter and the form much in the same way as taking a coffee-break at that moment would break it. Once again, one is given grounds for seriously doubting validity.

OTHER ASPECTS OF THE NEW EPISCOPAL RITE — ITS "SIGNIFICATIO EX ADJUNCTIS"

It may be argued that the other parts of the Post-Conciliar rite — its *significatio ex adjunctis* — function to correct the obvious defects of a highly indeterminate form. It behooves us then to examine the remainder of the ceremonies and see if such is the case. We will consider this under the two categories of additions and deletions:

What Has Been Added

Reading through the text of the new Ordination Rite for Bishops one finds the Consecrator's Homily given under the title "Consent of the People." This is a totally Protestant concept, for in Catholicism the bishop is appointed by the Pope (or his agent), and no consent on the part of the laity is required. Did Christ ask for the approval of anyone in appointing the Apostles?

---

43. Henry Davis, S.J., *Moral and Pastoral Theology*, New York: Sheed and Ward, 1935, vol. III, p.10. Dr. Ludwig Ott says much the same: "It is not necessary that they coincide absolutely in point of time; a moral coincidence suffices, that is, they must be connected with each other in such a fashion, that according to general estimation, they compose a unitary sign" (*Fundamentals of Catholic Dogma* [Rockford, IL: TAN, 1986]).

THE SACRAMENT OF ORDER   117

Continuing in the next paragraph we are informed that "in the person of the bishop, with the priests around him, Jesus Christ the Lord, who became High Priest forever, is present among you. Through the ministry of the bishop, Christ Himself continues to proclaim the Gospel and to confer the mysteries of faith on those who believe...." Such a statement is again misleading for, strictly speaking, the presence of Christ among us and the proclamation of the Gospel do not depend upon the bishop. However, this manner of expressing things has the advantage of being acceptable to Protestants.

Next we read that the bishop is a "minister of Christ" and a "steward of the Mysteries of God." He has been entrusted with the task of witnessing to the truth of the Gospel and fostering a spirit of justice and holiness. But this task is not particular to a bishop. Each and every Catholic is obliged "to give witness to the truth and to foster a spirit of justice and holiness." In a still later paragraph the bishop-elect is told that he is to be an "**overseer**." Once again we are left with an individual whose function as a Catholic bishop is in no way delineated. There is nothing in the entire statement that would offend Protestants, and indeed, the delineation of his function as "**overseer**" would delight them. And so this homily continues to the end without providing any positive *significatio ex adjunctis*.

What follows is the "Examination of the Candidate." Again, the bishop-elect is asked if he is "resolved to be faithful and constant and proclaiming the Gospel of Christ." The only part of this examination which could relate to his function as a Catholic bishop is the question as to whether or not he is "resolved to maintain the Deposit of Faith entire and uncorrupt as handed down by the Apostles and professed by the Church everywhere and at all times." He must respond in the affirmative, but then, so must every layman who wishes to call himself a Catholic. Moreover, it is obvious from the statements of the Post-Conciliar bishops that they hardly take this responsibility seriously.[44]

After the Litany of the Saints we find what is perhaps the only

---

44. Strict adherence to this response would require that they reject the heresies of Vatican II. Under such circumstances one can question whether they would be chosen by modern Rome to be "overseers."

saving statement in the entire Post-Conciliar rite. The principal consecrator at this point stands alone, with his hands joined and prays: "Lord, be moved by our prayers. Anoint your servant with the fullness of priestly grace and bless him with spiritual power in all its richness." This prayer is also found in the traditional rite where the Latin for the important phrase is "*cornu gratiae sacerdotalis*" (literally, "the horn of sacerdotal grace"). The statement however is ambiguous because the "horn of sacerdotal grace"—or even the mistranslation "fullness of priestly grace"—could be applied to the priesthood as much as to the episcopacy. Moreover, and most important, since it is made outside the sacramental form and apart from the matter, and it in no way specifies the power or grace conferred in the Sacrament.

What Has Been Deleted

In the present historical context, and in view of Pope Leo XIII's *Apostolicae Curae*, what has been deleted is of greater significance than what has been added. Because of the great length of the traditional rite (taking some two or three hours to say), I shall only discuss those passages which might influence the validity of the Sacrament.

The traditional rite is initiated by a request on the part of the senior assistant to the Consecrator: "Most Reverend Father, our holy Mother the Catholic Church asks that you promote this priest here present to the burden of the episcopate" [retained]. This is followed by an oath on the part of the ordinand in which he promises God "to promote the rights, honors, privileges and authority of the Holy Roman Church: and to "observe with all his strength, and cause to be observed by others, the rules of the Holy Fathers, etc. . . ." [omitted in the new rite and replaced by the Homily described above under the title of "Consent of the People"]. Next proceeds the "examination of the candidate" in which he is asked among other things if he will "keep and teach with reverence the traditions of the orthodox fathers and the decretal constitutions of the Holy and Apostolic See" [omitted, though he promises to "maintain the deposit of faith, entire and uncorrupt, as handed down by the Apostles and professed by the Church everywhere and at all times"]. Then he is asked to confirm his belief in each and every article of the Creed [omitted]. Finally he is asked if he will "anathematize every heresy that shall arise against the Holy Catholic Church" [omitted]. The deletion of the requirement to anathematize heresy is significant, for this is indeed one of the functions of a Bishop. Further, this function remains unspecified in the remainder of the Post-Conciliar rite.

In the traditional rite the consecrator instructs the bishop-elect in the following terms: "A bishop judges, interprets, consecrates, ordains, offers, baptizes and confirms." Now such a statement is indeed important for the *significatio ex adjunctis*. Its deletion in the new rite is most significant. Nowhere in the new rite is it stated that the function of the bishop is to ordain, or to confirm, much less to judge (to loose and to bind).

The consecratory prayer in the traditional rite of the Roman Church is different from that of the Antiochian-Syrian rite and provides the necessary "form" (including the essential words as specified by Pius XII). Its content or "substantial meaning" is sufficiently close to that of the Coptic, Antiochian and Syrian prayers as to require no further discussion. If in fact Paul VI had adopted the form used in the Eastern rites, absolutely no doubt would remain about validity.

In the traditional rite, after the consecratory prayer, the functions of a Bishop are once again specified. "Give him, O Lord, the keys of the Kingdom of Heaven... whatsoever he shall bind upon earth, let it be bound likewise in Heaven, and whatsoever he shall loose upon earth, let it likewise be loosed in Heaven. Whose sins he shall retain, let them be retained, and do Thou remit the sins of whomsoever he shall remit.... Grant him, O Lord, an episcopal chair...." This entire prayer has been omitted in the new rite.

THE RESULT OF THESE CHANGES IS THE PROTESTANTIZING OF THE ORDINAL; SOME WORDS OF LEO XIII TAKEN FROM HIS *APOSTOLICAE CURAE*

Clearly, almost every reference to a specifically Catholic understanding of the episcopate has been deleted from the Post-Conciliar rite. Included in these deletions are his function of ordaining priests, confirming, and his use of the "Keys." Admittedly the term "bishop" is retained, but outside the essential form, and in such a way as would in no way offend our Protestant brethren. As such there is no positive *significatio ex adjunctis*, but rather a negative one. With this in mind, let us consider some of the statements of Leo XIII in his *Apostolicae Curae* that irreformably declared Anglican Orders "null and void."[45]

> In vain has help been recently sought from the plea of the validity of Anglican Orders from the other prayers of the same Ordinal. For, to put aside other reasons which show this to be insufficient for the purpose of the Anglican rite, let this argument suffice for all. From them has been deliberately removed whatever sets forth the dignity and office of the Priesthood of the Catholic rite. That "form" consequently cannot be considered apt or sufficient for the Sacrament which omits what it ought essentially to signify.

> The same holds good of episcopal consecration.... Nor is anything gained by quoting the prayer of the preface, "Almighty God," since it, in like manner has been stripped of the words which denote the *summum sacerdotium*.

> The episcopate undoubtedly, by the institution of Christ, most truly belongs to the Sacrament of Order and constitutes the *sacerdotium* in the highest degree, namely that which by the teaching of the holy Fathers and our liturgical customs is called the *Summum sacerdotium, sacri ministerii summa*. So it comes to pass that, as the Sacrament of Order and the true *sacerdotium* of Christ were utterly eliminated from the Anglican rite, and hence the *sacerdotium* is in no wise conferred truly and validly in the episcopal consecration of the same rite, for the same reason, therefore, the episcopate can in no wise be truly and validly conferred by it and this the more so because among the first duties of the episcopate is that of ordaining ministers for the Holy Eucharist and Sacrifice.

---

45. Some liberal theologians argued that this Bull was not binding. Pope Leo XIII subsequently made it clear that the Bull was "irreformable."

Michael Davies, despite his dubious conclusion (in *The Order of Melchisedech*) that the new ordination rite is unquestionably valid, provides us with all the necessary evidence required to state that the intention of Paul VI was to make the new ordination rites acceptable to Protestants. He also provides us with the evidence that Paul VI's Ordinal was created with the help of the same henchmen that assisted in creating the *Novus Ordo Missae*—Archbishop Bugnini and the six heterodox (Protestant) "consultants." Francis Clark also stresses Paul VI's ecumenical intent. Indeed, he goes so far as to parallel it with Cranmer's intent in creating the Edwardian (Anglican) rite, namely that of destroying the sacerdotal character of Orders. He considers the Cranmerian result invalid, but that of the Post-Conciliar church as legitimate because it derives from a Pope.[46]

Let the import of such an intent be clear. Protestants deny the sacramental character of orders, and any attempt to create a rite that would satisfy them must resort to both ambiguity and deliberate obfuscation of doctrine. If Michael Davies' contention is correct, and I believe it is, Paul VI had no choice but to deliberately delete every reference to a specifically Catholic characterization of the Episcopacy. Let us once again turn to Leo XIII's *Apostolicae Curae*:

> For the full and accurate understanding of the Anglican Ordinal, besides what we have noted as to some of its parts, there is nothing more pertinent than to consider carefully the circumstances under which it was composed and publicly authorized.... The history of the time is sufficiently eloquent as to the animus of the

---

46. Francis Clark, S.J., *Eucharistic Sacrifice and the Reformation* (Devon: Augustine Press, 1981). In his second edition of *The Order of Melchisedech* Michael Davies again reiterates his opinion to the effect that there can be no question about the validity of the new rites for administering Holy Orders, because they have the approval of a pope. He quotes Francis Clark with special emphasis: "The wording of an ordination form, even if not specifically determinate in itself, can be given the required determination from its setting (ex adiunctis), that is, from the other prayers and actions of the rite, or *even from the connotation of the ceremony as a whole in the religious context of the age.*" Such a doctrinal position means that the new Church can ignore 2000 years of sacramental theology and declare anything it wishes to be a valid sacramental rite. It could for example declare "monkey-shines" or "abracadabra" to be a valid sacramental forms.

authors of the Ordinal.... As to the abettors whom they associated with themselves from the heterodox sects... for this reason, in the whole Ordinal not only is there no clear mention of the sacrifice, or consecration, of priesthood (*sacerdotium*), and of the power of consecrating and offering sacrifice, but, and as We have just stated, every trace of these things which have been in such prayers of the Catholic rite as they had not entirely rejected, was deliberately removed and struck out.

In this way, the native character—or spirit as it is called—of the Ordinal clearly manifests itself... **any words** in the Anglican Ordinal as it now is, **which lend themselves to ambiguity, cannot be taken in the same sense as they possess in the Catholic rite** [highlighting is mine]. For once a new rite has been initiated in which, as we have seen, the Sacrament of Order is adulterated or denied, and from which all idea of consecration and sacrifice has been rejected, the formula, "Receive the Holy Ghost," no longer holds good, because the Spirit is infused into the soul with the grace of the sacrament, and so the words "for the office and work of priest or bishop," and the like no longer hold good, but remain as words without the reality which Christ instituted.

CONCLUSION

If the Post-Conciliar rite, animated by a spirit of false ecumenism, follows the pattern established by its Cranmerian prototype; if it is, as Michael Davies contends, a move in the direction of a Common Ordinal; and if it deletes every phrase which characterizes a Catholic episcopacy, not only from the essential form, but from the entire rite, then it must logically be subject to the same condemnations that Leo XIII promulgated against Anglican Orders. In fact, there is not one statement in the above quotations from his Apostolic Bull which cannot be applied to it. If one adds to this the abrogation of the traditional form as specified by Pius XII's *ex cathedra* pronouncement, and the change in the "substance" or meaning of the essential words specified as its replacement, we are left with the unfortunate conclusion that the bishops ordained by the new rite may be in no way different from their Lutheran and Anglican counterparts. [The present "pope," Joseph Ratzinger, was consecrated according to the new rite.—ED]

And if the ordination of Post-Conciliar bishops is at best extremely doubtful, what is one to say of the ordination of "presbyters" under their aegis? In so far as the ordination rite for the priesthood has been criticized on similar grounds, we have a situation where doubt is added onto doubt. This in turn places all the other sacraments (except of course Baptism and Matrimony) on equally dangerous ground. The reader is reminded that, in the practical order, for a rite to be doubtful is the same as for it to be invalid. As Francis Clark says, "probabalism may not be used where the validity of the sacraments is in question," and as Father Jone states, "Matter and form must be certainly valid. Hence one may not follow a probable opinion and use either doubtful matter or form."[47]

Even worse than placing the various aspects of the Sacrament of Order and their dependent sacraments in doubt, is the question that these ritual changes raise about what is called the Apostolic Succession. The Bishops are the descendents of the Apostles and retain all the functions of the Apostles except that of Revelation. If their "descent" is nullified and voided, hopes for reconstituting the Church that Christ established in a saner age are also seriously circumscribed.

---

47. Rev. Heribert Jone, *Moral Theology* (Westminster MD: Newman, 1962).

3

THE DEMISE OF EXTREME UNCTION

> The Christian at least has the last sacraments administered a few hours in advance [of death].
>
> *Sigmund Freud*[1]

It is clear that we all must die, and indeed, in many ways this is the most important moment of our lives. It is at this time that one's entire life passes before one, and when final choices must be made, choices between despair and love, as so well exemplified by the two thieves crucified with Christ. It is a time when we need every available help—the prayers of loved ones, and above all the Sacraments which our holy mother the Church has for the past 2000 years so lovingly provided to the faithful. Catholics and clergy who have embraced the changes introduced after Vatican II have been deprived of the Sacrament of Extreme Unction which has been replaced by what is called the "blessing for the sick."[2] This is not to decry the "blessing of the sick," for blessings are always good. It is simply to state that what is proffered, Confession apart, is not a Sacrament. The seriousness of this defect cannot be exaggerated.

Catholics have always had the security of knowing that, when in

---

1. Letter to Fliess, quoted in Paul Vitz, *Sigmund Freud's Christian Unconscious* (Guilford: NY, 1988; and Grand Rapids: Eerdman's Publishing Company, 1993).

2. Conservative Novus Ordo priests speak of the importance of the final confession. In this of course they are correct, for that is the best they can offer the dying—assuming they are themselves properly ordained. Confession of course always preceded Extreme Unction in the case of those who were still conscious.

danger of death, the Church provided them with a saving Sacrament of a most powerful nature. Indeed, many a Catholic family is familiar with the story of some lapsed member, away from the Sacraments for years and even decades, who at the last moment asked for the priest in order to receive the "last rites." This is no longer a viable option.

What are the effects of Extreme Unction (usually provided after Confession and in association with the Holy Viaticum or the Sacred Species)? They are as varied as they are potent. Their "end" or "purpose" is said to be "the perfect healing of the soul," and it surely has the inherent power to attain its end in those who pose no obstacle to the grace it conveys. As the Council of Trent explains, "this effect is the grace of the Holy Ghost, Whose unction blots out sins, if any remain to be expiated, and the consequences of sin, and alleviates and strengthens the soul of the sick person, by exciting in him a great confidence in the divine mercy, sustained by which he bears more lightly the troubles and sufferings of disease, and more easily resists the temptations of the demon lying in wait for his heel[3]; and sometimes, when it is expedient for the soul's salvation, recovers bodily health." These effects are usually grouped under four headings.

The first effect is the remission of sins which follows from the passage in St. James: "If anyone be in a state of sin, his sins are forgiven him," and which is indeed confirmed by the very "form" of the Sacrament which states "*Indulgeat tibi Dominus... quidquid... deliquisti....* ("May God pardon thee whatever sins thou hast committed...."). Of course, it is true that mortal sins are forgiven by Confession, Absolution and Penance—but it is not unusual that a sick man, being weak or unconscious, cannot confess; yet providing he places no obstacle to the infusion of Grace into his soul (and implicitly has a proper intention), then through this Sacrament, even if he cannot confess, he is still washed clean of sin and regains his Baptismal purity. To such an individual Extreme Unction becomes the pillar of salvation. It can be argued that conditional Absolution obviates the need for this final Sacrament, but that would be to ignore its other effects.

3. The reference is to Genesis 3:15.

Secondly, this Sacrament remits temporal punishment due to us for our sins, which of course ordinary Confession and Absolution cannot do. It was, as Father Kilker says, "instituted for the perfect healing of the soul with a view to its immediate entrance into glory, unless indeed the all-knowing master of Life and Death should deem the restoration of bodily health more expedient. Consequently, it must accomplish the removal of all disabilities, it must render us fit to enter our heavenly home without delay. Were this not so, it would be absurd to say that the Sacrament is *consummativum spiritualis curationis*.[4] This doctrine must not however be construed to mean that when Extreme Unction is received, the remission of the entire temporal debt infallibly occurs. Often the subject blocks the completeness of the effect by defective and impeding dispositions. But, if the subject has in every way the correct disposition and devotion, it must be conceded that he receives the *plenissimam poenarum relaxationem*—the complete remission of temporal punishment.

The third and terribly important effect is what is called the *comfortatio animae*: or the "Comforting of the Soul." The approach of death with its distressing pains, its physical prostration and the associated mental disquietude, can truly be a most appalling experience. Man dreads few things as much as this "moment of truth." He reviews his past actions and, as it says in the Book of Wisdom, "they shall come with fear at the thought of their sins, and their iniquities shall stand against them to convict them." At the same time he recognizes that soon he must stand before the Judgment Seat of God. It is precisely at this time that the Devil uses all his powers and wiles to attack the soul. As the *Catechism of the Council of Trent* puts it: "Although the enemy of the human race never ceases, while we live, to meditate our ruin and destruction, yet at no time does he more violently use every effort utterly to destroy us, and if possible, to deprive us of all hope of divine mercy, then when he sees the last day of life approach." Now the third effect of this Sacrament is "to free

---

4. Rev. Adrian Kilker, *Extreme Unction, A Canonical Treatise* (London: Herder, 1927). The Latin is from St. Thomas Aquinas, *Summa Contra Gentiles.*, lib. 4., c. 73 de Ext. Unct. (trans. "the perfect healing of the soul").

the minds of the faithful from this solicitude, and to fill the soul with pious and holy joy." It further provides "arms and strength . . . to the faithful . . . to enable them to break the violence and impetuosity of the adversary, and to fight bravely against him. . . ." Who of us can be so presumptuous as not ardently to desire such assistance? Fourthly, it is a doctrine of our faith that one of the effects of Extreme Unction is the restoring of bodily health, if recovery is expedient for the soul's welfare. As a physician in practice I can testify to this effect without hesitation.

Lastly, though not strictly speaking a theological effect, the administration of the Sacrament, under traditional circumstances, made it perfectly plain to the individual concerned that he was facing death. He could no longer hide from himself the reality of his situation. He was forced, as it were, to the battlefield, and not allowed to drift away in some gently morphinized dream that "everything will be all right." And how often did physicians and relatives see the wonderful effects this Sacrament worked upon the souls of those who received it—turning as it were, their last moments on earth into a foretaste of that heavenly peace and glory that is, in fact, offered to every soul.

EXAMINING THE CHANGES IN THE FORM AND MATTER OF THE SACRAMENT

According to Father Kilker, "The remote matter of Extreme Unction is oil of olives. The 'proximate matter' is the oil of olives blessed by the Bishop. This the Council of Trent definitely defined. *Intellexit enim Ecclesia, materiam esse oleum ab episcopo benedictum* (Session XIV). There is no doubt about what St. James meant when he said "oil of olives" (5:14). Initially the oil of the sick could be blessed by priests and even saintly laymen, but ever since the Council of Châlons in 813, canon law requires that it be blessed by a Bishop. In the Eastern Church it is customary for the oil to be blessed by the priest in the house of the sick person.

In the Latin church it has ever been the custom to employ pure unadulterated olive oil, to which a fragrant oleoresin called *balm* or *balsam* has been added. In some Eastern rites the practice of adding a little water as a symbol of Baptism, or of a little wine in memory of the good Samaritan, or even of the dust of the sepulchre of some saint, has long been in vogue.

Now this oil is blessed by the Bishop at the magnificent Mass of Maundy Thursday in Holy Week—a Mass so sacred that the Bishop is traditionally attended and assisted by twelve priests, seven deacons and seven sub-deacons in order to say it properly. The prayer reads: *Emitte, quaesumus Domine, Spiritum sanctum tuum Paraclitum de coelis in hanc pinguedinem olivae, quam de viridi ligno producere dignatus es ad refectionem mentis et corporis....* ("Send forth, we beseech Thee O Lord, Thy Holy Ghost the Paraclete from heaven onto this fruit of the olive, which Thou hast deigned to produce from a green branch for the refreshment of mind and body....") For Catholics the remote matter of Extreme Unction remains oil of olives and the proximate matter, the anointing with oil blessed by a bishop.

What then is the "matter" specified by Paul VI, in his new *Rite of Anointing and Pastoral Care of the Sick* (promulgated November 30, 1972)?[5] The answer is any oil of plant origin—and, pray, what oil is ultimately not of plant origin [at least partially; see p. 97, n. 1—ED]? Axle-grease, Vaseline and Mazola oil can satisfy the requirement. Further, the oil can be blessed by any priest who has the "faculty," and this faculty has been extended by the "Bishop's Committee on the Liturgy" to any priest "where didactic or catechetical reasons prompt it." The blessing has of course also been changed. **No longer is the Holy Spirit invoked**, but rather, it now reads: "*May your blessing come upon all who are anointed with this oil, that they may be freed from pain and illness and made well again in body and mind and soul.*" **Notice also that the emphasis is almost entirely on the healing of illness, and not on the forgiveness of sins**.

Let us next consider the "Form" of the Sacrament, or the words that the priest uses when anointing the patient "in danger of death." The traditional words are: *Per istam sanctam unctionem et suam piissimam misericordiam indulgeat tibi dominus quidquid per... deliquisti* ("Through this Holy Unction or oil, and through the great

---

5. "*Sacram Unctionem Infirmorum*," Acta Apostolicae Sedis 65 (1973).

goodness of His mercy, may God pardon thee whatever sins thou hast by [evil use of sight—smell, touch etc.—depending on the organ anointed] committed.") Needless to say, this form also has been changed by the Post-Conciliar Church to *Per istam sanctam unctionem et suam piissimam misericordiam adiuvet te dominus gratia spiritus sancti, ut a peccatis liberatum te salvet atque propitius alleviet.* The semi-official translation given out through the Holy See Press Office is: "Through this holy anointing and His most loving mercy, may the Lord assist you by the grace of the Holy Spirit, so that when you have been freed from your sins, he may save you and in his goodness raise you up." Another translation taken from Father Keating's article is closer to the original: "Through this holy anointing and His great love for you, may the Lord who freed you from sin, heal you and extend his saving grace to you. . . ."[6] The official translation provided in *Documents on the Liturgy*, no. 408, is: "Through this holy anointing may the Lord in His love and mercy help you with the grace of the Holy Spirit. May the Lord who frees you from sin save you and raise you up."

Once again we must ask whether this change in the form is substantial—do the new words mean the same as the traditional formula? Pre-Vatican II theologians are virtually unanimous in stating that the essential words of the form—the words that convey its essential meaning and are therefore "substantial"—are *indulgeat tibi dominus*—"may God pardon thee." Most also insist upon *quidquid deliquisti* and *sanctam unctionem*. After all, as Leo XIII said, "the sacraments . . . ought . . . to 'signify the grace which they effect' if they are to 'effect what they signify'. And in the present situation this is the health of the soul which is effected by strengthening of the soul through grace and by the remission of sins. . . ." (*Summa*, III, Suppl. 29, 1). Now the new form **omits** all these critical words, and only asks that God "heal" one. While it is to be admitted that throughout history several valid forms have been in use, since the Council of Florence the form has been fixed. If some of these alternative forms used the words *parcat, remittat,* or even *sanat* in the place of *indulgeat,*

---

6. Charles J. Keating, "The Sacrament of Anointing the Sick," *Homiletic and Pastoral Review*, June, 1974.

this in no way affected the substance of the form. However, to **omit** the critical phrase entirely is to remove from the "form" its ability to absolve. What results is a change in "meaning," and to make a change of such a "substantial" nature almost certainly renders the form invalid. Even if the "blessing" is preceded by a valid absolution—which in many cases is also questionable—one is deprived of the other sacramental effects that are so important.[7] Should an older priest desire to use the traditional form, he should know that it is specifically forbidden by Paul VI's *Apostolic Constitution*.

The Post-Conciliar rite is named "Anointing of the Sick." Clearly then, if the Post-Conciliar "blessing" is upon the sick, the ersatz sacrament should no longer be limited to those "in danger of death." Twice during the Second Vatican Council the Fathers rejected suggestions that the requirement of "danger of death" for the reception of the Anointing be omitted. As Father Keating points out however, "the new rite does what the Council was not able to do".[8] In contrast to the negative wording of Canon 940 which states "Extreme Unction is not able to be offered except to the faithful, who, having attained the use of reason, fall into the danger of death from illness or old age," the new rite can be administered to those who are ill, but in no danger of death whatsoever. Furthermore, insofar as the Constitution on the Liturgy stresses that "whenever rites, according to their specific nature, make provision for communal celebrations involving the presence and active participation of the faithful, this way of celebrating them is to be preferred, as far as possible, to a celebration that is individual and quasi-private." Thus it follows that officially, this new so-called "sacrament" can be given communally. Indeed, in many parishes, it is the custom to gather all the mildly infirm and aged "senior citizens" together in the parish hall, and to bestow this "blessing" upon them—to be followed by coffee and cake!

7. Extreme Unction is usually preceded by Confession and Absolution.
8. Paul VI in his *Apostolic Constitution* quotes the Council as saying: "Extreme Unction, which may also and more properly be called 'the anointing of the sick', is not a sacrament for those only who are at the point of death. Hence, as soon as any one of the faithful begins to be in danger of death from sickness or old age, the fitting time for that person to receive this sacrament has certainly arrived." Once again we have the use of doublespeak.

It is to be admitted that the Apostle James specified the "sick." "Is any man sick among you? Let him bring in the priests of the church and let them pray over him, anointing him with oil in the name of the Lord" (James 5:14–14). But it is a matter of common sense that one cannot and should not call the priests for every trivial complaint. The standard practice of the Church throughout history has been to understand by the "sick," those in danger of death—those about to undergo major surgery, those who have had a heart attack etc. The application of the sacrament to a more general category cannot but trivialize it in the minds of the faithful. And indeed, one sees this in that nurses of presumably Catholic background rarely if ever bother to call a priest even when a patient in the hospital is truly in danger of death.[9] Such is not to be wondered at when they are taught that "Anointing of the Sick is a ritual moment which makes visible and present to the sick and the whole community an image of who we are as Church, that is, a community of mutual healing and support."[10]

In actual practice several other "modifications" are allowed for. According to one study, "the sick person and all those present may receive communion under both kinds.... If the sick person is not confined to bed, he may receive the sacrament of anointing in the church or some other fitting place, where there is a suitable chair or place prepared for him and enough room for his relatives and friends to take part." The same document continues to state that "in

---

9. The reader is reminded that the author has been a practicing surgeon for some 30 years. It is pertinent to quote the comments of Father Baumann, Director of Marydale Diocesan Retreat House and Chairman of the committee for the Continuing Education of Priests:

> The Sacrament of the Anointing of the Sick should not be a Last Sacrament any more than Baptism, Confirmation, Matrimony or Holy Orders.... We used to have some notion that it could effect a forgiveness of sin, and on occasion, might even restore physical health. Today we see the Sacrament NOT [his emphasis] as a preparation for death but as an aid to a more beautiful life—first and immediately on earth. (*The Messenger*, Sept. 12, 1982)

10. Father Thomas Richstatter, O.F.M., "The New Rite for Anointing the Sick," *Catholic Update*, St. Anthony Messenger Press, 1984. Father Richstatter is a recognized authority and his texts are fairly standard teaching sources in today's seminaries.

hospitals the priest should consider other sick people: whether they should be included in the celebration, or if they are not Christians whether they might be offended." And so, even in its mitigated form the "president" is to be careful not to offend the Protestants, even if it means depriving a Catholic soul of what he (hopefully) believes is a critical sacrament![11]

In the traditional rite the priest arrived in a subdued manner, carrying the Blessed Sacrament in his pyx, and spoke only when necessary. Those who knew and understood his function knelt before him (for he carried the Blessed Sacrament), and those caring for the patient prepared a table by the bed with lighted candles and a crucifix. Whenever possible the priest was accompanied by an acolyte who rang a bell so the faithful would not accidentally slight our Lord. (When the Blessed Sacrament passes by, any healthy Catholic should get down on both knees until it has passed.) On arriving he would say three short appropriate prayers, the Confiteor, (and if appropriate, listen to the patient's confession and give him Absolution[12]), and then immediately administer the Viaticum. Then with his right hand extended over the head of the patient he said "In the name of the Father + and the Son + and the Holy Ghost +, be there quenched in thee all power of the devil, through the laying on of my hands, and through the invocation of the glorious and holy Virgin Mary, Mother of God, her illustrious spouse Joseph, and all the holy Angels, Archangels, Patriarchs, Prophets, Apostles, Martyrs, Confessors, Virgins, and all the Saints, Amen." Then with his thumb dipped in the Holy Oils, he anointed the sick in the form of the Cross on parts described in the rite above. This was followed with a

---

11. *Anointing the Sick, a Study in Pastoral Liturgy*; prepared by the St. Thomas More Center for Pastoral Liturgy; published by Mayhew-McCrimmon Ltd., Southend-on-Sea, England; used in the Sydney Australia Archdiocese; quoted by Hutton Gibson in his *Paul VI's Legacy: Catholicism?* (Cochin, India: Leo Panakal, 1974). An American version is available from *Catholic Update*, published by the St. Anthony Messenger Press (Cincinnati, Ohio), entitled *The New Rite for Anointing the Sick*, by Father Thomas Richstatter, O.F.M.

12. If the patient is incapacitated, the priest will ask him/her if they have sinned against any of the commandments and then list each of them in turn. All the patient has to do is nod his head or even blink his eyes.

short responsory prayer (including the Lord's Prayer) and three additional, highly specific prayers for the sick person. Because he was carrying Our Lord's Body, the priest did not stop to chat or have coffee, but returned as quickly as possible to the sacristy.

In the new rite the priest arrives—no longer necessarily even dressed as a priest—and greets one and all in a friendly manner. Then instead of doing what he came for, he makes a speech to let all know why he came. This is followed by a "penitential rite" in place of the Confiteor. According to the instructions "whenever possible, Viaticum should be received within mass" (which of course poses no difficulty as the Novus Ordo only requires a table). There follows a short litany which may be transferred to the time after the anointing, or recited "at some other point." Now he lays his hands on the sick person in silence, for the various above mentioned prayers are no longer required. As for the anointing, it is limited to the forehead and hands, and this is done with the new "blessing" of dubious sacramental efficacy. This is followed by a prayer "best suited to the person's condition." (Hutton Gibson suggests "Now I lay me down to sleep.") The service ends with the Lord's Prayer and a blessing.

Lest this description seem exaggerated, allow me to give the suggested manner of acting according to Father Richstatter, a well known expert on liturgical practice. After suggesting that Confession or the Viaticum (Eucharist) not be administered at the same time as the Sacrament for the Sick, he describes the new way of doing things:

> The rite starts much as Mass does: with prayers to gather us into the presence of Christ and of one another, and to recall our continuing need for healing. Holy water may be used to remind us that we have been baptized into the Christ who suffered for us and has transformed our suffering into victory. All sacraments begin with readings from the Bible. The number and length of the readings (and of the homily and general intercessions) will depend on the circumstances. The rite is similar to the first part of Sunday Mass.
>
> After the litany of intercessions the priest will lay his hands on your head. Together with all present he will pray silently for your

healing. Next he will bless God for the gift of oil: "God of all consolation... make this oil a remedy for all who are anointed with it; heal them in body, in soul and in spirit, and deliver them from every affliction." The priest will anoint you with the blessed oil. First he will make the sign of the cross with the oil on your forehead, saying: "Through this holy anointing may the Lord in his love and mercy help you with the grace of the Holy Spirit." All respond: "Amen." The priest will ask that you present the palms of your hands to him and he will anoint them with the sign of the cross: "May the Lord who frees you from sin save you and raise you up." All respond: "Amen." You may find it helpful to rub your hands together and pray that as the oil penetrates and soothes your skin, so may the healing of Christ penetrate and heal any weakness or affliction.

Yet another change! In former times the priest would anoint and administer Extreme Unction "conditionally" to a person who was already dead—up to a limited time of about three hours. This was only reasonable because the patient could die while awaiting the arrival of the priest, and because no one presumed to know at just what point the soul departed from the body.[13] (I became aware that this was no longer the case when working on accident victims in the emergency room. Priests would not come if the patient was already dead, even if he or she had just died—or they would offer to come to console the family.) Nowadays, "when a priest is called to attend those who are already dead, he should not administer the Sacrament of anointing. Instead, he should pray for them, asking that God forgive their sins and graciously receive them into the Kingdom." One

---

13. The physician can certify that the body has died. The older medical and theological literature gave ample testimony to the fact that patients occasionally would recover after being pronounced dead by competent physicians. Rigor mortis, which occurs 3 to 6 hours after apparent death, was considered a point of no possible return. Current medical practice has the technology to refine the point of bodily death with greater accuracy—absence of electrical activity in the brain and heart [The resuscitation of patients after "brain death," while rare, continues to be reported—ED]. However, this is still to speak of the body and not the soul (cf. Rev. Juan B. Ferreres, S.J., *Death, Real and Apparent, in relation to the Sacraments* [St. Louis: Herder, 1906]).

would think that even if the president didn't personally believe in the sacramental effects produced, he would administer the rite to console the next of kin. In any event, those who believe in the efficacy of this new rite better be sure they call the president in time.

It is interesting in passing to quote Paul VI's description of the new rite. According to him "the celebration of this sacrament consists especially in the laying on of hands by priests of the Church, the offering of the prayer of faith, and the anointing of the sick with oil made holy by God's blessing." But have no fear, for Paul VI continues: "This rite signifies the grace of the sacrament and confers it." Despite his assurances, one may reasonably be allowed to doubt if the new rite conveys anything more than a blessing.

It should not be thought that the Church has any objection to the blessing of the sick. Indeed the Roman ritual contains three such blessings: There is an extended blessing with a relic of the true Cross in honor of St. Benedict and St. Maurice, and there is an "ordinary" blessing for both adults and for children.[14] This is but further evidence that there was no need to change the Sacrament into yet another such blessing.

The blessing of the sick is one thing and the Sacrament of Extreme Unction quite another. This is brought home to us by the story of St. Raymund Nonnatus (August 31) who, after a life of great sacrifice, prayer and holiness was, must to his embarrassment, raised to the Cardinalate by Pope Gregory IX. On his way to Rome he fell ill, and begged for the sacrament with great fervor. The priest, however, was long delayed, and St. Raymund was refreshed with the saving Viaticum from the hands of an angel, who appeared to him in the likeness of a member of his own order.

Clearly the changes made in this sacrament, or rather the destruction of this Sacrament and its replacement with a blessing, either reflect a lack of belief in the Sacrament, or else are made to mollify the Protestants who deny the Sacraments that are dependent upon a validly ordained priest. One argument put forth to justify the destruction of Extreme Unction is that the traditional administration of the Sacrament frightens the patient. As a surgeon of some

---

14. There is even a blessing for sick animals.

30 years of active practice, I have never known a patient who was not aware of his imminent end, and I have never known one who was frightened by the arrival of a priest for this purpose. On the contrary, patients that believe have often expressed their anxiety at the delay of the priest's arrival. I have often encouraged Catholic patients to receive the Sacrament, and have never known them to refuse or be frightened by the request. Families and relatives may express concern, but can be easily reassured. Even those whose faith is weak to the point of not fully believing in the efficacy of the Sacrament greatly benefit.

Returning to more serious considerations, let us remember that none of us can escape the necessity of facing death. If we are to believe in the "effects" of the Sacrament, then it behooves us also to believe in the need for its "validity." Validity in turn demands a certain integrity in matter and form and hence it is our right to have this integrity retained by the Church that claims to be founded by Christ and the Apostles. No traditional Catholic admitted to the emergency room "in extremis" and asking for a priest, would settle for a Baptist minister—even if he should say the proper words of the form. Yet in fact, of what more use is a priest who uses an incorrect and doubtful form? One must further express great wonderment at the new breed of priest who feels free to "play around" with such a powerful Sacrament. The bestowal of Extreme Unction must be one of the paramount and most satisfying aspects of a priest's life, and is moreover something which in charity and in justice he is bound to provide. And what is one to think of a "Church" that would dupe its obedient and faithful followers, rob them of this pearl, and pay them off with a facile blessing? Indeed, we live in dangerous times and the world itself is *in extremis*. Unless we take a stand on such issues, we will have little grounds for complaint when on our own death beds we prepare to face our Lord and Judge without the assistance of these necessary graces.

4

CONFIRMATION

Confirmation has been called the "compliment and perfection of Baptism," and Scripture tells us that it was conferred by the Apostles: "They laid their hands upon them, and they received the Holy Ghost" (Acts 8:17).

The effects of Confirmation are twofold. First of all, it impresses upon the soul a special character which cannot be effaced. This sacramental character makes us soldiers of Christ, and we are thus bound to defend the faith under all circumstances, even at the cost of our lives.

Secondly, through Confirmation we receive the Holy Ghost with the abundance of His gifts and graces. He gives us the grace of strength, which confirms evermore within us Faith, Hope and Charity, and thus we are able to confess Jesus Christ by word and deed, and to advance in piety, despite the temptations of the world, the flesh and the devil. "In this sacrament," says St. Thomas, "is given the plenitude of the Holy Ghost for the strengthening of grace."

To fully understand the difference between the graces bestowed in Baptism and Confirmation, one has but to consider their varied effects on the lives of the Apostles. After Baptism and prior to Pentecost, they had lain hidden, timid, fearful and had even denied and deserted Our Lord when threatened. After the descent of the Holy Ghost, they were like lions breathing fire, and not even the threat of death could hinder them from preaching the Gospel.

Those of us who have received this Sacrament may see few such dramatic effects in our lives: however, an analogy will give us encouragement.

A man endowed with marvelous strength is not always conscious of that strength until the time comes to use it. So it is with the

Sacrament of Confirmation. On special occasions the strength of the Sacrament is experienced, just as it was experienced by the early Christians in times of persecution. Moreover, this is infallibly experienced, providing that sin places no obstacle in the way, for just as sin hinders the grace of a Sacrament in its actual reception, so also does it hinder the effects of the same grace at the moment in which it should be exercised.

And so it is that Confirmation bestows upon Christians in substance what the Holy Ghost bestowed upon the Apostles at Pentecost, and enables them to defend the faith against whatever assails it in every age.

Let us for a moment consider the words off St. Thérèse of Lisieux with regard to this Sacrament:

> A short time after my First Communion, I went again into retreat for my Confirmation. I had very carefully prepared myself for the coming of the Holy Spirit. I could not understand why so little attention was often paid to this Sacrament of love.... How happy my soul was! Like the Apostles I happily awaited the promised Comforter. I rejoiced that soon I should be a perfect Christian, and have eternally marked upon my forehead the mysterious cross of his ineffable Sacrament. On that day I received the strength to suffer, a strength which I much needed, for the martyrdom of my soul was soon to begin.

A SHORT HISTORY OF CONFIRMATION

Scriptural reference has already been provided. In the second century Tertullian states "after having come out of the laver (Baptism), we are anointed thoroughly with a blessed unction according to the ancient rule.... Next to this, the hand is laid upon us, through the blessing calling upon and inviting the Holy Spirit." St. Cyprian teaches "anointed also must he of necessity be, who is baptized ... a person is not born by the imposition of hands when he receives the Holy Ghost, but in baptism; that being already born he may receive the Spirit...." St. Ambrose told the catechumens who had just been baptized and anointed "thou hast received the spiritual seal, the spirit of wisdom and of understanding, the spirit of counsel and of fortitude, the spirit of knowledge and of piety, the spirit of holy fear; and keep what thou hast received. God the Father has sealed thee.... God the Father has confirmed thee: and the Spirit has given the pledge in thy heart...."

Pope Innocent III wrote "The anointing of the forehead with chrism signifies the laying on of the hand, the other name for which is Confirmation, since through it the Holy Spirit is given for growth and strength." He further said, "We regard Confirmation by the bishop, that is, the laying on of hands, to be holy and to be received with reverence." Innocent IV mentions that the apostles conferred the Holy Spirit through the laying on of the hand, "which Confirmation or the anointing of the forehead with chrism represents."

HOW IMPORTANT IS THIS SACRAMENT?

The Church has always taught that the Sacrament of Confirmation was not necessary for salvation. However, Confirmation was instituted for the battles in this life, and is required by precept because Our Lord instituted it as a means of grace. All are obliged, therefore, to receive it, if they are able to do so.

The Council of Laodicea in 370 stated that "it behooves those who are illuminated to be anointed after Baptism with the supercelestial chrism, and to be made partakers of Christ." St. Peter Damian, a Doctor of the Church, insists that the obligation to receive it is a serious one. Benedict XIV taught that the obligation bound under pain of sin, if no grave inconvenience was involved in its reception. Clement XIV approved a decree in 1774 which stated that "this Sacrament cannot be refused or neglected without incurring the guilt of mortal sin, if there be an opportune occasion of receiving it."

THE MINISTER OF THE SACRAMENT

Some historians have claimed that Confirmation grew out of Baptism—citing the fact that in the Eastern Church both are given at the same time as evidence. Let us listen then to one of the most important authorities of the Eastern Church, St. John Chrysostom.

He tells us that:

> Philip was one of the seven, the second [in rank] after Stephen. Hence, when he baptized, he did not communicate to the neophytes the Holy Ghost, because he had not the power to do so. This gift was peculiar to the twelve, a prerogative of the Apostles; whence we see [even now] that the bishops and none other do this.

In the Western Church, the ordinary (normal) minister of the Sacrament of Confirmation is the bishop. Since Pius XII's decree *Spiritum Sancti Munera* of September 14, 1946, it has been common law in the Latin Church that all pastors or their equivalents may confer this sacrament on their subjects in danger of death. In the Eastern Churches today, the ordinary minister of the Sacrament is the parish priest, and the Sacrament is frequently administered immediately after Baptism. It goes without saying that the Priest or Bishop must have been validly ordained.

THE MATTER OF THE SACRAMENT

Chrism blessed by the bishop on Holy Thursday is considered to be the "remote matter" of the Sacrament. The Church has always insisted that only olive oil and balm may be used for this purpose. The Post-Conciliar Church now allows for the use of any "vegetable oil."[1] The reader is referred to the Chapter on Extreme Unction for a fuller discussion of the nature of this oil, and the blessing required to "sanctify" it. (The need for balsam or balm—a fragrant oleoresin exuded from certain plants and trees—to be added to the olive oil was debated by theologians over the centuries, and was considered until 1971 as "of precept" but not essential for validity.)

There is some difference of opinion about what is called the

---

1. "Olive oil or another oil extracted from plants." *Documents on the Liturgy*, no. 3864. Chrism is also important in Baptism and Extreme Unction. One wonders why axle grease could not be considered an oil extracted from plants. Cases of priests using Vaseline as chrism have occurred. [Vaseline and axle grease are by-products of the refinement of petroleum, which is thought to have developed from an ancient biomass of both plant and animal origin.—ED]

"proximate matter." Some theologians hold that it lies in the imposition of hands, while others maintain that it lies in the anointing with chrism. Still others hold that both are required, and some that either is sufficient.

Because of the differences of opinion most theologians now hold that both the imposition of hands and the anointing with chrism are necessary. Indeed, in the traditional rite, the bishop performs both actions simultaneously with an individual imposition of hands for each confirmand as the anointing is being done. A prior imposition of hands takes place at the beginning of the ceremony when the bishop extends his hands over the confirmands as a group. In the Eastern Rites, only the second imposition of hands is used, and it is this one that pertains to the "proximate matter."

In the new Post-Conciliar rite established by Paul VI's Apostolic Constitution *Divinae Consortium Naturae* (15 August, 1971), and based on his personal reply to a query (*Documents on the Liturgy*, no. 306), only the initial blessing over all the confirmands has been retained. The individual laying-on of hands at the time of the actual anointing has been suppressed. He stated that anointing with chrism "sufficiently expresses the laying on of hands."

This decision is interesting in view of the statement by Father Pourrat that "In the Apostolic Age, the matter of Confirmation was the imposition of hands; after the second century, it was, besides, the anointing with holy chrism."[2] Thus the new rite constitutes a clear-cut departure from both Scriptural and Patristic custom.

THE FORM OF THE SACRAMENT

During the course of history different forms for the Sacrament of Confirmation have been used—they have presumably all been substantially (i.e. in their meaning) similar. The current form has been in use since at least the 12th Century and was specified as such by both St. Thomas Aquinas and St. Bonaventura, though St. Albert the Great and Alexander of Hales specified slightly different but

---

2. Father P. Pourrat, *Theology of the Sacraments* (St. Louis, Herder, 1914), fn., p. 85.

substantially similar ones. The Council of Florence and the Council of Trent both specified that the formula was "I sign thee with the Sign of the Cross, and I confirm thee with the chrism of salvation. In the name of the Father, and of the Son and of the Holy Ghost." (*Signo te signo Crucis, et confirmo te Chrismate salutis. In nomine Patris, et Filii et Spiritus Sancti.*)

The form used in the Eastern Churches differs slightly: "The sign [or seal] of the gift of the Holy Ghost." (The Latin for this would be *signaculum doni spiritus Sancti.*) This probably dates back to the First Council of Constantinople (381), and certainly dates back to the Trullan Council of 692. (This is not to say that it was not in use prior to that time, but only that we can historically trace its use back to these dates.)

Now the essential words must clearly be found in what the Western and Eastern formulas have in common. Father Joseph Pohle discusses this in his pre-Vatican II text *The Sacraments: A Dogmatic Treatise*:[3]

> Which particular words constitute the substance of the formula is a purely theoretical question that can easily be decided if we admit the Greek formula[4] to be essentially equivalent to the longer Latin one.... Manifestly, the formula of Confirmation must express two concepts, viz.: (1) the act of signing or sealing (*signo te*) and (2), the grace of the Holy Ghost (*confirmo te*). Neither the invocation of the Most Holy Trinity nor the words *signo crucis* and *chrismate salutis* are essential. So far as we know, all the forms ever used embodied these two leading ideas, at least implicitly.
>
> (The blow on the cheek, the *alapa*, did not become customary until the twelfth century. It was apparently devised in imitation of the blow by which knighthood was conferred in the Middle Ages and obviously complemented the concept that the recipient of the Sacrament was now a soldier of Christ.)

---

3. St. Louis: B. Herder, 1917.
4. The Greeks refer to the Sacrament of Confirmation as "the chrism of Holy Ointment," or "the seal of the gift of the Holy Ghost."

THE POST-CONCILIAR CHANGES IN THE FORM

When we come to the new rite of Confirmation as established by Paul VI's Apostolic constitution *Divinae Consortium Naturae* (15 August, 1971), we find the following statement:

> The Sacrament of Confirmation is conferred through the anointing with chrism on the forehead, which is done by laying on of the hand and through the words *"accipe signaculum doni Spiritus Sancti"* (officially translated as "Be Sealed with the Gift of the Holy Ghost").

Paul VI tells us that he has adopted this formula from the Byzantine Rite, stating, "We therefore adopt this formula, rendering it almost word for word . . . by which the Gift of the Holy Spirit Himself is expressed and the outpouring of the Spirit which took place on the day of Pentecost is recalled." He is of course correct, for the Greek form, as noted above, is *signaculum doni Spiritus Sancti*. Why, however, did he add *accipe*, which changes the meaning of the words from the active sense of something the Bishop imposes on the recipient, to the passive request for him to accept what is offered?

The answer is that by the use of this one word, the recipient is merely **asked** to receive the gifts of the Holy Ghost, and this is a purely **subjective** act on the recipient's part. By doing this Paul VI introduced a formula which is much more acceptable to the Protestants who would be horrified at the idea that an indelible character is imprinted *ex opere operato* on the recipient.

There is yet a further problem with Paul VI's *Divinae Consortium Naturae*. In it he states that the rite of Confirmation "recalls" what took place on Pentecost. This is a faulty notion of a Sacrament. The gifts of the Holy Ghost are bestowed once again through the rites of the Church, and not simply "recalled."

WHY THE CHANGES?

Paul VI tells us that the reason for the revision "which concurs with the very essence of the rite of confirmation" was in order that "the intimate connection of this sacrament with the whole Christian initiation may stand out more clearly." And the result, he assures us, is that "the rite and words of this sacrament "express more clearly the holy things they signify and the Christian people, as far as possible, are able to understand them with ease and take part in them fully, actively, and as befits a community." It is for the reader to judge whether this end has been achieved.

CONCLUSION

Once again we have a Sacrament whose form and matter have been significantly tampered with. While one cannot officially state that it has been invalidated—indeed, only the teaching magisterium of the Church could ever come to such a conclusion and obligate us to accept it as being "of faith." However, one can certainly state that with the change in the remote matter of olive oil to any vegetable oil, with the suppression of the laying on of hands and the statement that the signing of the forehead with the cross suffices for this, and with the subjective change in the form of the sacrament, an element of doubt has been raised. We are no longer supplied with the necessary *medium certum*.

5

WHAT HAPPENED TO CONFESSION?

Repentance for our faults can alone take the place of innocence, and . . . to show ourselves repentant, we must begin by declaring them.   Voltaire

Few Catholic customs have been subjected to greater criticism than that of going to Confession. One can do no better than to initiate this discussion with the sneering comment of George Bernard Shaw to G.K. Chesterton after his conversion: "Your portly kneeling figure" in the confessional would be "incredible, monstrous, comic." More enlightened was Chesterton's answer: "When a Catholic comes from confession, he does truly, by definition, step out into that dawn of his own beginning... in that brief ritual God has really remade him in His own image. He may be grey and gouty, but he is only five minutes old."

All of us "who are over 30" remember the long confessional lines that plagued us every week in our childhood. Saints like the Curé of Ars were known to have spent 17 hours continuously in that "dark box"—and those that suspect some "voyeuristic" pleasure in such a function would do well to meditate on the fact that man's inventiveness in sin is limited, and that priests have always complained that listening to pettiness of man's repetitive sins is the least pleasant and most boring of all their obligations.

All this has changed. As of this writing, only 6% of those who consider themselves Catholic and who go to Church regularly go to Confession on a monthly basis and only 1% more often than that. According to the Notre Dame study in 1983, 26% of those formally affiliated to their parishes never go to confession at all. Now all this is occurring at a time when higher percentages of practicing Catholics are receiving the Eucharist on a regular basis. Studies show that among those who go to Confession once or twice a year or never at all, more than 80% are communicants. Are we to assume that sin has lessened? One may be permitted to doubt this.[1]

A recent report by the American Bishops' Committee for Pastoral Research and Practice considers the results of such polls "puzzling." Religious liberals conclude that the old forms are no longer serving the believers' needs. Others suggest that the more obvious explanation is a lessened fear of hell and a decreased awareness about the nature of sin and the purpose of the Confessional.[2]

CONFESSION IS NOT A PSYCHIATRIC SESSION

Considerable confusion has been spread abroad by liberal Catholics who attempt to explain away Confession as a "way of getting rid of guilt," and hence as a Catholic variety of psychotherapy. It should be clear that, while the forgiveness of sins carries in its train the removal of guilt—at least that obvious guilt that relates to the sin involved—this is a far cry from the analyst's couch. The Catholic penitent is just that—a penitent. He admits that he is guilty of sin and his forgiveness is among other things totally dependent upon a "firm purpose of amendment." The psychoanalyst who by definition passes no moral judgment on his patient, functions to uncover the root causes for a patient's sense of guilt. This sense of guilt the psychiatrist deals with is in no way objective; it is not an offence the patient is aware of. The psychiatrist functions to help the patient uncover suppressed or false reasons for this sense of guilt. If and when he does this, he then attempts to teach the patient how to live with those "negative" (never evil) traits within his and every per-

---

1. Many surveys gloatingly inform us that 80 to 95% of Catholics are using artificial methods of birth control. No religious distinctions can be found among parties getting divorced or abortions.

2. Many of these comments are drawn from a *New York Times* article, March 31, 1990.

son's soul. The psychiatrist never forgives—it is the patient who must forgive himself. The psychiatrist never demands retribution, for this also is left to the patient—indeed, if the patient felt the need to perform some penitential act it would be viewed by the analyst as evidence of a persisting guilt complex. The psychiatrist does not demand any amendment of life other than that which the patient may himself recognize the need of.

A BRIEF HISTORY OF CONFESSION

As a result of Adam's "fall," the material and animal principle in man declared war against the spiritual and intellectual—the net result of which is, as St. Paul expressed it, that "I find a law, that when I have a will to do good, evil is present with me. For I am delighted with the law of God according to the inward man, but I see another law in my members, fighting against the law of my mind, and captivating me in the law of sin" (Rom. 7:22–23). While such is the underlying principle leading to sin, the Ten Commandments clearly codify those offences against God and one's fellow man.

We see also, that even among the Jews, Confession was a "sacrament." In Num. 5:6–7 we read, "when a man or woman shall have committed any of all the sins that men are wont to commit, and by negligence shall have transgressed the commandment of the Lord, and offended, they shall confess their sin and restore the principal itself, and the fifth part over and above, to him against whom they have sinned. But if there be no one to receive it, they shall give it to the Lord, and it shall be the priest's besides the ram that is offered for expiation, to be an atoning sacrifice."[3]

As with the other sacraments, Confession was established by Our Lord when he said "Receive ye the Holy Ghost, whose sins you shall forgive, they are forgiven" (2 Cor. 2:6–8. Cf. also John 1:9; James 5:16).

---

3. According to Rabbi David Kimchi, not only was such confession necessary, but, without it, sacrifices could be of no avail; for he remarks: "All the efficacy of sacrifices consists in the confession of sins and in repentance." (Quoted by Rev. L. De Goesbriand, *The History of Confession* [NY: Benzinger, 1889])

And from the foundation of the Church the Fathers have encouraged Confession. As St. Clement of Rome said in the First Century: "For whatsoever things, therefore, we have transgressed by any of the suggestions of the adversary, let us supplicate pardon." Tertullian says of this Sacrament that "Confession of sins lightens their burthen, as much as the dissembling of them increases it; for confession savoureth of satisfaction, dissembling of stubbornness... if thou drawest back from confession, consider in thine heart that hell-fire which confession shall quench for thee; and first imagine to thyself the greatness of the punishment, that thou mayest not doubt concerning the adoption of the remedy." St. Cyprian teaches: "We have an Advocate and an Intercessor for our sins, Jesus Christ, our Lord and our God, if only we are penitent that we have sinned in time past, and confessing and understanding our sins whereby we now offend the Lord, we promise, for the future at least, to walk in his ways, and to fear his commandments." St. Cyril of Jerusalem instructs us to "Put off the old man, who is corrupted according to the deceitful lusts[4], by means of confession, that you may put on the new man." St. Ambrose tells us that "Sins are remitted by the word of God, of which the Levite is the interpreter, and also the executor; they are also remitted by the office of the priest, and the sacred ministry."

We see in these early examples all the principles required for a proper confession: the admission of sin to a priest, a firm purpose of amendment; the acceptance of a penance (sacrifice), the need for reparation or restitution where appropriate; and absolution given by the priest as an *alter Christus*.

TO WHOM DO WE CONFESS?

It should be clear that through the medium of the priest—who functions as an *alter Christus* or "another Christ"—it is to Christ Himself that we confess, and similarly, the priest forgives us in the same capacity. This is made strikingly clear in the Eastern Rites where the priest and the penitent approach Christ's icon on the

---

4. "Lusts" in theological writing do not necessarily imply sexual sins. One can for instance, "lust" after money.

iconostasis; the priest drapes his stole over the penitent who then confesses to both the priest and before the iconographic representation of our Lord.

DO WE NEED A PRIEST TO CONFESS TO?

St. Augustine addresses this issue. To quote him directly:

> Let no person say, I do penance in secret in the presence of God; it suffices that he who is to grant me pardon should know the repentance which I feel in the depth of my heart. If such were the case, it would be without reason for Jesus Christ to say, Whatsoever you shall loose on earth shall be loosed in heaven, or that He should have confided the keys to His Church. It is not, then, sufficient to confess to God; we must also confess to those who have received from Him the power of binding and loosing.[5]

And again:

> There are some who imagine it is sufficient for their salvation to confess to God, from whom nothing is concealed, and who reads the secrets of all hearts, for they are unwilling, either from motives of shame, or pride, or contempt, to show themselves to the priests, although our Lord has appointed them to discern between the different kinds of leprosy. Disabuse yourself of such an opinion, and be not ashamed to confess to the vicar of the Lord. For we must submit to the judgment of those whom He has not disdained to put in His place. When, then, you are sick, send for a priest to come to you and disclose to him all the secrets of your conscience. Do not permit yourself to be led astray by the false religion of those who tell you, in visiting you, that confession made to God alone, without the intervention of the priest, is capable of saving you. We do not deny that it is often necessary to address ourselves to God, and make our confession to Him, but, before all things, we have need of the priest. Regard him as an Angel sent by God; open to him the innermost secrets of your

---

5. St. Augustine, *Sermon II, in psalm i.*, n. 3.

heart; reveal to him whatever causes you most confusion; be not ashamed to declare to one man what you have not blushed to commit in the presence of many. Make, then, an entire confession, without dissimulation or excuses for your fault. Be simple and exact; make no evasions or circumlocutions, which only obscure and embarrass the truth. Note the circumstances of your sins, the places, occasions, and the persons, without however naming them.[6]

The Eastern Churches hold to the same opinion. The *Confessio Orthodoxa* directed against Cyril Lucar by Peter Mogilas (1642), which was signed by all the Orthodox patriarchs of the time, enjoys among them the value of a creed. It contains the following statement:

> This contrition of the heart must be followed by an oral confession of each and every sin, because the confessor cannot forgive anything if he does not know what there is to be forgiven and what sort of penance he is to impose.

THE SEAL OF CONFESSION

Brief mention must be made of what is called the "Seal of Confession," or the obligation of the priest never under any circumstances to reveal what he hears in confession. The most trifling disclosure, either direct or indirect, is contrary to the very essence of confession.

> The seal of confession is of divine right; it rests on the institution of the Sacrament of Penance, on the obligation laid upon us to confess our sins; hence no power can dispense from the law, *not even in the case of danger to the commonweal.*[7]

Civil law has recognized this seal and priests have given up their lives to protect it. Priests who have gone insane, have on being questioned about what they heard in confession, refused to answer.

---

6. Quoted in Rev. L. De Goesbriand, *The History of Confession*, op. cit.
7. Quoted from *De Réal* by L. De Goesbriand.

Priests who have left the Church and apostatized from the faith have somehow kept the seal. It is an extraordinary fact that over almost 2000 years of recorded history, no one can point to a documented case where this seal has been violated.

WHAT IF NO PRIEST IS AVAILABLE?

God does not ask the impossible. Obviously, if no priest is available, one cannot confess to one. However, when in danger of death, a Catholic can request any validly ordained priest to hear his confession. According to Father Augustine, such applies "even [to a priest] who is a member of a schismatic or heretic sect, or apostatized or censured...." Such a priest "may validly absolve anyone in danger of death, even in the presence of an approved confessor."[8] A further note has been added to this ruling by a decision of the Holy Office: "provided no scandal is given to the faithful, no danger of perversion threatens the sick person, and finally, provided that it may be reasonably presumed that the schismatic minister will absolve according to the rite of the Church."

If even such is not available the person can make what is called an ACT OF CONTRITION.

> O My God, I am heartily sorry for my sins, not only because I fear the loss of heaven and the pains of hell [up to now we have an act of imperfect contrition], but most of all because I have offended Thee My God, who art infinitely good and worthy of all my love. [It is this higher motivation—for the love of God, if sufficiently intense—that makes an act of contrition perfect.] I resolve, with the help of Thy grace, to amend my life, to confess my sins and to do penance" [i.e., make satisfaction].

It should be added that for the dying individual

The Papal benediction with attached plenary indulgence may be gained by saying the Holy Name of Jesus. If unable to say it, the

---

8. Rev. Charles Augustine, *A Commentary on the New Code of Canon Law* (1917) (St. Louis: Herder, 1925).

person must at least think it, and with contrition kiss a blessed crucifix.[9]

THE COMPONENTS OF THE SACRAMENT OF PENANCE: THE MATTER OF THE SACRAMENT

The acts of the penitent are the proximate matter of the sacrament and as such similar to the anointing with chrism in Confirmation or the use of water in Baptism. Sins are not atoned for simply by fulfilling the sentence of a judge; the Confession of the sinner and the will of an offended God must also be taken into consideration. In view of this three acts are required of the penitent: Contrition, Confession, and Satisfaction.

CONTRITION is deliberate sorrow for sins which includes the purpose of confessing and making satisfaction for them. The Council of Trent declared that "Contrition . . . is a profound sorrow and detestation for sin committed, with a resolution of sinning no more. The word Contrition comes from the Latin *contritum* or *contritio* which signifies a crushing, breaking or undoing of something—thus it represents that crushing or breaking of man's attachment to sin.

Natural sorrow or remorse (such as is based on some worldly motive such as shame) is not sufficient because the Sacrament of Penance pertains to the supernatural order.

ATTRITION or "imperfect contrition" combined with the reception of penance is sufficient for the forgiveness of sin. Such for example, as illustrated above in the "act of contrition," is the fear of hell. While this is the least noble of supernatural motives, it is undeniably supernatural because the existence of hell is accepted on divine faith. Further, attrition includes a detestation of sin, which is a means of avoiding hell. This kind of sorrow is likened to the fear entertained by a slave.

Perfect contrition however can remit all sin. This is true even when confession is impossible (i.e., when a confessor is unavailable), provided that the desire for the sacrament is included in the contrition, for contrition breaks the attachment of the will to sin.

---

9. Louis LaRavoire Morro, *My Catholic Faith* (Kenosh, WI: My Mission House).

(Contrition does not extend to original sin, which is something that exists apart from the individual's will, nor to future sins that may or may not be committed.)

In point of fact, no sin can be forgiven without contrition—in sacramental penance attrition becomes contrition through the power of the Sacrament. The reason for this is that the will cannot both cling to and detest the same sin at the same time.

Attrition or Contrition should be **true and formal** (i.e., not pretended); it should be **supernatural**, (i.e., be inspired by and dependent upon grace and motivated by some consideration known by the light of faith); it must be **supreme** (i.e., the penitent must regard sin as the greatest of evils—this does not require an intense feeling of sorrow, but rather a conviction of the evil of sin); and it must be **universal**, (i.e., extend to all one's mortal sins).

A purpose of amendment is implicit in true contrition, for it is the resolve not to sin again. Without the resolve not to sin again there is no true contrition. Yet this purpose of amendment, which is more than a mere wish of avoiding sins, is not a promise or vow never to sin again.

Theologians list three qualities that should be present. The intention must be **firm** (at least at the time it is made), it must be **efficacious** (there must be the intent to avoid the occasions for the sin and the ordinary safeguards against sin—both *caution* and *prayer*. There must also be the *intent to repair* as far as is possible the damage done by the sin). And finally, it must be **universal** (i.e., the resolve to avoid all mortal sins).

CONFESSION is defined as the telling of the personal sins one has committed after Baptism to an authorized priest for the purpose of obtaining absolution.

Confession is necessary for salvation for anyone who after Baptism has the misfortune to fall into mortal sin. This general obligation which arises from divine law is made more specific by the law of the Church: "Every one of the faithful of either sex, upon reaching the age of discretion is bound to confess sincerely all sins at least once a year" (Canon 906).

It is commonly taught that the divine precept of confession would oblige anyone who is in actual or probable danger of death. The precept would also become binding in the face of special circumstances, as for example, when one is about to marry or be confirmed, when one is in need of special graces to overcome temptations, or when one is not in a state of grace and wishes to receive Communion.

Confession should be discreet, free, sincere, courageous, marked by shame, sorrowful, humble, truthful, open, simple, entire, accusatory, manifestive of a readiness to obey the confessor, secret, frequent and prompt.

SATISFACTION is the last and final aspect of penance. It is an act of virtue which pertains to justice. In making satisfaction for sin, the compensation need not be quantitatively, but only proportionately equal. (We can never make adequate satisfaction for a mortal sin which offends an infinite God and therefore in some way is an infinite offence.) But God accepts this satisfaction (i.e., the penance given) as sufficient to regain divine friendship. As the Council of Trent teaches, "It befits divine mercy that sins not be forgiven us without any satisfaction, lest having thus found an occasion for thinking sins to be light, we fall into graver sins (such as insulting and contemning the Holy Spirit), storing up wrath for ourselves on the day of wrath."

Satisfaction can be made in God's sight through the grace of Christ in several ways:

(1) By freely undertaking penance for sin
(2) By patiently bearing the temporal punishment sent by God
(3) By doing the penance assigned by the priest in confession

The three principal acts of penance are almsgiving, fasting and prayer which are said to primarily uproot the concupiscence of the eyes, concupiscence of the flesh and pride of life. It should be clear that the penance imposed is a means whereby the penitent satisfies the temporal punishment due to his sins. The eternal punishment due to mortal sin is forgiven by the Sacrament itself; the penance is designed to remit temporal punishment.

Normally the priest is obliged to assign a penance. (He might not do so with a dying patient.) Similarly the penitent must perform the penance, which is an integral part of the sacrament. (There is no special obligation to fulfill the penance before receiving Holy

Communion, though this is certainly the best course to follow in practice.)

ANOTHER IMPORTANT ASPECT OF CONFESSION

Not greatly stressed in texts on Sacramental Theology is another important aspect of Confession—namely spiritual direction. Not infrequently, after having absolved the penitent of his sins, the priest will give a brief instruction to the penitent on the spiritual life, for it is understood that the virtuous life is not an end in itself, but predispositive to the spiritual life.

THE FORM OF THE SACRAMENT

The form of the Sacrament has changed over the centuries. Father Villien lists many of these in his *History and Liturgy of the Sacraments*.[10] Thus for example an early Pontifical from Tours, after stating that Christ had instituted the Sacrament, and after invoking various saints and the Blessed Virgin, states: *ipse vos absolvat per ministerium nostrum ab omnibus peccatis vestris, quaecumque cogitatione, aut locutione, aut operatione negligenter egistis, atque a vinculis peccatorum vestrorum absolutos perducat ad regnum coelorum. Per Dominum....* ("may He absolve you through our ministry from all your sins, be they negligences of thought, word or deed, and when you have been absolved from the chains of your sins may he lead you to the kingdom of heaven. Through our Lord....") The traditional form for Absolution which uses the indicative formula "I absolve you from you sins in the name of the Father and the Son, and the Holy Spirit" has been in use from at least the thirteenth century, is in conformity with that specified by St. Thomas Aquinas and was affirmed by the Council of Trent. One will note in passing that the substance of the formula remains unchanged.[11]

---

10. A. Villien, *The History and Liturgy of the Sacraments* (London: Burns Oates, 1932).

11. The deprecative formula is still used in the Greek Church, but since the ninth or tenth century the Latin Church has insisted on the indicative formula. To quote Pohle-Preuss, "The indicative formula of absolution now used in the Latin

156 THE PROBLEMS WITH THE OTHER SACRAMENTS

THE POST-CONCILIAR CHANGES IN CONFESSION

The Concilium responsible for changing the sacraments attempted to alter the traditional form of absolution to "In the name of our Lord Jesus Christ and by the power of the Holy Spirit I absolve you from your sins and restore you to the peace of the Church," which, as Annibale Bugnini points out, "calls attention to the ecclesial aspect of reconciliation." This change was blocked by the Congregation of the Doctrine of the Faith on the grounds that it removed the Trinitarian phrase.[12] The integrity of the form is preserved. But what of other changes?

It is interesting to quote Annibale Bugnini about these. According to him:

> The structure [of the sacramental rite] is the same as in the older rite, but has been enriched and revised. The penitent is now welcomed; he makes the sign of the cross and is urged to trust in God's mercy. This opening rite is followed by a reading from the word of God (optional), personal confession, expression of repentance, prayer of absolution, praise of God's mercy, and dismissal of the penitent.

The various formulas put on the lips of the priest and penitent are either taken from or thoroughly inspired by the Scriptures. The presence of God's word as read during or before the sacramental rite urges us to repentance and to proclamation of God's mercy. By means of it the power of God to save is proclaimed in the very midst of human sin. It is a highly significant innovation to have God's word present even in this manner of celebrating reconciliation.

Another interesting feature is the "restored" gesture of laying on of hands (or at least the right hand), which accompanies the formula for absolution. Such an action requires the removal of the

---

Church is prescribed by Eugene IV (1439), by the Council of Trent, and by the Roman Ritual. Hence probably no other is now valid." *The Sacraments*, vol. III (NY: Herder, 1918).

12. Annibale Bugnini, *The Reform of the Liturgy, 1948–1975* (Collegeville, MN: Liturgical Press, 1990). Why they were so resistant to change in this sacrament after their laxity in the others is hard to understand.

screen between priest and penitent, which of course is not essential to the rite, but does provide privacy and anonymity.[13] Many new churches provide rooms where priest and penitent can openly face each other, and some have abolished confessionals to force the use of open confession.

There is also much talk of celebration—to again quote Bugnini, "The rite is easily adaptable to situations in which there are a large number of penitents. On the other hand, it also becomes possible, especially at times when there is less pressure, to have a true celebration that is spiritually rich and profitable." What this means is that ideally the sacrament should be part of a community celebration.

The new rite, now called the Sacrament of Reconciliation, was introduced by Paul VI's *Reconciliationem inter Deum et Homines* (December 2, 1973). It has three forms: (1) individual reconciliation; (2) communal celebration followed by individual reconciliation for the forgiveness of "grave" sins, and (3) general absolution for use when the numbers of penitents are such as to preclude individual Confession (as in time of war or disaster). The first, apart from the "welcoming," and the reading from the "Word of God," closely resembles what we have always known as the Sacrament of Confession. In the practical order, the "welcoming" and reading from the word of God, being optional, are rarely carried out. The older generation goes to confession in the same manner it always has. The last and third form has always been an option in the Church when large numbers of the faithful were in danger of death and sufficient priests are not available for individual confession—such occurs in time of war or pestilence. The privilege has been extended to cover the situation where there is a genuine shortage of priests.

THE SECOND WAY OF RECONCILIATION

The second form is the most innovative and the one recommended for use whenever possible. Paul VI gives some of the reasons when he introduced the new Rite of Penance, December 2, 1973:

---

13. The use of confessionals dates from about the 17th century. Prior to that time priests sat in a chair and the penitent sat or kneeled beside them.

> In the Sacrament of Penance the faithful obtain from God's mercy pardon for having offended him, and at the same time reconciliation with the Church, which they have wounded by their sins....

The hidden and gracious mystery of God unites us through a supernatural bond: on this basis one person's sin harms the rest even as one person's goodness enriches them. Penance always therefore entails reconciliation with our brothers and sisters who remain harmed by our sins.

We see in these brief quotations, not so much a deviation from orthodoxy, as a shift in emphasis. In line with this Paul VI added to the usual way of confessing, what he calls "the second way of reconciliation" which is a communal preparation followed by individual confession and absolution which "combines the two values of being a community act and a personal act." **"It is the preferable form of reconciliation for our people when it is possible... we hope it may become the normal way of celebration."**

Further clarification of this change in emphasis is provided by the Decree of Cardinal Jean Villot and Annibale Bugnini found in the front of the new *Roman Ritual*. In it they state that this "new rite, beside [being] the rite for Reconciliation of Individual Penitents, [is] a Rite for Reconciliation of Several Penitents [and it] has been drawn up to emphasize the relation of the Sacrament to the community."

This shift in emphasis is made more specific by Paul VI's Address to a General Audience given April 1974 (*Documents on the Liturgy*, no. 369):

> We must not be indifferent and certainly not distrustful toward the invitation the Church is now addressing to us to reform our way of thinking and therefore also our religious practice relative to the sacrament of penance, which from now on we will do better to speak of as the sacrament of reconciliation. By that we mean, first, reconciliation with God; this is something we are familiar with even if it will always be a reason for endless and joyous wonder. We mean also reconciliation with the Church.... It is at this point that a new matter for reflection begins, offered to our ecclesial

consciousness by the publication of the new Rite of Penance....
The reflection is this: just as every personal failure has its impact
on our own essential and vital relationship with God, so too that
failure has its impact on our relationship with the community,
which in an analogous sense is also essential and vital....

In the practical order this "second way of reconciliation" has not
often been used, and this for the simple reason that it takes longer
and requires the presence of several priests to hear individual confessions after the communal rite.

FOOLING AROUND WITH THE MATTER

The form of the Sacrament remains the same in all three. But what
about the matter? We said above that the acts and dispositions of the
penitent constitute the proximate matter for the Sacrament. At first
it might seem that it was impossible to change this. But is such the
case? The matter can be changed by altering the way the penitent
views his sins. This has been achieved in several ways:

(1) *Sin is No Longer "Mortal" but "Grave"*

While one can find the term "mortal" in earlier Post-Conciliar documents, the promulgation of *Reconciliationem inter Deum et Homines* reverts exclusively to the term "grave," which term is also found
in the new code of Canon Law. The term "grave" has the advantage
of not upsetting an older generation, while obscuring the distinction between venial and mortal for the younger generation. The
same document also explains that "the ultimate purpose of penance
is that we should love God deeply and commit ourselves completely
to him.... Penance always therefore entails reconciliation with our
brothers and sisters who remain harmed by our sins." The Penitent,
having expressed his grave sins is now asked by the priest to "express
his sorrow ... in these or similar words."

(2) *The New Act of Contrition:*

My God, I am sorry for my sins with all my heart. In choosing to do
wrong and failing to do good, I have sinned against you whom I
should love above all things. I firmly intend, with your help, to do

penance, to sin no more, and to avoid whatever leads me to sin. Our Savior Jesus Christ suffered and died for us. In his name, my God, have mercy.

At first sight there seems little wrong with this prayer. But notice that, unlike the traditional "Act of Contrition," there is no mention of either heaven or hell; there is no recognition of the rewards or punishments due to man for sin, and in line with the definition of penance given above, no sense of the need to make satisfaction.

Even more serious is the absence of any distinction between perfect and imperfect contrition. With the decreasing number of priests available, the lack of knowledge about how to make a proper act of contrition when one dies is bound to have serious consequences.

Annibale Bugnini spoke of "the various formulas put on the lips of the priest and penitent are either taken from or thoroughly inspired by the Scriptures," being "a highly significant innovation to have God's word present even in this manner of celebrating reconciliation." When we review the various formulas provided we see the same pattern throughout with the occasional additional concept that God should "help us to live in unity with our fellow Christians."

THE REAL REASON FOR THE DECREASED USE OF CONFESSION

Many older Catholics continue to go to confession as they always did. They can see little difference in their practice, and indeed, in the practical order nothing has changed. This category of Catholic suffers from the attrition of age and is one of the reasons for the decreased use of Confession.

Younger Post-Conciliar Catholics pose a different problem. For them religion has to a great extent been reduced to the social obligation of helping their neighbor. They are no longer taught about heaven and hell, and no longer have a proper understanding of the nature of sin, contrition and penance. Nor do they see the priest as a man set apart, an *alter Christus* appointed to guide their souls. Under such circumstances, it is hardly surprising that they fail to storm the doors of the confessional.

6

BAPTISM

INTRODUCTION

Many Protestant sects do not object to Baptism or deny that it is a sacrament instituted by Christ. Hence it would seem there was little reason for the Post-Conciliar Church to engage in extensive revisions of this rite. Nevertheless, the documents relating to the new rite of Baptism, or as it is called, "The Rite of Christian Initiation" (RCIA), involve 47 pages of small print with only a single passing reference to original sin while stressing that "baptism is the sacrament by which men and women are incorporated into the Church, built up together in the Spirit into a house where God lives, into a holy nation and a royal priesthood. It is a sacramental bond of unity linking all who have been signed by it." (Sacrosanctum Concilium Divine Worship, Christian Initiation, General Introduction, no. 4, 1973.)

What are the instructions of Conciliar Baptism? "Initiation into the Christian community" is relevant and important. "Removal of original sin" is comparatively irrelevant and unimportant. This is the sum total of Post-Conciliar baptismal teaching. It appears that this teaching is not strictly speaking an error, because it does not directly deny original sin; it only derogates it almost to the status of irrelevancy. Nor can we say that promotion of "initiation" is an error. "Initiation into the Christian community" is simply irrelevant. It has no more spiritual significance than initiation into a college fraternity. A premature baby dying in the arms of its heartbroken mother will never know the "Christian community" nor does its tiny soul care about the "Christian community". Its soul hungers, as do all human souls, for the presence of God Almighty.

I am indebted to Rev. Father Dominic Savio Radecki, CMRI, for the following in-depth study of the Post-Conciliar revisions of the rite of Baptism.

Rama P. Coomaraswamy

THE NEW RITE OF BAPTISM
by Fr. Dominic Radecki, CMRI

THE DIVINE POWER IN BAPTISM

Jesus Christ instituted the Seven Sacraments of the Catholic Church, one of which is Baptism. The Son of God, Who has the power to cure the sick and transform bread and wine into His Body, Blood, Soul and Divinity, continues to exercise His divine power through the sacraments.

Considering what is essential for Baptism in the light of reason and common sense, one might ask the question, "How can water flowing over a few inches of a baby's skin cleanse a stain that is on the infant's soul?" Do you remember how Our Lord restored sight to a blind man? While the man stood before Him, Christ applied a dab of clay to his eyes and commanded him to wash in the Pool of Siloe. He went, he washed, and he saw.

How was sight restored to the blind man? Did light come into those sightless eyes because of the clay or the water? No. Otherwise, there would have been no more blind men in Judea. His sight was restored not because of the clay or the water, but through the divine power of Our Lord working through these elements. This action can be compared to electricity acting through wires. One cannot perceive anything happening, but a transmission of power is really taking place. Therefore, it is not the water or the words of Baptism, but the power of Christ working through these elements which He has so chosen that gives sanctifying grace to the soul and removes original sin.

MATTER, FORM, MINISTER AND INTENTION

In order to have a glass of orange juice, you must first have oranges. If you have a glass of juice which is made from another substance, it really is juice, but it cannot be orange juice. Just as oranges are essential to orange juice, the Catholic Church teaches that there are elements essential to every sacrament: valid matter, valid form, valid minister and the proper intention of the minister. If any one of these is lacking, the sacrament is invalid and does not take place.

The Council of Florence (AD 1438–1443) describes the elements necessary for the validity of the sacraments: "All these sacraments are brought to completion by three components, by things as matter, by words as form and by the person of the minister effecting the sacrament with the intention of doing what the Church does; if any one of these three is lacking, the sacrament is not effected."[1]

The **matter** of a sacrament is some sensible action or thing, which is the sacrament's material element. In the case of Baptism it is the baptismal water and its proper application. The **form** of a sacrament consists of the essential words. In Baptism these words are: "I baptize you in the name of the Father, and of the Son, and of the Holy Spirit (Ghost)."

The **minister** of a sacrament is the person conferring the sacrament, who in the case of Baptism can be anyone with the right intention. This means that the person who confers the sacrament must have the **proper intention**; he or she must have the intention of doing what the Church does (what Christ ordered to be done). St. Thomas Aquinas teaches, "His intention is required, whereby he subjects himself to the principal agent; that is, it is necessary that he intend to do that which Christ and the Church do."[2]

THE ESSENTIALS OF BAPTISM

The valid administration of Baptism depends upon the use of the correct rite and matter, together with the proper intention of the person administering it. Priests and bishops are the ordinary, lawful ministers of solemn Baptism. Nevertheless, "in case of urgent necessity any human being, irrespective of sex or faith, can validly baptize. This teaching is based on the fact that Baptism is necessary for salvation. It is not a mere question of ecclesiastical discipline but a

---

1. Denzinger-Bannwart (hereafter, DB), n. 695.
2. St. Thomas Aquinas, *Summa Theologica*, 3a, q. 64, art. 8, ad. 1.

dogma, and can be rightly understood only in the light of Christ's explicit command, as interpreted by Tradition."³

This truth is expressed by the Fourth Lateran Council (1215): "The Sacrament of Baptism . . . properly conferred, no matter by whom [*a quocunque rite collatum*], is useful for salvation."⁴ The Council of Florence explains the phrase "*a quocunque*" as follows: "In case of necessity, not only a priest or a deacon, but a layman or woman, nay even a pagan and a heretic, can [validly] baptize, provided only that he observes the form prescribed by the Church and has the intention of doing what the Church does."⁵

This is confirmed by *The Catechism of the Council of Trent*:

> Those who may administer Baptism, in case of necessity . . . are included all, even the laity, men and women, to whatever sect they may belong. This power extends, in case of necessity, even to Jews, infidels and heretics; provided, however, they intend to do what the Catholic Church does in the act of her ministry.⁶

Thus, anyone can validly baptize, provided that he or she uses water, pouring it at the same time as he or she recites the essential words, with the intention of doing what the Church does or what Christ intended. "The theological reason for the validity of Baptism when conferred by a heretical minister is to be sought in the maxim so constantly urged by St. Augustine: 'It is Christ who baptizes.'"⁷ This means that the minister of Baptism, whether he himself is virtuous or sinful, baptized or unbaptized, Catholic or heretic, does not confer his own Baptism, but the Baptism of Christ.

However, if the person who is baptizing does not intend to do what Christ and the Church does, the Baptism is invalid. In 1690, Pope Alexander VIII **condemned** the proposition that "Baptism is valid when conferred by a minister who observes all the external rite and form of baptizing, but within his heart resolves, I do not intend

---

3. Msgr. Joseph Pohle, *The Sacraments, Vol. I*, p. 259.
4. DB, n. 430.
5. DB, n. 696.
6. Page 173.
7. Msgr. Joseph Pohle, *The Sacraments, Vol. I*, p. 174.

what the Church does."[8] The Council of Trent (1545–1563) reaffirms this when it teaches, "If anyone shall say that in ministers, when they effect and confer the sacraments, the intention at least of doing what the Church does is not required: let him be anathema."[9]

Our Lord instituted the sacrament of Baptism and entrusted it to the Apostles. They faithfully administered it and, in turn, handed it down to their successors. Thus, for nearly 2,000 years the Catholic Church has never changed the essential matter, form and intention of the minister in this sacred rite as instituted by Christ. It wasn't until the Second Vatican Council (1962–1965), which was influenced by Pierre Teilhard de Chardin's view of original sin, that the purpose of Baptism began to be questioned.

In the Post-Conciliar Church Baptism eventually became the Rite of Christian Initiation, a change which emphasizes entrance into the community of the people of God and virtually ignores the power of Baptism to remit original sin. This would leave us to question whether those who administer this new rite intend to do what the Catholic Church does. If they do not, then the "Baptism" administered is invalid. Let us examine the evidence.

CHANGES RESULTING FROM VATICAN II

The Second Vatican Council, better known as Vatican II, mandated changes in the sacraments. Vatican II's *Constitution on the Sacred Liturgy* ordered that the rite for the baptism of infants and adults be revised.[10] The Vatican newspaper, *L'Osservatore Romano*, reported that "the reform of the liturgy, carried out in accordance with the Constitution of the Second Vatican Council, has also introduced certain modifications in the **very essence**[11] of the sacramental rites."[12]

These changes to the ritual in the form of alterations, deletions

---

8. DB, n. 1318.
9. DB, n. 854.
10. Walter Abbott, S.J., *The Documents of Vatican II,* pp. 159–160.
11. Emphasis added.
12. *L'Osservatore Romano,* Nov. 7, 1974.

and insertions were made in order to express the new theology and beliefs of the Second Vatican Council. The new rite for the baptism of infants was introduced on June 1, 1970. The Rite of Christian Initiation of Adults (RCIA) was issued on January 6, 1972. The Modernists behind these changes of Vatican II also sought to **reshape** the traditional Catholic teaching on original sin and sanctifying grace.

The official documents relating to the new rite of Baptism (47 pages in small print) have only a single passing reference to original sin: "Baptism, the cleansing with water by the power of the living word, washes away every stain of sin, original and personal."[13] At the same time they are replete with phrases such as "through the sacraments of Christian initiation men and women are freed from the power of darkness..."[14] and "they receive the Spirit of adoption which makes them God's sons and daughters, and, with the entire people of God, they celebrate the memorial of the Lord's death and resurrection."[15]

Is this new rite of Baptism a valid sacrament? Absent an official declaration as to the invalidity of the new sacramental rite, we can still affirm the principle that any substantial change in a sacramental rite **invalidates** the sacrament.

Although numerous changes were introduced into the new Rite of Christian Initiation of Adults and the new Rite of Baptism for Children, the essential words, "I baptize you in the name of the Father, and of the Son, and of the Holy Spirit (Ghost),"[16] have been retained. However, this, of itself, does not assure the validity of the new rite because, following the Second Vatican Council, radical priests sometimes experiment with the essential rites of the sacraments, including that of Baptism. Instead of using the correct words, some priests make up their own form and alter the essential words or change key elements. Others perform the ceremonies, such as the pouring of baptismal water, improperly. These alterations,

13. *Documents on the Liturgy: 1963–1979*, p. 721.
14. United States Catholic Conference, *Rite of Baptism for Children*, no. 1.
15. Ibid., no. 4.
16. *The Rite of Baptism for One Child and Several Children according to texts approved by the National Conference of Bishops in the United States and confirmed by the Apostolic See*, p. 10.

deletions and insertions render many baptisms either doubtfully valid or certainly invalid.

In addition, there is great reason to fear that there is no baptism when very little water is applied or if it is poured carelessly. The baptism is also doubtful or invalid if the essential words are preceded by others which modify or change their meaning, or if they are spoken a considerable time before or after the application of water.

[For this reason such baptisms are in question, in addition to those administered by Protestant preachers who either] merely fillip [flick water] over a child's head; ... dip the tips of two fingers in a bowl, and then lay them on the forehead; ... sprinkle lightly towards the person's face, the head being covered with a bonnet; [this is why] a well-founded doubt arises in many cases whether an ablution of any kind can be said to have been performed.

Hence it has become customary to baptize, under condition, converts from Protestant sects, when positive evidence of the proper performance of the rite is wanting; which, being furnished, we abstain from [conditionally] baptizing, because we hold the baptism to be valid, independently of the faith of the minister.[17]

The greatest threat to the validity of Baptism in the new Church of the Second Vatican Council comes from a possible defective intention on the part of the minister because many priests have accepted the heresies of Pierre Teilhard de Chardin on original sin. Some openly proclaim their disbelief in original sin and, consequently, deny the purpose of Baptism as established by Christ. Some consider the regenerative power of Baptism (the removal of original sin) unimportant or irrelevant. It thus becomes doubtful as to whether these priests have the proper intention when conferring Baptism.

To understand the seriousness of this and the extent of the problem, it is really necessary to understand the theology and influence of Teilhard. Beginning from the 1920's to the present his heretical

---

17. Archbishop Francis Kenrick, *A Treatise on Baptism*, p. 151.

beliefs and writings, such as his denial of original sin and the existence of Adam and Eve, were widely circulated among clergy and laity. Just as Martin Luther ignited the flames of the Protestant Revolution and poisoned the general populace, so too, Teilhard's erroneous teachings infected the Second Vatican Council. As a result, a new liturgy and a new church were formed.

THE WRITINGS OF PIERRE TEILHARD DE CHARDIN

Pierre Teilhard de Chardin (1881–1955) was a French Jesuit priest who taught a combined form of Darwinian evolution and revolutionary "Catholic" theology. According to evolutionary theology, which Modernists profess, the notion of **an unchangeable Deposit of Faith** is denied because nothing is exempt from substantial change. Henri Rambaud summarized Teilhard's Modernist beliefs when he clearly stated: "His faith was not that of the Catholic Church and he knew it. After all, he had studied enough to know that the Faith of the Church is a faith in the words of Jesus Christ and that consequently this faith cannot change substantially."[18]

[In 1907, Pope St. Pius X described the insidious nature of Modernists such as Teilhard, who] put themselves forward as reformers of the Church, and, forming more boldly into line of attack, assail all that is most sacred in the work of Christ, not sparing even the Person of the Divine Redeemer, Whom, with sacrilegious audacity, they degrade to the condition of a simple and ordinary man.[19]

Further on in this encyclical Pope St. Pius X quotes Pope Gregory XVI, who, in 1834, also condemned Modernism in *Singulari Nos*:

"Blind" they are, and "leaders of the blind" puffed up with the proud name of science, they have reached that pitch of folly at which they pervert the eternal concept of truth and the true meaning of religion; in introducing a new system in which "they are seen to be under the sway of a blind and unchecked passion

---

18. Henri Rambaud, *The Strange Faith of Teilhard de Chardin*, p. 23.
19. *Encyclical Letter on the Doctrine of the Modernists*, no. 2.

for novelty, thinking not at all of finding some solid foundation of truth, but despising the holy and apostolic traditions, they embrace other and vain, futile, uncertain doctrines, unapproved by the Church, on which, in the height of their vanity, they think they can base and maintain truth itself."[20]

Teilhard's teachings are totally opposed to traditional Catholic belief. Most of his writings, including a prolific body of correspondence, remained unpublished during his lifetime because it was clear to Rome and various Church authorities that his teachings were erroneous. They therefore attempted to muzzle him as much as possible and prevent his writings from being circulated.

In 1927 Rome refused an imprimatur on [Teilhard's] book, *Le Milieu Divin*. In 1933 he was ordered not to teach in Paris. In 1933 Rome refused him permission to publish *L'Energie Humaine*. In 1944 his *Phenomene Humain* was banned. In 1948, summoned by his Superior General to Rome, he sought permission once more to publish his *Phenomene Humain*—and was refused. Again in 1949 and 1955, his printings and activities were restricted. *In December of 1957, a decree from the Holy Office ordered the withdrawal of his works from Catholic libraries, seminaries, religious institutions and bookshops.*[21] Most of the essays never saw print until after his death because many of his ideas were considered too unorthodox by various authorities in the Church... His outspokenness on many traditionally expressed doctrines of the Church, such as original sin, sincerely disturbed his superiors and so, in 1925, he received instructions, "sympathetically given," to concentrate on scientific work and return to China.[22]

"In reality, Teilhard was being silenced by a virtual exile from Europe."[23] He died suddenly on Easter Sunday, 1955 in New York City. His last words were, "This time, I feel it's terrible."[24]

20. Ibid., no. 13.
21. Fr. Charles Coughlin, *Bishops Versus Pope*, pp. 215–216.
22. R. Wayne Kraft, *The Relevance of Teilhard*, p. 20.
23. Hugh McElwain, O.S.M., *Introduction to Teilhard de Chardin*, p. 8.
24. Pierre Leroy, S.J., *Teilhard de Chardin: The Man*, p. 33.

"He was not allowed to publish his most significant works during his lifetime and, in fact, they have never been published with a *Nihil Obstat* and *Imprimatur* [official declarations that the books are free of doctrinal or moral error]."[25] Shortly before the Second Vatican Council began, on June 30, 1962, the Holy Office issued a *monitum* (warning) "against the ambiguities and even grave errors against Catholic doctrine" in his writings.[26] "In 1963 the Vicariate of Rome, in a decree, required that Catholic bookshops in Rome should withdraw from circulation the works of de Chardin, and also those books which favor his erroneous doctrines."[27]

The Catholic Church rejects Teilhard's writings because they are filled with fundamental errors in philosophy and theology. His new faith *claims* to be the Catholic faith, but it completely abandons many doctrines revealed by God and taught by the Catholic Church. Teilhard laid the groundwork for the new, ecumenical religion formed after the Second Vatican Council.

Commenting on his new faith, Henri Rambaud writes: "It is not, in any case, the faith of the Catholic Church, and it is small wonder that through the Holy Office, the organ qualified to speak in her name, the Church has thought it necessary to declare that she does not recognize herself in Teilhard's writings."[28]

COMPARISON TO THE WRITINGS OF ST. THOMAS AQUINAS

In the 13th century, St. Thomas Aquinas (1225–1274) reconciled the reasoning process of Aristotle (384–322 BC), one of the greatest Western philosophers, with Catholic doctrine. The writings of this Dominican theologian and philosopher have influenced generations of scholars. "Since he resembled the angels, not only in innocence but also in intellect, he received the appropriate name of Angelic Doctor

---

25. Ibid., p. 29.
26. T. Lincoln Bouscaren, S.J., *Canon Law Digest*, Vol. 5, pp. 621–622.
27. J. W. Johnson, *Evolution?*, p. 120.
28. Henri Rambaud, *The Strange Faith of Teilhard de Chardin*, p. 11.

[of the Church], which was confirmed by [Pope] St. Pius V."[29] His theological proofs, including his demonstration of God's existence, are considered irrefutable, since they are based on deduction.

The writings of St. Thomas Aquinas and Teilhard de Chardin are at two opposite ends of the spectrum. Thomistic philosophy is clear, precise, ordered and logical. The teachings of Teilhard are obscure, erratic, disordered and illogical; this is readily apparent when reading his various works. Adding to the confusion, Teilhard fabricated a large number of words (e.g., *Christogenesis, noösphere, lithosphere, radial energy, totalization, Omega point, pleromization* and many others) to describe different stages in his evolutionary theory.

A MODERN FALSE PROPHET

Dietrich von Hildebrand refers to Teilhard and other Modernists in his *Trojan Horse in the City of God*:

> It is sad enough when people lose their faith and leave the Church; but it is much worse when those who in reality have lost their faith remain within the Church and try—like termites—to undermine Christian faith with their claim that they are giving to Christian revelation the interpretation that suits modern man.[30]

Our Lord foretold in Sacred Scripture that cunning men, inspired by the devil, would lead multitudes astray. Jesus Christ repeatedly warned His flock against their wily attacks:

> Beware of false prophets, who come to you in sheep's clothing but inwardly are ravening wolves. By their fruits you will know them.[31] And take care that no one leads you astray.[32] And many false prophets will arise, and will lead many astray.[33]

---

29. *Breviarium Romanum*, (Spring edition), p. 743.
30. Page 265.
31. Matt. 7:15–16.
32. Matt. 24:4.
33. Matt. 24:14.

It is obvious that Teilhard is a false prophet:

> Let us recall the marks of these false prophets. He is a false prophet who denies original sin and mankind's need of redemption and thereby undermines the meaning of Christ's death on the Cross. He is not a true Christian who no longer sees that redemption of the world through Christ is the source of true happiness and that nothing can be compared to this one glorious fact.[34]

TOTAL REJECTION OF THE CATHOLIC FAITH

Teilhard's evolutionary theology is nothing less than a repudiation of core, traditional Catholic doctrines which attacks the very foundation of the Church. In his essay, *Stuff of the Universe*, written in 1953, Teilhard makes no secret as to the amount of Christian doctrine he was prepared to throw overboard; the very core of dogma had to be reshaped. He wrote:

> In return for a valorization and amortization of the stuff of things, a whole series of readjustments must be made, I am well aware (if we wish frankly to Christify evolution), in a number of representations or attitudes which seem to us definitely fixed in Christian dogma. In consequence, and by factual necessity, one might say that a hitherto unknown form of religion—one that no one could have imagined or described, for lack of a universe large enough and organic enough to contain it—is burgeoning [growing vigorously] in the heart of modern man, from a seed sown by the idea of evolution.[35]

Such a theory is incompatible with all the basic doctrines of Catholicism, some of which are Creation, original sin, sanctifying grace, the divinity of Christ, the Redemption, the seven sacraments, the Holy Sacrifice of the Mass, Heaven and Hell. In accepting Teilhard's theory, one would have to abandon or completely transform the teachings of the Catholic Church. One can see how his evolutionary theology paved the way for the Great Apostasy—the

---

34. Dietrich von Hildebrand, *Trojan Horse in the City of God*, p. 265.
35. Pierre Teilhard de Chardin, *Activation of Energy*, pp. 282–283.

abandonment of the faith by the majority of Catholics as described by St. Paul in 2 Thessalonians 2:3–4.

Teilhard clearly believed that evolution was superior to the Deposit of Faith. He wrote: "Is evolution a theory, a system or a hypothesis? It is much more: it is a general condition to which all theories, all hypotheses, all systems must bow and which they must satisfy henceforward if they are to be thinkable and true. Evolution is a light illuminating all facts, a curve that all lines must follow."[36]

Dietrich von Hildebrand comments on Teilhard's appeal, based on his novel beliefs and "scientific" claims:

> Many Catholics view Teilhard de Chardin as a great scientist who has reconciled science with the Christian faith by introducing a grandiose new theology and metaphysics that take modern scientific findings into account and thus fit into our scientific age. Though I am not a competent judge of Teilhard as a scientist, this opinion may be questioned without expertise. For one thing, every careful thinker knows that a reconciliation of science and the Christian faith has never been needed, because true science (in contradistinction to false philosophies disguised in scientific garments) can never be incompatible with Christian faith.[37]

The following discussion provides us with great insight into the mind of Teilhard:

> [Dietrich von Hildebrand once conversed with him regarding St. Augustine. Teilhard] exclaimed violently: "Don't mention that unfortunate man; he spoiled everything by introducing the supernatural." This remark confirmed the impression I had gained of the crass materialism of his views, but it also struck me in another way: the criticism of St. Augustine—the greatest of the Fathers of the Church—betrayed Teilhard's lack of a genuine sense of intellectual and spiritual grandeur.[38]

---

36. Pierre Teilhard de Chardin, *The Phenomenon of Man*, p. 218.
37. Dietrich von Hildebrand, *Teilhard de Chardin: A False Prophet*, p. 10.
38. Von Hildebrand, p. 9.

PIERRE TEILHARD DE CHARDIN'S TEACHINGS ON ORIGINAL SIN

In the early 1920's "some of the ideas which he had expressed in his lectures about original sin and its relation to evolution, were regarded as unorthodox by his religious superiors, and he was forbidden to continue teaching."[39]

> [In 1922, an article on original sin written by Teilhard] came to the eyes of Cardinal Merry del Val, who was alert to the suspicion of heresy as a foxhound is alert to the scent. He made sharp representations to the General of the Jesuits, Father Ledochowski, who had already been warned from other sources.... Teilhard was asked to promise that he would neither say nor write anything "against the traditional position of the Church on the matter of original sin".... Rome was implacable. He was finally requested to subscribe to six propositions.... On the advice of friends—and not without considerable reluctance—he signed it.[40] [Sadly, Teilhard did not keep his promise, but continued to express his heretical views on original sin, both in his words and in his writings.]

In Teilhard's new evolutionary theology there is no place for sanctifying grace or the supernatural. The Catholic Church's doctrines of the Redemption and original sin have no real meaning in his new religion. Even Teilhard was aware of the incompatibility of Divine Revelation with his teachings when he wrote, "Sometimes I am a bit afraid, when I think of the transposition to which I must submit my mind concerning the vulgar notions of creation, inspiration, miracle[s], original sin, Resurrection, etc. in order to be able to accept them."[41]

A number of Teilhard's writings contain theories conflicting with

---

39. Pierre Teilhard de Chardin, *The Phenomenon of Man*, Introduction by Sir Julian Huxley, p. 23.
40. Robert Speaight, *The Life of Teilhard de Chardin*, p. 136.
41. Letter of December 17, 1922 as quoted in *Rome et Teilhard de Chardin*, p. 47, by Philippe de la Trinité.

the Catholic doctrine of original sin. "In dealing with original sin ... he occasionally offered explanations that were rightly judged to be unsatisfactory."[42] His teachings regarding original sin varied and the form he gave them was certainly untenable. Because Teilhard's views regarding original sin were heretical, his ideas regarding Baptism had to be reformulated as well.

As early as July 20, 1920, in his unpublished essay, *Fall, Redemption, and Geocentrism*, Teilhard stated:

> ... original sin, taken in its widest sense, is not a malady specific to the earth, nor is it bound up with human generation. It simply symbolizes the inevitable chance of evil (*Necesse est ut eveniant scandala.* ["It must be that scandals come."]) which accompanies the existence of all participated beings.... Original sin is the essential reaction of the finite to the creative act. Inevitably it insinuates itself into existence through the medium of all creation. It is the *reverse side* of all creation.... Strictly speaking, there is no first Adam. The name disguises a universal and unbreakable law of reversion or perversion—the price that has to be paid for progress.[43]

Teilhard's illogical and disjointed thought process reveals itself in a letter written from Tientsin on January 27, 1927:

> Ah, the great symbol of Baptism, in which ordinary men see no more than the drop of water that cleanses, and miss the river that sweeps away! In everything that I have happened to read on the World, I seem never to have found an accent, a cry, that has not already escaped me. I repeat: Spirit is the most violent, the most incendiary of Matters.[44]

Since Teilhard believed that the Catholic doctrine of original sin was intellectually confining, he viewed baptism in an unconventional way. In 1933, in the essay *Christology and Evolution*, he wrote:

---

42. Henri de Lubac, *The Religion of Teilhard de Chardin*, p. 120.
43. Pierre Teilhard de Chardin, *Christianity and Evolution*, pp. 40–41.
44. Pierre Teilhard de Chardin, *Letters to Two Friends, 1926–1952*, p. 56.

The full mystery of baptism is no longer to cleanse but (as the Greek Fathers fully realized) to plunge into the fire of the purifying battle "for being"—no longer the shadow, but the sweat and toil, of the Cross.... I am familiar with the solemn decrees of the Council of Trent on the subject of original sin. I am aware of the infinite network of formulas and attitudes through which the idea that we are the guilty children of Adam and Eve has percolated into our Christian life.

[After declaring that he understands the traditional Catholic doctrine, Teilhard goes on to reject original sin, saying:] ... for all sorts of reasons—scientific, moral and religious—the classic *depiction* of the Fall has already ceased to be for us anything but a strait-jacket and a verbal imposition, the *letter* of which can no longer satisfy us either intellectually or emotionally. In its *material representation*, it no longer belongs either to our Christianity or to our universe.[45]

Teilhard realized that there would be difficulty in winning acceptance for his erroneous theory on original sin. At one point he wrote, "I do not think that in the history of the Church anyone has 'pulled off' such an adjustment of dogma as that of which we're speaking—though similar attempts have been made and carried half-way."[46]

Teilhard also stated:

From the point of view of the Christian scientist, acceptance of Adam and Eve necessarily means that history is cut off short in a completely unreal way at the level of the appearance of man; but what is more, when we reach the more immediately living domain of belief, original sin, in its present representation, is a constant bar to the natural development of our religion. It clips the wings of hope: we are incessantly eager to launch out into the wide open field of conquest which optimism suggests, and every time it drags us back inexorably into the overpowering darkness of reparation and expiation.

45. Pierre Teilhard de Chardin, *Christianity and Evolution*, pp. 85–86.
46. Pierre Teilhard de Chardin, *Lettres intimes a August Valensin, Bruno de Solages, Henri de Lubac, 1919-1955*, p. 84.

BAPTISM 177

The more I study the matter, the more I am forced to accept this evidence that original sin, conceived in the form still attributed to it today, is an intellectual and emotional strait-jacket. What lies behind this pernicious quality it possesses, and to whom can we look for release?

To my mind, the answer is that if the dogma of original sin is constricting and debilitating it is simply because, as now expressed, it represents a survival of obsolete static views into our now evolutionary way of thinking.[47]

This lies in direct contradiction to what the Catholic Church has always explicitly taught:

All men are obliged to make atonement, since, according to the teachings of the Christian faith, our souls have been disfigured, as a result of the pitiable fall of Adam, by original sin. We are subject also to our passions and corrupted in a truly sad way, and so have made ourselves worthy of eternal damnation.

It is true that the proud philosophers of this world [including Teilhard] deny the above truth, raising up in its place the ancient heresy of Pelagius, which conceded to human nature a certain inborn goodness which, by our own powers, raises us up to ever higher levels of perfection; but these false theories, born of human pride, have been condemned by the Apostle, who admonished us that we were by nature children of wrath.

As a matter of fact, from the very creation of the world, mankind has recognized, in one way or another, the obligation of making reparation, and impelled, as it were, by a natural instinct, has tried to placate God by offering Him public sacrifices.[48]

In a letter written to Teilhard, Pere Marechal states:

But this new explanation [he is referring to Teilhard's theory of original sin] modifies, it seems to me, the essential basis, and not simply the formulation of the "defined" dogma. More precisely

---

47. Pierre Teilhard de Chardin, *Christianity and Evolution*, pp. 79–80.
48. *Breviarium Romanum*, (Summer edition), p. 381.

still, it suppresses the dogma, by declaring that it is superfluous. What in fact it does is to replace original sin by the distant ontological root of physical and moral evil. Now, this root, this metaphysical possibility of evil, inherent in the creature qua creature, [as such] neither calls for nor rules out the state of supernatural justification, and therefore cannot take on, with the "privation of original justice", the relationship of active principle with effective consequence which the Council of Trent asserts so clearly of the sin of Adam. The whole Christian economy of "justification" is upset. The hypothesis put forward would lead to saying that mankind as such has never lost its initial right to grace and that the deprivation of grace is to be seen, in each individual, simply as the effect of a fault of which he is now guilty. All that would remain under the name "original sin" would be simply the natural imperfections of the created being, "the radical condition that causes the creature to be born from the multiple" (p. 10 of the ms. *Christologie et evolution*)—in other words, a philosophical truth.[49]

It is certain that Teilhard ended his life no longer believing in original sin. On April 8, 1955, two days before he died, Teilhard wrote to Fr. Andre Ravier as follows: "In the Universe of Cosmogenesis where Evil is no longer catastrophic (that is to say, not an accident) but evolutive (that is to say, the statistically inevitable by-product of a Universe in course of unification in God). . . ."[50]

Teilhard's theory of evolution demanded polygenism (many first parents). In his book, *Mons Univers*, he rejected the creation of the Biblical first man, Adam, and the first woman, Eve. He taught that we are not descendants from a singular pair of first parents, but that there were many "first parents" who evolved from primates at one time. In such a hypothesis original sin is impossible. Teilhard expressed this belief in his book, *The Phenomenon of Man*, in which he wrote, "Thus *in the eyes of science*, which at long range can only see things in bulk, the 'first man' is, and can only be, *a crowd*, and his infancy is made up of thousands and thousands of years."[51] From

49. Emile Rideau, *The Thought of Teilhard de Chardin*, pp. 543–544.
50. Quoted in *Janus*, no. 4., Dec. 1964, p. 32.
51. Page 186.

this it would follow that to accept polygenism is to reject the doctrine of original sin.

In 1950, Pope Pius XII directly condemned polygenism in his encyclical *Humani Generis*:

> The faithful cannot embrace that opinion which maintains either that after Adam there existed on this earth true men who did not take their origin through natural generation from him as from the first parent of all, or that Adam represents a certain number of first parents. Now it is in no way apparent how such an opinion can be reconciled with that which the sources of revealed truth and the documents of the Teaching Authority of the Church propose with regard to original sin, which proceeds from a sin actually committed by an individual Adam and which through generation is passed on to all and is in everyone as his own.[52]

In the same encyclical he teaches: "Catholic faith obliges us to hold that souls are immediately created by God."[53] Teilhard's theories are contrary to this belief.

Joseph Kopp, the author of *A New Synthesis of Evolution*, says that Church doctrine and Teilhard's theories are irreconcilable:

> We must be quite clear about this: whoever postulates an "intervention" on the part of God in His own work does not just modify de Chardin's concepts, he destroys the very core of his philosophy. To speak of "the introduction of the human soul through a special act of creation" is to remove all meaning from de Chardin's theory of purposeful evolution of the biosphere toward man. Also his theory of the evolution of the noösphere[54] which, as we shall see, becomes completely unintelligible if one accepts the idea of intervention. We have to accept Teilhard's view of an upward-developing creation up to and including man or reject his entire philosophy.[55]

---

52. Note 37.
53. Ibid., n. 36.
54. "Teilhard's notion of a total network of thinking minds." Dietrich von Hildebrand, *Teilhard de Chardin: A False Prophet*, p. 41.
55. Joseph Kopp, *Teilhard de Chardin: A New Synthesis of Evolution*, pp. 43–44.

180   THE PROBLEMS WITH THE OTHER SACRAMENTS

It is impossible to reconcile Teilhard's teachings on original sin with the "through one man sin entered into the world"[56] to which the Council of Trent referred specifically when formulating its decree on original sin: "If anyone does not profess that the first man Adam immediately lost the justice and holiness in which he was constituted when he disobeyed the commandment of God ... let him be anathema."[57]

The Church presents no alternative interpretation of the traditional expressions "Our First Parents," "The Garden of Eden," "The Fall" and "Original Sin" that would allow Teilhard's hypothesis to be even vaguely theologically acceptable. His concept of original sin is completely contrary to Christian revelation and Church teaching. There is a radical difference between the doctrine of the Catholic Church and the theological fiction of Teilhard.

The teachings of Teilhard lead ultimately to a denial of the divinity of Christ and prepare his followers to accept a new, ecumenical religion. Dietrich von Hildebrand expresses this clearly:

> Teilhard's Christ is no longer Jesus, the God-man ... the Redeemer; instead, He is the initiator of a purely natural evolutionary process and, simultaneously, its end—the Christ-Omega.... In his basic conception of the world, which does not provide for original sin in the sense the Church gives to this term, there is no place for the Jesus Christ of the Gospels; for if there is no original sin, then the redemption of man through Christ loses its inner meaning.[58]

PIERRE TEILHARD DE CHARDIN, VATICAN II AND THE NEW RITE OF BAPTISM (INITIATION)

Although Pierre Teilhard de Chardin died many years before the new rite of Baptism was introduced, the Second Vatican Council, John XXIII, Paul VI and the liturgical "reformers" were influenced

---

56. Romans 5:12.
57. DB, n. 788–789.
58. Dietrich von Hildebrand, *Teilhard de Chardin: A False Prophet*, p. 21.

by his teachings. Toward the end of the council, *Time* magazine noted the trend and reported, "Although the faithful have twice been warned about dangers [to faith] in his work, Popes John XXIII and Paul VI have privately acknowledged his greatness."[59] Several archbishops and cardinals used Teilhard's terminology in their addresses on the floor of the Second Vatican Council. His erroneous teachings were also adopted by many of the bishops and *periti* (advisors of the council).

The idea of an ecumenical church stems directly from the teachings of Teilhard. "Teilhard had a tremendous vision of the Church as a community of Christian love, where people live together as individuals, yet united in love—total, unbounded, without limit—within the world; a sign of the presence of God, finally and fully as LOVE."[60]

His concept of Baptism was simply an initiation into this community. In Teilhard's religion there is no place for the supernatural life of grace that is infused into souls through Baptism. For him, union with God consists principally in assimilation into the evolutionary process.

Teilhard's heretical teachings have been widely circulated through the seminaries, rectories, schools, religious houses and libraries of the New Church. His teachings manifest a definite apostasy from the Catholic Church. "Father de Lubac, S.J., speaking at the Institute on Renewal in the Church said in Toronto in 1967 that clearly 'the Church is facing a grave crisis.' 'Under the name of 'the new church', 'the post-conciliar church', he added, 'a different church from that of Jesus Christ is now trying to establish itself.'"[61] Teilhard had laid the foundation of this new church.

THE INTENTION OF THE MINISTER OF BAPTISM

The heretical teachings of Teilhard regarding original sin have been assimilated and adopted by many priests. This has caused many

---

59. October 16, 1964, p. 92.
60. Hugh McElwain, O.S.M., *Introduction to Teilhard de Chardin*, p. 71.
61. Dietrich von Hildebrand, *Teilhard de Chardin: A False Prophet*, p. 5.

others to have false views and beliefs on Baptism. Can such priests and people validly administer Baptism?

The Church teaches that even heretics can baptize validly **if they intend to administer the Baptism of Christ** and use the right matter and form in administering it. "The validity of Baptism does not depend on the minister or the kind of person he may be, but on the fact that, wishing to administer the Baptism of Christ, he uses the correct rite."[62]

St. Augustine said that anyone who follows the rite instituted by Christ administers Baptism validly.[63] Fr. John Murphy, in his book, *The Sacrament of Baptism*, remarks:

> After the Fathers, this question was gradually developed, and by the time of St. Thomas it was universally held by theologians that anyone, man or woman, baptized or unbaptized, could validly baptize. It must, of course, be clearly understood that a right intention, that is, an intention of doing what the Church of Christ does, is always necessary for the validity of the sacrament.[64]

Baptism administered by a non-Catholic is valid if he or she uses the correct rite and intends to administer the Baptism of Christ. The Baptism is valid because of the **principle of simple error**. Although this principle is somewhat difficult to understand, it is a decisive factor in judging the validity of some baptisms and marriages.

"Error is a false judgment of the mind. The error is *simple* if it remains in the mind without passing over into the will, and so without modifying the act which the will elicits."[65] Theologians make a distinction between the error in the mind and the intention in the will.

The Church makes a distinction, then, between the belief in a person's mind and the intent in his will. As a result, a person who administers Baptism may have false beliefs in his mind about the

---

62. Fr. John Murphy, *The Sacrament of Baptism*, p. 55.
63. *De Baptismo contra Donatistas*, bk. 7, 53, 102.
64. Pages 55–56.
65. T. Lincoln Bouscaren, S.J., *Canon Law: A Text and Commentary*, p. 559.

nature, effects and efficacy of Baptism yet still can administer it validly because he wills to do so. For example, in an emergency, a mother may ask a non-Catholic doctor or nurse to baptize her dying infant. As long as the person performs the ceremony correctly and he or she intends to perform the Baptism of Christ, in accord with the mother's desire, the sacrament is valid.

In the example above, simple error may be in the mind of the person because he has a poor or even erroneous understanding of Baptism. Yet, as long as he does not have an actual intention in his will contrary to the general intention of Christ and His Church, the Baptism is valid. On the other hand, if the person who administers Baptism, by a special act of his will, does not intend to do what Christ wanted and instituted, the sacrament is invalid.

The topic of the minister's intention in Baptism and the principle of simple error are covered in a lengthy article by Ulric Beste in the April 1950 edition of the *American Ecclesiastical Review*. Beste begins by listing the essential elements of a sacrament:

> It is then certain and admitted by all that, besides the matter and form prescribed by Christ, also the proper intention on the part of the minister is required for validity in the administration of Baptism. However, as is commonly taught by theologians, this intention need not necessarily be explicit or express, nor determinate and distinct or well-defined; it is quite sufficient that it exist confusedly and implicitly in the mind of the minister.
>
> Indeed, no more is necessary than that he intends to perform what the Church performs, or what Christ instituted and ordered to be done, or what he ordinarily sees pastors or Christians do in their churches. This remains true although interiorly in his heart and mind he feels and is convinced that this is a vain and meaningless ceremony and that the Church in performing it certainly errs and posits a purely inefficacious act.
>
> The acceptance of such an intention is evident from the practice of the Church, for she will not order or allow rebaptism for the sole and simple reason that a Jew or Saracen, pagan or heretic, who frequently know little or nothing about the purpose and

powers of Baptism, administered the sacrament, provided of course the duly requisite matter and form were employed.[66]

Beste continues by saying of the minister of Baptism:

> Error and mistaken notions about Baptism, holding it to be but an external sign of aggregation without any effect upon the soul, even when systematically taught as a tenet of a sect and obstinately declared by a minister immediately before the act of baptizing (whether as part of the ceremonial of Baptism or not), do not yet destroy the intention of doing what the Church does, or what Christ instituted; his general intention prevails over and, as it were, absorbs the private or qualified mental attitude of the minister towards Baptism due to false doctrines and heretical ideas; error can coexist with a right intention.[67]

> [In the same article he asserts:] The reason is that the minister's general intention to do what Christ instituted predominates and absorbs false ideas and opinions. Error is rooted in the intellect, while intention is an act of the will. The Sacred Congregation does not tire to repeat and insist in its pronouncements that error about the effect of a sacrament does not make it impossible for a minister to have the necessary intention to perform what Christ has instituted.[68]

The principle of simple error also comes into play in the sacrament of Matrimony. The Code of Canon Law applies this same principle to marriage cases. Canon 1084 describes simple error regarding the unity or the indissolubility or the sacramental dignity of marriage. In order that such error may vitiate [nullify] the consent, it must be transferred to and be made part of the intention by a positive act of the will, as is stated explicitly in canon 1086, section 2: "But if either party or both parties by a positive act of the will should exclude marriage itself, or all right to the conjugal act, or any essential property of marriage, he contracts invalidly."[69]

---

66. Ulric Beste, O.S.B., *American Ecclesiastical Review*, April 1950, p. 257.
67. Ibid., p. 270.
68. Ibid., p. 272.
69. John Abbo, S.T.L., J.C.D., *The Sacred Canons, Vol. II*, pp. 305, 309.

Thus, in Matrimony, simple error may exist in the mind of the bride or groom, yet it does not nullify consent unless a positive act of the will excludes an essential property of marriage. In Baptism "false notions and errors with regard to the nature, efficacy, and effects of the sacrament are compatible with a minister's true and sincere intention of doing what the true Church does or what Christ had instituted."[70]

False notions and errors with regard to the nature, efficacy and effects of the sacrament may remain in the **mind**. This simple error of the mind is compatible with a proper intention in the will. As long as the minister of Baptism does not have an actual prevailing intention in his will contrary to the general intention of Christ and His Church, the sacrament is valid.

However, if the minister of the sacrament of Baptism **by a special act of the will** elicits a contrary intention to the general intention to do what Christ wanted and instituted and what the Church does, the sacrament would be invalid. Therefore, **in the face of an actual prevailing intention to the contrary** to what Christ wanted and instituted and the Church does, this general intention would be nullified and destroyed.

The decisions and pronouncements of the Church make this principle stand out clearly, as illustrated in this example:

> At one time in France a dispute had arisen whether those baptized by the Calvinists should be rebaptized. [Pope] St. Pius V settled the controversy by defining that Baptism was not to be repeated. It should be noted that the Calvinists . . . denied Baptism to have any efficacy to regenerate. Yet the instruction makes it clear that erroneous views in the minister "circa intelligentiam formae vel aliquem effectum" [concerning the understanding of the form or some effect, i.e., what the sacrament does] do not render the sacrament invalid, provided the right matter and form instituted by Christ were used with the general intention to perform what Christ instituted; that this general intention prevails over the particular error or wrong private interpretation. Error and heretical opinion

---

70. Ulric Beste, O.S.B., *American Ecclesiastical Review*, April 1950, p. 273.

about the nature and effects of Baptism can therefore coexist with a sincere intention of doing what Christ did or had instituted.[71]

The following quotes of Ulric Beste, taken together as a unit, clarify the Church's teaching on this important topic:

> False views and beliefs based upon the heretical opinions and teachings, changes and alterations ... so long as the sect and its ministers think that they are performing and repeating that rite of Christ, the Church justly and reasonably presumes and must presume that they want to do what Christ wanted and instituted and the true Church does, whatever the minister in a particular case may think about the true nature, necessity and efficacy of the sacrament.[72]

> It is possible, of course, that a minister [would] carry his heretical ideas from the realm of his intellect into that of his intention [his will], in such a way that, although pronouncing the words of the essential form in Baptism, he wills and intends to administer a mere external rite or ceremony shorn of all spiritual meaning and efficacy [and therefore not what was intended by Christ.] But to bring that about he must elicit a positive act whereby he specifically and definitely excludes and rules out all regeneration when performing the essential rite of Baptism. [This would make the sacrament invalid.][73]

CONCLUSION

In the light of what has been said here, we may conclude by asking whether the baptisms performed in the Post-Conciliar Church are valid or not. The safest course is to investigate each case. We should follow the wise guidelines given in the *American Ecclesiastical Review*: "If the inquiry brings to light that Baptism was conferred either invalidly or not at all, the sacrament is to be administered absolutely; if the point of validity or invalidity remains doubtful,

---

71. Ibid., pp. 268–269.
72. Ulric Beste, O.S.B., *American Ecclesiastical Review*, April 1950, p. 273.
73. Ibid., p. 273.

the sacrament is to be conferred conditionally."[74] In view of the fact that Baptism is necessary for salvation, "the repetition of the sacrament ought to be done where its validity is doubted—or rather, so long as its validity is not morally certain."[75]

BIBLIOGRAPHY
TO 'THE NEW RITE OF BAPTISM'

Abbo, S.T.L., J.C.D., John and Jerome Hannan, A.M., S.T.D., J.C.D. *The Sacred Canons*, Vol. II. St. Louis: Herder Book Co., 1952.

Abbott, S.J., Walter. *The Documents of Vatican II*. New York: Guild Press, 1966.

Aquinas, St. Thomas. *Summa Theologica*, Vol. Two. New York: Benziger Brothers, Inc., 1947.

Beste, O.S.B., Ulric. *American Ecclesiastical Review*, Vol. 122. April 1950. Washington, D.C.: Catholic University of America Press.

Bouscaren, S.J., LL.B., S.T.D., T. Lincoln and Adam Ellis., S.J., M.A., J.C.D. *Canon Law: A Text and Commentary*. Milwaukee: Bruce Publishing Co., 1953.

Bouscaren, S.J., LL.B., S.T.D., T. Lincoln and James O'Connor, S.J., A.M., S.T.L., J.C.D. *Canon Law Digest*, Vol. 5. Milwaukee: Bruce Publishing Co., 1963.

Breviarium Romanum, (Spring edition). Regensburg: Friderici Pustet, 1957.

Breviarium Romanum, (Summer edition). Regensburg: Friderici Pustet, 1957.

Coughlin, Fr. Charles. *Bishops Versus Pope*. Bloomfield Hills, MI: Helmet and Sword, 1969.

Denzinger, Henricus. *Enchiridion Symbolorum*. Freiburg: Herder and Co., 1937.

---

74. Ibid., pp. 260–261.
75. Ibid., pp. 268–269.

Documents on the Liturgy: 1963–1979. Collegeville: The Liturgical Press, 1982.

Hildebrand, Dietrich von. *Teilhard de Chardin: A False Prophet*. Chicago: Franciscan Herald Press, 1968.

———. *Trojan Horse in the City of God*. Manchester: Sophia Inst. Press.

Holy Bible. Chicago: Catholic Press, Inc., 1951.

Johnson, J. *Evolution?* Los Angeles: Perpetual Eucharistic Adoration, 1987.

Kenrick, Archbishop Francis. *A Treatise on Baptism*. Mianwali Nagar: SSM Books, 2008. Reprinted from the 1852 edition.

Kopp, Joseph. *Teilhard de Chardin: A New Synthesis of Evolution*. Glen Rock: Paulist Press, 1965.

Kraft, R. Wayne. *The Relevance of Teilhard*. Notre Dame: Fides Publishers, 1968.

Leroy, S.J., Pierre. 'Teilhard de Chardin: The Man'. *L'Osservatore Romano*. November 7, 1974, Vatican City.

Lubac, Henri de. *The Religion of Teilhard de Chardin*. New York, Desclee, 1967.

McElwain, O.S.M., Hugh. *Introduction to Teilhard de Chardin*. Chicago: Argus Communications, 1967.

Murphy, D.D., Ph.D., John. *The Sacrament of Baptism*. New York: Macmillan, 1929.

Pius X, Pope St. *Encyclical Letter on the Doctrine of the Modernists*. Boston: St. Paul Editions, 1954.

Pius XII, Pope. *Humani Generis*. Washington, D.C.: National Catholic Welfare Conference, 1950.

Pohle, Ph.D., D.D., Msgr. Joseph. *The Sacraments*, Vol. I. St. Louis: Herder, 1957.

Rambaud, Henri. *The Strange Faith of Teilhard de Chardin*. Surrey: Anglo-Gaelic Civic Association, 1966.

Rideau, Emile. *The Thought of Teilhard de Chardin*. New York: Harper and Row, 1967.

Rite of Baptism for One Child and Several Children according to texts approved by the National Conference of Bishops in the United States and confirmed by the Apostolic See. Collegeville: The Liturgical Press, 1970.

Speaight, Robert. *The Life of Teilhard de Chardin*. New York: Harper and Row, 1967.

Teilhard de Chardin, Pierre. *Activation of Energy.* New York: Harcourt Brace Jovanovich, 1970.

———. *Christianity and Evolution.* San Diego: Harcourt Brace and Company, 1971.

———. *Human Energy.* New York: Harcourt Brace Jovanovich, 1969.

———. *Lettres intimes à August Valensin, Bruno de Solages, Henri de Lubac, 1919–1955.* Paris: Aubier Montaigne, 1972.

———. *Letters to Two Friends, 1926–1952.* New York: The New American Library, 1968.

———. *The Phenomenon of Man.* London: Collins, 1959.

Tridentine Fathers. *The Catechism of the Council of Trent.* New York: Joseph Wagner, Inc., 1934.

7

MARRIAGE

It is virtually impossible to invalidate the Sacrament of Marriage providing the partners involved have the correct intention. This is because, as the Council of Florence declared, "the efficient cause of Matrimony (i.e., as a Sacrament) invariably is the mutual consent expressed by words in the present tense." Pius IX taught that "among Christians there can be no marriage [correct intention assumed] which is not at the same time a Sacrament... and consequently the Sacrament can never be separated from the marital contract" (*Allocution*, Sept. 27, 1852).

According to Pohle-Preuss, Bellarmine, Suarez, Sanchez and other theologians of equal stature, "both the matter and form of the Sacrament are contained in the marital contract itself; being the words of consent spoken by the contracting parties, or the signs used. The words or signs constitute the matter of the Sacrament in so far as they signify the mutual surrender of the bodies (*traditio*), and its form in so far as they signify the acceptance (*acceptio*) of the same."[1]

To simplify the issue, one can state that the mutual consent of the contracting parties to give themselves to each other (the contract) is the matter of the Sacrament, and the giving of consent in the present tense, the form. This is consistent with the teaching of St. Thomas Aquinas that "the words in which the matrimonial consent is expressed constitute the form of this Sacrament; not the sacerdotal blessing, which is a sort of sacramental."[2] (The Contract as such is not distinguishable from the words of consent.)

---

1. Pohle-Preuss, *The Sacraments*, op. cit.
2. *Summa.*, Suppl., q. 42, art. 1, ad 1.

What then is the role of the priest? According to Pohle-Preuss, "the contracting parties to a marriage administer the Sacrament to each other. The priest is merely the minister of the (accidental) celebration and the representative and chief official witness of the Church. This explains why his presence is required by ecclesiastical law."

The conditions for validity are four. The recipients must be baptized, they must be of different sexes, there must be no diriment impediment in the way of their marriage (such as previous valid marriage) and they must have the intention of doing what the Church does—i.e. of contracting a Christian marriage. (Normally, a marriage must be solemnized before a priest—however, if no priest is available and is unlikely to be available for a long period of time (as occurs for example in certain parts of Mexico), the marriage can occur without him, though it must be solemnized by a priest when one becomes available.)

Proper intention is of course required on the part of the recipients of this Sacrament. That intention may be implicit, but the contrary intention should not be present. A valid marriage contract must be "till death do us part," must consider the primary purpose of marriage to be the procreation of children and their education in the faith.[3]

POST-CONCILIAR MARRIAGE

Space does not allow for a full consideration of the new catechesis on the nature of marriage. Two fundamental principles however have been abrogated and each of them of sufficient importance to possibly vitiate the marriage contract and thus the exclude the sacramental nature of the union. Moreover, the Post-Conciliar minister

---

3. True consent should be absolute and express the intention of the will with regard to everything that is essential to marriage: the exclusive and perpetual right over each other's bodies with regard to sexual union and procreation. (The intent to limit the number of children would be sinful, but not invalidating, unless this determination was the *sine qua non* for the marriage.) Protestant marriages are valid though of course there can be no requirement on their part to bring up their children in the Catholic Faith. The finer technicalities of canon law are beyond the purpose of this book.

(president, priest?) must inform the persons about to be married both before the ceremony and during the ceremony of these changes.[4]

(1) THE HIERARCHICAL NATURE OF MARRIAGE

It is clear from Ephesians, chapter 5, that marriage is a hierarchical structure. Paul explicitly taught that the partners in marriage should be "subject to one another, in the fear of Christ." He further taught, "Let women be subject to their husbands, as to the Lord: because the husband is the head of the wife, as Christ is head of the Church ... as the Church is subject to Christ, so also let wives be to their husbands in all things."[5] This principle is repeated in innumerable places in both the Old and New Testaments; it is concurred with by Peter who says "in like manner also let wives be subject to their husbands" (1 Pet. 3:1). Likewise, this principle has been repeatedly confirmed by the popes. Pope Pius XI considered the submission of women to man as a fundamental law of the family, established and fixed by God. Pope Pius XII specified that "to reestablish an hierarchy within the family, something indispensable to its unity as well as to its happiness, to grandeur, this was one of Christianity's greatest undertakings, since that day when Christ proclaimed, before the Pharisees and the people, 'what therefore God hath joined together, let no man put asunder.'"

The teaching of the new Rome is first seen in the pastoral constitution *Gaudium et Spes* (declared by Paul VI to the supreme form of the ordinary Magisterium): "Just as of old God encountered his people with a covenant of love and fidelity, so our savior, the spouse of the Church, now encounters Christian spouses through the sacrament of Marriage. He abides with them in order that by their mutual self-giving, spouses will love each other with enduring fidelity, as he

---

4. *Documents on the Liturgy 1963–1979* (Collegeville, MN: The Liturgical Press, 1982), no. 2973.
5. Clearly this is associated with the need for the husband to love his wife as the Christ loved the Church, for him in fact to be an *alter Christus* in the family which is in turn patterned after the Church.

loved the Church and delivered himself for it." Here the teaching of Ephesians has been decisively abridged. Only what is agreeable has been taken from it, namely "love." The subordination of women and, correlatively, that of the Church to her Head, is simply disregarded. Drawing on this statement the Synod of Wurzburg declared in 1975 that the husband and wife were to be seen as partners, and that "the allotment of roles between husband and wife, which was strongly patriarchal in character, has been corrected."

This is also the teaching of John Paul II who holds that love creates equality. In his Apostolic Letter *Familiaris Consortio* issued in 1981 he teaches that "above all it is important to underline the equal dignity and responsibility of women and men ... in creating the human race "male and female," God gives man and woman an equal personal dignity, endowing them with the inalienable rights and responsibilities proper to the human person." The same "responsibilities" for man and woman exclude man from being the head of the family. This was made even more explicit in the Charter of Family Rights promulgated by Rome in 1983 where it states that "the husband and wife have the same dignity and the same rights with respect to their marriage." Again, in a statement published in "*L'Osservatore Romano*, John Paul II explains away the Pauline injunction on the grounds that "the author [Paul] does not hesitate to accept those ideas which were proper to the contemporary mentality and to its forms of expression.... Our sentiments are certainly different today, different also are our mentality and customs, and finally, different is a woman's social position vis-à-vis the man."[6] All this is a far cry from the statement of the German bishops in 1953 to the effect that:

> Anyone who, as a matter of principle, denies the responsibility of the husband and father as head of the woman and of the family, puts himself in opposition to the Gospel and the doctrine of the Church.[7]

---

6. *L'Osservatore Romano*, German edition of 8/27/82.
7. *Hirtenwort der deutschen Erzbishoefe und Bichoefe zur Neurodnung des Ehe- und Familienrechte*, printed as a supplement to *St. Korads Blatt*, No. 10, 1953.

(2) VATICAN II CHANGES A DE FIDE TEACHING ON MARRIAGE

The second significant change in the theology of marriage pertains to the two ends of marriage. The traditional Church taught *de fide* that:

> The primary end of Marriage is the procreation and education of offspring, while its secondary purposes are mutual help and the allaying (also translated "as a remedy for") concupiscence. The latter are entirely subordinate to the former.

Now in saying that this teaching is *de fide*[8] one is saying that Catholics must believe this to be true. Vatican II however places the Catholic couple in an untenable position because it teaches, with (apparently) equal authority, that the two ends of marriage are equal, and further lists the secondary end before the primary one.[9] With the traditional teaching couples whose love for any reason had grown cold, still stayed together for the sake of the children. Now, should the first listed reason for marriage no longer persist, divorce or separation is justified. No longer does the procreation and education of children come first. And to further facilitate the possibility of divorce, one of the new and Post-Conciliar indications allowed by the Rota (marriage court) is "psychological immaturity." Needless to say, it is only the saint who is not psychologically immature.

What are the consequences of entering marriage with this understanding (or misunderstanding) about the hierarchical nature of this state of life—to say nothing of the perversion of its purpose? Without presuming to speak in absolute terms, let us consider the opinion of Father Klaus Moersdorf, a theologian and expert in Canon law. It is his opinion that the hierarchical relationship between man and woman is fraught with a crucial importance for marriage. According to him, "this idea corresponds to the previously

---

8. So declared by the Holy Office with the approval of Pius XII (*Acta Apostolicae Sedis* 36, 1944, 103).

9. I say, "untenable position," because they are forced to deny one or the other *de fide* teachings when they know that the Holy Ghost who guarantees the truth of *de fide* teachings cannot contradict himself.

mentioned teachings of the popes.... A marriage is realized through the uniformity of the will of both people. Both parties of the marriage have to be in agreement in order to affirm the essential content of the marriage contract, which is to say the one who wishes to conclude a marriage must be ready to accept three characteristics of marriage. These are: the right to the body, the indissolubility of marriage and the unity of marriage."

The unity of marriage signifies, according to Father Moersdorf, the union of one man with one woman, and therefore a single couple (monogamy), and that the man and the woman be united in a hierarchical order by a holy unity. According to this author, for the realization of a valid marriage, it is indispensable that the contracting parties recognize and fulfill these three conditions. "If the necessary understanding and will for the conclusion of a marriage are seriously lacking, the marriage will not be valid."

Consequently, it is to be feared that if a marriage is concluded in the spirit of a partnership, and if at least one of the parties rejects the superiority of the man, that marriage is not validly concluded. That means that such partners live together without being united by the marriage bond and without receiving the graces which the sacrament of marriage effects. Dr. Seibel, a professor of sociology and a theologian of some repute states that "a marriage, deprived of its head, is 'decapitated' in the true sense of the word, which is to say that it is 'dead'. At any rate, a marriage which is strictly a partnership can in no case be considered as a Christian marriage."[10]

[An essay on the nature of Catholic Marriage is offered in the section "ADDITIONAL ESSAYS", below.]

CONCLUSION

The Sacraments are of critical importance to the spiritual life of Catholics. They were instituted by Christ as means of grace, and their integrity is independent of man's innovative needs. "Lord, by

---

10. Cf. Paragraph 50, "The Church in the Modern World," *The Documents of Vatican II*; for John Paul II's teaching on marriage see Wigand Siebel's *Philosophie et Théologie de Karol Wojtyla*, SAKA: Bâle, Switzerland.

Your divine sacraments you renew the world. Let your Church draw benefit from Your sacred rites, and do not leave her without temporal aids either. This we ask through Jesus Christ our Lord." (Collect for Matins, Friday, Fourth Week in Lent).

There is no doubt but that the Post-Conciliar Church has played fast and loose with the Sacraments. Whether or not the result has rendered some of them invalid is for the reader to try to figure out. Similarly, and what in the practical order amounts to the same thing, is the question as to whether or not they have been rendered doubtful. If either is the case, their usage is sacrilegious and to be avoided.

All these changes have been carried out for two basic reasons—*aggiornamento* ["bringing up to date," i.e., reconciliation with the world—ED] and ecumenism. Both reasons are intrinsically absurd and damaging to the Faith. There has never been a need for the revealed teachings of Christ to adapt themselves to the modern or any other world. The very concept denies the intrinsic nature of Catholic truth which is why it has always been necessary for the world to adapt itself to the teachings of Christ. Proof of the invalidity of this principle is provided by the fact that Christ made no attempt to adapt His teachings to the Jews or the Romans of his era; and that it was necessary for the Prodigal Son to return to the bosom of his father. As for the motivation of ecumenism, one can make but three comments. First: the very exclusive nature of Catholicism militates against ecumenism. Christ did not die on the Cross so that mankind could choose its own religious views. Secondly, ecumenism inevitably requires the watering down of Christian teaching, for it is only the lowest common denominator that can bring all our "separated brethren" into that false unity of "the people of God" which is desired. And lastly, the very idea of ecumenism implies tolerance to error. It has never been necessary to be tolerant of the truth, and charity to error (as opposed to individuals who are in error) has never been a characteristic of the Catholic Faith.

By their fruits ye shall know them. We have now had some 35 years of the Post-Conciliar establishment with her new sacramental forms. Clearly, by every possible criterion imaginable, the results have been disastrous. The changes introduced by the documents of

Vatican II would have been all but ignored if not implemented through the media of the sacraments—for indeed the *lex credendi* is reflected in the *lex orandi*—our beliefs are reflected in the manner in which we pray. This if nothing else should raise doubts in the minds of the faithful, not only about the sacramental changes, but also about the principles that inspired them.

There are those who will feel that these criticisms have been picky. What after all does a word here or there mean? One can only answer that words indeed do have meaning, or if not, then why have the sacraments at all? Despite the claims of modernists, the sacraments are not "rites of passage." Consider the words of Pope Leo XIII with regard to doctrine:

> Nothing is more dangerous than the heretics who, while conserving almost all the remainder of the Church's teaching intact, corrupt WITH A SINGLE WORD, like a drop of poison, the purity and simplicity of the faith which we have received through tradition from God and through the Apostles.

If such could be said of doctrine, how much more can it be said of the sacraments? Many will argue that obedience requires our acceptance of these changes. But consider the teaching of Suarez:

> [a Pope] also falls into Schism if he himself departs from the body of the Church by refusing to be in communion with her by participating in the sacraments.... The Pope can become schismatic in this manner if he does not wish to be in proper communion with the body of the Church [i.e., the Church as she has always existed], a situation which would arise if he tried to excommunicate the entire Church, or, as both Cajetan and Torquemada observe, IF HE WISHED TO CHANGE ALL THE ECCLESIASTICAL CEREMONIES, FOUNDED AS THEY ARE ON APOSTOLIC TRADITION.

This clearly raises the question of authority. Do the Post-Conciliar "popes" have the authority to introduce these changes which are by their own admission "innovations," and reflective of a "new ecclesiology"? Such a question cannot be answered within the framework of the present study, but it is one that every person who has doubts about the validity of the new sacraments must ask and eventually resolve.

What is clear however is that traditional Catholics who have doubts about the validity of the new sacramental forms, have every right to avoid them in practice, and to seek out and demand unquestionably valid sacraments. This issue is at the heart of the Catholic resistance.

ADDITIONAL ESSAYS

Three additional essays are appended to the text of this book. It is hoped that they will deal with several problems which are related to the Sacraments and which frequently come up for discussion. The first is on Baptism of Desire, the second on Marriage, and the last is a conclusion which provides us with true hope in face of all the devastation.

I

IS BAPTISM OF DESIRE AND BLOOD A CATHOLIC TEACHING?

And Jesus said to them . . . Can you drink the chalice that I drink of: or be baptized with the baptism wherewith I am baptized?
　　　　　　　　　　　　　　　Mark 10:38

Let not the son of the stranger, that adhereth to the Lord, speak, saying the Lord will divide and separate me from his people. . . . For thus saith the Lord . . . they that shall keep my sabbaths, and shall choose the things that please me, and shall hold fast my covenant: I will give to them in my house, and within my walls, a place, and a name better than sons and daughters: I will give them an everlasting name which shall never perish.
　　　　　　　　　　　　　　　Isaiah 6:3

It is one God who justifies the circumcision by faith and the uncircumcision through faith.
　　　　　　　　　　　　　　　Romans 3:3

The continued debate among traditionally-minded Catholic groups with regard to Baptism of Desire and Baptism of Blood can only be resolved by examining the constant teaching of the Church throughout the ages. With this in view, the various arguments which bear on this matter will be reviewed in a semi-historical sequence. Melchior Cano has pointed to the ten sources or *locis theologicis* from which Catholic doctrine can be determined:

(1) Holy Scripture
(2) Oral Tradition
(3) The Authority of the Catholic Church
(4) The Authority of the Councils
(5) The Authority of the Roman Church
(6) The Authority of the Holy Fathers
(7) The Authority of the Scholastic Theologians
(8) The Worthiness of Natural Reason
(9) The Authority of the Philosophers
(10) The Authority of History.

It will be seen in what follows that we have documented the Church's teaching on the issue of Baptism of Desire from all but the 4th and 9th of these loci. In a certain sense one can state that the issue is outside the realm of philosophy. That the Councils have not addressed the issue is understandable if one considers the fact that issues raised in the Councils were always relative to matters in dispute. The validity of Baptism of Desire has, before the present century, never been in doubt. It should be clear that many of the examples we point to fall within the province of "the ordinary and universal Magisterium" of the Church.

Theologians have spoken of the triple form of baptism—namely water, desire and blood. St. Paul in Hebrews 6:2 speaks of the doctrines of baptism in the plural (*doctrinae baptismatum*), implying the possibility of more than one form—the sacrament of course being one by its nature as in "one faith, one baptism."[1] And indeed, Scripture provides us with examples in both the Old and New Testament. In the Old Testament we have the example of Job who was "from the North Country," and not a Jew. In the New Testament we have the slaughter of the innocents, and later the case of the Centurion as in Matt. 8:1–13. Scripture also tells us that the good thief went to heaven, despite the fact that he was not baptized with water. However, those who argue for the absolute need of baptism by water will respond by noting that the Church was not officially "founded"

---

1. The Thomistic commentator Billuant has a pertinent discussion regarding this three-fold baptism.

till the day of Pentecost—and that hence baptism by water only became a requirement subsequent to that time. In support of this position they will quote Matt. 28:19 where Christ says "Going therefore, teach ye all nations, baptizing them in the name of the Father, and of the Son and of the Holy Ghost." This opinion is not grounded on any teaching of the Church. In point of fact, this statement was made before Pentecost—though after the Resurrection. And further, the argument forgets that Christ told Nicodemus, prior to His Crucifixion, that "unless a man be born again of water and the Holy Ghost, he cannot enter into the kingdom of God."[2] Also pertinent is the teaching of St. Paul with regard to Circumcision, which he likened to Baptism. In Rom. 2:25–27 he teaches: "Circumcision profiteth indeed, if thou keep the law; but if thou be a transgressor of the law, thy circumcision is made uncircumcision. If, then, the uncircumcised keep the justices of the law, shall not this uncircumcision be counted for circumcision?"

Granting for the sake of argument that these Scriptural examples fail to close the debate, let us look to the constant practice and teaching of the Church for further clarification.

TERTULLIAN: Born in the year 160 and writing about the year 200, this author, despite his later defection to Montanism, is usually considered as a "Church Father" and certainly one of the earliest exponents of orthodox Catholic doctrine. The following passage is taken from his writings under the section *"De Baptismo"* in the *Enchiridion Patristicum*:

> In truth we also have a second laver which is the same as the first, namely that of blood, concerning which Our Lord said, "And I have a baptism wherewith I am to be baptized" (Luke 12:50) after He had already been baptized; for He came by water and blood as John wrote, that He might be baptized by water and glorified by blood, likewise too that He might make us called by water and chosen by blood; He poured forth these two baptisms from the wound dug in His side so that those who believed in His blood

---

2. Most theologians hold that the Sacrament of Baptism was instituted at the time Christ was baptized by John and the Blessed Trinity indicated its presence.

might be cleansed by water and those who were cleansed by water might bear His blood; this is the baptism which takes the place of the laver which has not been received and restores what was lost.

ST. ALBAN AND HIS FELLOW MARTYR: The Venerable Bede tells us in the Ecclesiastical History of the Church of the English Nation tells us the story of an early English Martyr. The story is well summarized by Dom Gueranger (whom St. Theresa of Lisieux considered to be a saint) in his *Liturgical Year*:

> When the mandates of the emperors Diocletian and Maximian were raging against the Christians, Alban, as yet a pagan, received into his house a certain priest fleeing from persecution. Now, when he [Alban] beheld how this priest persevered day and night in constant watching and prayer, he was suddenly touched by divine grace, so that he was fain to imitate the example of his faith and piety; and being instructed by degrees, through his salutary exhortations, forsaking the darkness of idolatry, he with his whole heart became a Christian.
>
> The persecutors, being in search of this cleric, came to Alban's house, whereupon, disguised in the cleric's apparel—namely, in the caracalla—he presented himself to the soldiers in the place of his master and guest; by them he was bound with thongs, and led off to the judge. This latter finding himself thus deceived, ordered that the holy confessor of God should be beaten by the executioners; and, perceiving at last that he could neither overcome him by torments, nor win him over from the worship of the Christian religion, he commanded his head to be struck off.
>
> Alban having reached the brow of the neighboring hill, the executioner who was to dispatch him, admonished by a divine inspiration, casting away his sword, threw himself at the saint's feet, desiring to die either with the martyr, or instead of him. Alban, being at once beheaded, received the crown of life, which God hath promised to them that love him.
>
> The soldier who had refused to strike him, was likewise beheaded: concerning whom it is quite certain that, albeit he was not washed in the baptismal font, still was he made clean in the

laver of his own blood and so made worthy of entering into the kingdom of heaven. Alban suffered at Verulam, on the tenths of the Kalends of July. And the judge, astonished at the novelty of so many heavenly miracles, ordered the persecution to cease immediately, beginning to honor the death of the saints [only St. Alban and the soldier had been executed], by which [death] he had before thought that they might be diverted from the Christian faith.

As Martin Gwynne points out, this last paragraph is taken verbatum from the writings of Bede, and Bede is a Doctor of the Church. Moreover, St. Alban, who died on June 22 in the year 303, is considered to be the proto-martyr of the English Church.[3]

ST. EMERENTIANA: Those familiar with the traditional Breviary (dropped from the Novus Ordo "missals") will know the story of this virgin and martyr. The idea that the Church would have her religious commemorate such a person who was unbaptized—according to those who deny Baptism of Desire and Blood—on a yearly basis for some 1800 years, is to say the least "offensive to pious ears." Let us quote the Breviary directly:

Emerentiana, a Roman virgin, step-sister of the blessed Agnes, while still a catechumen, burning with faith and charity, when she vehemently rebuked idol-worshippers who were stealing from Christians, was stoned and struck down by the crowd which she had angered. Praying in her agony at the tomb of holy Agnes, baptized by her own blood which she poured forth unflinchingly for Christ, she gave up her soul to God.

---

3. Martin Gwynne has discussed this issue in his *Briton's Catholic Library*, Letter no. 5. Some of the material in this essay is drawn from this source. It should be made clear that Mr. Gwynne's approval for this journal is not to be presumed, nor do its editors give their unequivocal support to the opinions of Mr. Gwynne. Thomas Hutchinson in his *Desire and Deception* explains away this episode by first telling us a miraculous fountain provided St. Alban with the water required for baptism, and then wondering if St. Bede, "writing four centuries after the fact, using ancient documents, didn't miss something."

This virgin and martyr died in Rome about the year 350. A church was built over her grave. According to *The Catholic Encyclopedia* (1908), some days after the death of St. Agnes, Emerentiana, who was still a catechumen, went to the grave to pray, and while praying she was suddenly attacked by the pagans and killed with stones. Her feast is kept on January 23 and she is again commemorated on Sept. 16 under the phrase *in caemeterio maiore* (where she is buried). She is represented in the iconography of the church with stones in her lap and a palm of lily in her hands. Some have argued that she was baptized—but such is absurd as she is both called a catechumen, and the Church states in her liturgy that she was "baptized in her own blood."[4]

Yet another example, enshrined in the Breviary in the office of Nov. 10, is that of ST. RESPICIUS:

> During the reign of the emperor Decius, as Tryphon was preaching the faith of Jesus Christ and striving to persuade all men to worship the Lord, he was arrested by the henchmen of Decius. First, he was tortured on the rack, his flesh torn with iron hooks, then hung head downward, his feet pierced with red hot nails. He was beaten by clubs, scorched by burning torches held against his body. As a result of seeing him endure all these tortures so courageously, the tribune Respicius was converted to the faith of Christ the Lord. Upon the spot he publicly declared himself to be a Christian. Respicius was then tortured in various ways, and together with Tryphon, dragged to a statue of Jupiter. As Tryphon prayed, the statue fell down. After this occurred both were mercilessly beaten with leaden tipped whips and thus attained to glorious martyrdom.

ST. AMBROSE, another doctor of the Church, provides us with the fourth example. He has the following to say with regard to the death of Valentinian II, who was murdered at Vienne in the year 371. Valentinian II was the son of the Emperor Valentinian I, Emperor of

---

4. Thomas Hutchinson explains this away by assuring us that if at the time of her martyrdom "she had truly not been baptized, it must be expected that someone would have done it while she lay dying."

the West, and his second wife Justina. Valentinian I and Justina had been displaced by Magnus Maximus, and had sought support from the Arian Theodosius, who was Emperor of the East. As a result, Valentinian II for many years sat on the fence and tried to bring about a compromise in the arguments between the Arians and the Orthodox. In this he was opposed by St. Ambrose. When his mother died, Valentinian II abandoned Arianism, became a catechumen, and invited St. Ambrose to come to Gaul and administer baptism to him. He was however assassinated before this could happen and his body was brought to Milan where the saint delivered his funeral oration *De Obitu Valentiniani Consolatio* which dwelt on the efficacy of baptism of desire. The following is extracted from this oration:

> But I hear that you are distressed because he did not receive the sacrament of baptism. Tell me, what attribute do we have besides our will, our intention? Yet, a short time ago he had this desire that before he came to Italy he should be initiated [baptized], and he indicated that he wanted to be baptized as soon as possible by myself. Did he not, therefore, have that grace which he desired? Did he not have what he asked for? Undoubtedly because he asked for it he received it. Whence it is written, "The just man, by whatsoever death he shall be overtaken, his soul shall be at rest" (Wisdom 4:7).[5]

ST. AUGUSTINE, another Doctor of the Church, has also spoken to this issue. In his *City of God* he makes his position more than clear:

> Those also who die for the confession of Christ without having received the laver of regeneration are released thereby from their sins just as much as if they had been cleansed by the sacred spring of baptism. For He who said, "Unless a man be born again of

---

5. Thomas Hutchinson informs us that St. Ambrose was using a political ploy, and that he made this statement in a "highly charged atmosphere of grief, fear, and popular anger surrounding the funeral." He then assures us that St. Ambrose in fact "knew" that Valentinian had indeed been baptized, but was "not at liberty to reveal the circumstances of the event, which presumably were bound up with the Emperor's mysterious death."

water and the Holy Ghost, he cannot enter into the kingdom of God" (John 3:5), by another statement made exceptions to this when He said no less comprehensively: "Everyone... that shall confess me before men, I will confess before my Father who is in Heaven." (Matt. 10:32).

Lest anyone claim that this was an isolated opinion of Augustine's, we also give the following drawn from his "*De Baptismo*" and found in the *Enchiridion Patristicum*, a source which provides Catholic scholars with approved texts on doctrinal issues (para. 1629).[6]

> I do not doubt that a Catholic catechumen, burning with Divine charity, is superior to a baptized heretic. But even inside the Catholic Church we consider a good catechumen better than a bad man who has been baptized; and for this reason we do no injury to the sacrament of baptism, which the one has not yet received and the other has, nor do we consider the sacrament of the catechumen superior to the sacrament of baptism by considering a particular catechumen more faithful and better than a particular person who has been baptized. For the centurion Cornelius was better when he was not yet baptized than was Simon [Magus] after he had been baptized. For the former was filled with the Holy Ghost even before baptism, while the latter was full of the evil spirit even after baptism....
>
> That the place of baptism can sometimes assuredly be taken by suffering, the blessed Cyprian takes as no mean proof the words addressed to the thief who was not baptized: "This day thou shalt be with me in paradise" (Luke 23:43). In considering which again, I find that not only suffering for the name of Christ can supply that which was lacking in respect of baptism [*id quod ex baptismo deerat*], but also faith and conversion of heart if perchance in straitened times it is impossible to arrange for the celebration of the mystery of baptism:

---

6. Published by B. Herder and printed by Typographus Editor Pontificus. Needless to say, this text carries a *Nihil Obstat* and *Imprimatur*, dated 1911 in my edition. Hutchinson tells us that "St. Augustine appears at one point to have misread his old mentor's views."

IS BAPTISM OF DESIRE AND BLOOD A CATHOLIC TEACHING? 209

Since reference to ST. CYPRIAN (martyred in the year 257) has been made by St. Augustine, it seems appropriate to quote him directly. Again, we use as our source the *Enchiridion Patristicum* (paragraph 1328):

> Some people, as if by human argument they could rob of its truth the teaching of the Gospel, present us with the case of catechumens, demanding whether, if one of these, before he was baptized in the church, were captured and killed in the confession of his belief, he would forfeit his hope of salvation and the reward of his confession because he had not previously been born again by water. Men of this kind, who laud and abet heretics, are well aware that those catechumens who first hold inviolate the faith and truth of the Church and advance, with full and sincere knowledge of God the Father and Christ and the Holy Ghost, to fight off the devil from the Divine battlements are certainly not thereupon deprived of the sacrament of baptism seeing that they have been baptized with the greatest and most glorious baptism of blood, concerning which Our Lord said that He had another baptism wherewith to be baptized (Luke 12:50). The same Lord, however, affirms in the gospel that those who are baptized by their own blood and sanctified by their sufferings, are consummated and receive the grace of the Divine promise. This is implied by His words when he spoke to the thief who believed in and confessed His passion, promising that he would be with him in paradise.

At this point we will return to examples taken from history—specifically drawing on the Bollandists who are the official hagiographers of the Church. We take two examples drawn from *Les Petits Bollandistes*:[7]

The first is the story of the brother martyrs SAINTS DONATIEN AND ROGATIEN, who were martyred during the reign of Maxim-

---

7. Hagiography is the study of the lives of the saints. The Bollandists, a branch of the Jesuits organized under the initial direction of Father Bolland (with papal approval), have taken it as their special function to research the lives of the saints and provide official versions of both their acts and writings.

ian about the year 287 and who are the patron saints of the city of Nantes in France.

> There was a young man in Nantes called Donatien. Born into an illustrious family, he was even more illustrious for his faith.... He had received baptism, and fortified by the holy mysteries, he publicly proclaimed the triumph of Jesus Christ and spread the divine wheat that had been so fruitful in his own heart, in the hearts of the Gentiles around him.
>
> He gained his elder brother Rogatien who was still an idolator to the Christian faith at a time of great peril, for it was a period when the profession of Christianity was proscribed. But such considerations did not deter Rogatien from adhering to the truth and committing himself to following Jesus Christ, even unto death. In order to have the strength to undertake this dangerous combat, he sought out the sacrament of baptism with great ardor, but in the absence of a priest (*sacerdotis absentia fugitiva*)—for the priests had been forced to flee the land—he could only be baptized in his own blood.

Rogatien and his brother were placed in the same jail and Rogatien had only one sorrow—that he had not received baptism. Continuing the story as provided by the Bollandists:

> But the faith which he had in God led him to hope that the kiss of his brother would take the place of the sacred bath [baptism]. Donatien, informed of the sorrow of his brother, made the following prayer to God: "Lord Jesus Christ, with whom desires have the same merit as works, when it is absolutely impossible to fulfill the wishes of someone who is completely devoted to you, as is the case with your servant Rogatien, grant if the judge persists in his obstinacy, that his pure faith may take the place of baptism, and that his blood may become the sacred oils."

The following morning both brothers were slain, and "Donatien, having gained his brother to Jesus Christ, had the consolation of seeing him respond with dignity to the graces of his vocation; Rogatien, baptized in his own blood, showed himself in no way inferior to his brother, and the two achieved an illustrious victory and were united in the happy flock that is never to be separated from the immortal Lamb, the author and consummator of their beatitude." There are many churches in the districts around Nantes dedicated to these two saints.

There is yet another saint that the Bollandists tell us of—ST. VICTOR OF BRAGA in Portugal—a saint who is commemorated in the Breviary on April 11. According to our source, "St. Victor of Braga was as yet only a catechumen when he refused to adore an idol and confessed with great courage his belief in Jesus Christ. He was decapitated after many tortures and thus had the good fortune to be baptized in his own blood—this about the year 300 during the reign of Diocletian."

Returning once again to the doctors of the Church, we find the following statement in the writings of ST. CYRIL OF JERUSALEM who died in the year 386:

> If anyone does not receive baptism, he does not have salvation, excepting only martyrs who gain the kingdom even without water.[8]

ST. GREGORY NAZIANZEN who, according to *The Catholic Encyclopedia* (1908), is one of the greatest theologians of the Church, has the following to say about Baptism:

> I know also that there is a fourth kind of baptism [i.e., apart from the baptism of Moses, of John, and of Jesus], namely that which is acquired by martyrdom and blood, by which Christ Himself was also baptized, and which indeed is nobler than the others, because it is contaminated by no subsequent defilements.[9]

Yet another authority is that of ST. JOHN CHRYSOSTOM, (died 407) who *The Catholic Encyclopedia* (1908) describes as generally considered "the most prominent doctor in the Greek Church and the greatest preacher ever heard in the Christian pulpit," makes the following statement in his *Panegyric on St. Lucianus*:

---

8. *Enchiridion Patristicum*, 811.
9. Ibid., 1139.

Do not be surprised that I should equate martyrdom with baptism; for here too the spirit blows with much fruitfulness, and a marvelous and astonishing remission of sins and cleansing of the soul is effected; and just as those who are baptized by water, so, too, those who suffer martyrdom are cleansed with their own blood.

Yet another authority is that of ST. FULGENTIUS who died in the early part of the sixth century:

From the time when Our Savior said "Unless a man be born again of water and the Holy Ghost, he cannot enter into the kingdom of God," without the sacrament of baptism, apart from those who pour forth their blood for Christ in the Catholic Church without baptism, no one can receive the kingdom of Heaven, nor eternal life.[10]

It might seem that most of our examples are taken from the lives of the martyrs and that hence we only defend a baptism of blood and not one of desire. However, in the practical order, one who desires baptism and is not martyred or assassinated, usually is in no way impeded from obtaining it. Thus it is that the desire for baptism is almost always demonstrated and proven only by the complementary baptism of blood—and indeed, the theologians almost always discuss them together. Let us demonstrate this by turning to ST. THOMAS AQUINAS whose authoritative teaching few will debate:

As stated in question 62, fifth article, baptism of water has its efficacy from Christ's Passion, to which a man is conformed by baptism, and also from the Holy Ghost as first cause. Now although the effect depends on the first cause, the cause far surpasses the effect, nor does it depend on it. Consequently, a man may, without baptism of water, receive the sacramental effect from Christ's Passion, in so far as he is conformed to Christ by suffering for Him. Hence it is written (Rev. 7:14): "These are they who are come out of great tribulation, and have washed their robes and made them white in the blood of the Lamb." In like manner a

---

10. Ibid., 2269.

man receives the effect of baptism by the power of the Holy Ghost, not only without baptism of water, but also without baptism of blood: forasmuch as his heart is moved by the Holy Ghost to believe in and love God and to repent of his sins: wherefore this is also called the baptism of repentance. Of this it is written (Isaiah 4:4): "If the Lord shall wash away the filth of the daughters of Sion, and shall wash away the blood of Jerusalem out of the midst thereof, by the spirit of judgment, and by the spirit of burning." Thus, therefore, each of these other baptisms is called baptism, forasmuch as it takes the place of baptism.

Summa, Part III, Question 66, Eleventh Article

St. Thomas completes this article by quoting the passage from St. Augustine we have ourselves quoted above. He then moves on to the next question (66):

> Augustine [*Ad Fortunatum*], speaking of the comparison between baptisms says: "The newly baptized confesses his faith in the presence of the priest; the martyr in the presence of the persecutor. The former is sprinkled with water, after he has confessed; the latter with his blood. The former receives the Holy Ghost by the imposition of the bishop's hands; the latter is made the temple of the Holy Ghost."
>
> As stated above (article 11), the shedding of blood for Christ's sake, and the inward operation of the Holy Ghost, are called baptisms, in so far as they produce the effect of the baptism of water. Now the baptism of water derives its efficacy from the Holy Ghost, as already stated. These two causes act in each of these three baptisms; most excellently, however, in the baptism of blood. For Christ's Passion acts in the baptism of water by way of desire; but in the baptism of blood by way of imitating the (Divine) act. In like manner, too, the power of the Holy Ghost acts in the baptism of water through a certain hidden power; in the baptism of repentance by moving the heart; but in the baptism of blood by the highest degree of fervor of dilection and love, according to John 15:13 "Greater love than this no man hath, that a man lay down his life for his friends."

ST. THOMAS AQUINAS discusses the matter again in his Commentary on the Gospel of St. John (section 444):

> Two questions arise here. First, if no one enters the kingdom of God unless he is born again of water, and if the fathers of old were not born again of water (because they were not baptized), then they have not entered the kingdom of God. Secondly, since baptism is of three kinds, that is, of water, of desire and of blood, and many have been baptized in the latter two ways (who we say have entered the kingdom of God immediately, even though they were not born again of water), it does not seem to be true to say that unless one is born again of water and the Holy Spirit, he cannot enter the kingdom of God. The answer to the first is that rebirth or regeneration from water and the Holy Spirit takes place in two ways: in truth and in symbol. Now the fathers of old, although they were not reborn with a true rebirth, were nevertheless reborn with a symbolic rebirth, because they always had a sense perceptible sign in which true rebirth was prefigured. So according to this, thus reborn, they did enter the kingdom of God, after the ransom was paid. The answer to the second is that those who are reborn by a baptism of blood and fire, although they do not have regeneration in deed, they do have it in desire. Otherwise neither would the baptism of blood mean anything nor could there be a baptism of the Spirit. Consequently, in order that man may enter the kingdom of heaven, it is necessary that there be baptism of water in deed, as is the case of all baptized persons, or in desire, as in the case of the martyrs and catechumens, who are prevented by death from fulfilling their desire, or in symbol as in the case of the fathers of old.[11]

PETER LOMBARD, the master of the sentences, also held this doctrine. To quote him directly:

> With regard to this issue it should be noted that Our Lord said in John 3 that "unless a person be reborn of water and the Holy

---

11. Once again, Thomas Hutchinson assures us that St. Thomas Aquinas failed to study St. Ambrose as carefully as he had studied Aristotle, and that in his teaching about Baptism of Desire he was plain and simply wrong.

Spirit, he cannot enter the kingdom of heaven." Now this is generally true ... it is to be understood of those who are capable of receiving but despise baptism. For them, apart from baptism by water and the Holy Spirit there is no salvation. But this same regeneration can be achieved, not only by baptism of water, but also by repentance [and hence desire] and by blood. Hence it follows that many apostolic authorities teach that baptism can be of water, repentance or blood ... and this is only reasonable.... Whence Augustine asks: which is greater, faith or water? Unquestionably everyone would respond "faith." Therefore, if what is the lesser can sanctify, why cannot the greater, namely faith, with regard to which Christ said, "He who believes in me, even though he should die, liveth'? *Lib. IV, De Sacramentis.*

Again, ST. BONAVENTURE teaches that

There are three distinct forms of Baptism, namely that of fire, that of water and that of blood. Baptism of fire is that provided by repentance and the grace of the Holy Spirit, and purifies from sin. In Baptism of water we are both purified from sin and absolved of all temporal punishment due to sin. In Baptism of blood we are purified from all misery.[12]

Yet another mediaeval theologian of authority, HUGH of ST. VICTOR, has spoken to the issue. As his statement is rather lengthy, it is added as an appendix.

Let us next turn to the authority of a pope, namely that of POPE INNOCENT II who reigned from 1130-1143. He wrote to the Bishop of Cremona in a letter entitled *Apostolicam Sedem*:

We assert without hesitation (on the authority of the holy Fathers Augustine and Ambrose) that the "priest" whom you indicated (in your letter) had died without the water of baptism, because he persevered in the Faith of Holy Mother Church and in the confession of the name of Christ, was freed from original sin and attained the joys of the heavenly fatherland. Read [brother] in the eighth book of Augustine's *City of God* where among other things

12. *Centiloquij*, Tertia Pars, and *De Sacramentorum Virtute*, lib. VI.

it is written: "Baptism is administered invisibly to one whom not contempt of religion, but death excludes." Read again the book also of the blessed Ambrose concerning the death of Valentinian where he says the same thing. Therefore, to questions concerning the dead, you should hold the opinions of the learned Fathers, and in your church you should join in prayers and you should have sacrifices offered to God for the "priest" mentioned.[13]

Similarly, in a letter to a Bishop Berthold of Metz on August 28, 1206 he stated:

You have, to be sure, intimated that a certain Jew, when at the point of death, since he lived only among Jews, immersed himself in water while saying: "I baptize myself in the name of the Father, and of the Son, and of the Holy Spirit, Amen." We respond that, since there should be a distinction between the one baptizing and the one baptized, as is clearly gathered from the words of the Lord, when he says to the Apostles: "Go baptize all nations in the names etc." (cf. Matt. 28:19), the Jew mentioned must be baptized again by another, that it may be shown that he who is baptized is one person, and he who baptizes another.... If, however, such a one had died immediately, he would have rushed to his heavenly home without delay because of the faith of the sacrament, although not because of the sacrament of faith.[14]

We next provide a brief quotation taken from the *Dictionnaire de Theologie Catholique*—not that the quotation adds any significant

---

13. As Mr. Gwynne points out, the original letter to which the pope was responding has been lost. The title "priest" obviously was not applied to a person in holy orders and probably implies his "priestly" act of sacrifice. The letter *Apostolam Sedem* written by Celestine II (1143–1144) was sent to the Bishop of Cremona and is quoted in *The Seraph*, March, 1993.

14. Thomas Hutchinson assures us on his own authority that these quotations taken from Denzinger only represent "a private communication regarding a prudential and disciplinary judgment," and that "there is no question of the lack of infallibility of such a document." Now Denzinger's work is entitled *Enchiridion Symbolorum, Definitionum et Declarationum de Rebus Fidei et Morum*. Is everything in Denzinger which Mr. Hutchinson doesn't agree with to be declared fallible and hence erroneous?

information, but rather it demonstrates that this weighty and orthodox text, published around the turn of the century, is in full concordance with all that has so far been said.

> Nevertheless, regardless of the absolute necessity of baptism for salvation, are there not other means [than that of water] of providing for it? The Fathers [of the Church] admit to baptism of blood or martyrdom, and in a certain measure the baptism of desire, as a means of replacing the baptism of water.[15]

THE COUNCIL OF TRENT is often appealed to by those who would deny baptism of blood and desire. The argument put forth is based on the second canon of the Council which states:

> If anyone should say that true and natural water is not necessary for baptism and should therefore twist into some metaphor the words of Our Lord Jesus Christ "unless a man be born again of water and the Holy Ghost," let him be anathema.

Now, there is nothing in such a statement which contradicts what has been said throughout this essay. As is always the case, one must take things in their proper context. This particular anathema was directed against Calvin who argued that water was simply a metaphor for the grace of the Holy Ghost. Thus, reference to the Decree on Justification promulgated by the Council of Trent is necessary for the full understanding of the doctrine in question. Quoting from Fr. Heinrich Denzinger, yet another unquestionably Catholic source, we make note of the following:

> This ... translation [i.e. from the state of original sin to the state of grace "of the adoption of sons" (Rom. 8:15)] after the promulgation of the Gospel cannot take place without the laver of regeneration or the desire for it. ...
>
> *Enchiridion Symbolorum,*
> *Definitionum et Declarationum*
> *de Rebus Fidei et Morum,* §796

---

15. Section on Baptism—*Bapteme d'apres les Peres Grecs et Latins.*

Some have argued against Baptism of Blood and Desire on the basis of the *Catechism of the Council of Trent* where it is stated that "the Sacrament of Baptism can be said to exist only when we actually apply the water to someone by way of ablution, while using the words appointed by our Lord." This statement of course is only meant to apply to the "normative" form of baptism with water, and was never meant to be taken out of context as an absolute statement in and of itself. Proof of this is provided by the fact that in the Definition of Baptism given in the same section of this *Catechism* we find the following statement—"For He gave power to men to be made the sons of God, to them that believe in His name, who are born, not of blood, nor of the will of the flesh, nor of the will of man, but of God," footnoted by a reference to St. Thomas Aquinas as quoted above, and to a section in St. Alphonsus Liguori's *Moral Theology*. It is worthwhile seeing what the latter has to say on this issue.

According to ST. ALPHONSUS LIGUORI:

> Truly Baptism of Blood is the pouring forth of blood, undergone for the sake of the faith, or for some other Christian virtue, as teaches St. Thomas, Viva, Croix along with Aversa and Gobet, etc. This is equivalent to real baptism because [it acts] as if it were *ex operato*, and like Baptism remits both sin and punishment. It is said to be *quasi*—"as if"—because martyrdom is not strictly speaking like a sacrament, but because those privileged in this way imitate the Passion of Christ as says Bellarmine, Suarez, Sotus, Cajetan, etc., along with Croix; and in a firm manner, Petrocorensis.
>
> Therefore martyrdom is efficacious, even in infants, as is shown by the Holy Innocents which are indeed considered true martyrs. This is clearly taught by Suarez along with Croix and to oppose such an opinion is indeed temerarious. In adults it is necessary that martyrdom be at least habitually accepted from supernatural motives as Coninck, Cajetan, Suarez, Bonacina and Croix, etc., teach....

Such also is the teaching of ST. CATHERINE OF SIENNA. Christ addressed the issue of Baptism in response to her question in the following terms:

I wished thee to see the secret of the Heart, showing it to thee open, so that thou mightest see how much more I loved than I could show thee by finite pain. I poured from it Blood and Water, to show thee the baptism of water which is received in virtue of the Blood. I also showed the baptism of love in two ways, first in those who are baptized in their blood shed for Me which has virtue through My Blood, even if they have not been able to have Holy Baptism, and also those who are baptized in fire, not being able to have Holy Baptism, but desiring it with the affection of love. There is no baptism of desire without the Blood, because Blood is steeped in and kneaded with the fire of Divine charity, because through love was it shed. There is yet another way by which the soul receives the baptism of Blood, speaking, as it were, under a figure, and this way the Divine charity provided, knowing the infirmity and fragility of man, through which he offends, not that he is obliged, through his fragility and infirmity, to commit sin, unless he wish to do so; by falling, as he will, into the guilt of mortal sin, by which he loses the grace which he drew from Holy Baptism in virtue of the Blood, it was necessary to have a continual baptism of blood. This the Divine charity provided in the Sacrament of Holy Confession, the soul receiving the Baptism of blood, with contrition of heart, confessing, when able, to My ministers, who hold the keys of the Blood, sprinkling It, in absolution, upon the face of the soul. But if the soul is unable to confess, contrition of heart is sufficient for this baptism, the hand of My clemency giving you the fruit of this precious Blood.... Thou seest then that these Baptisms, which you should all receive until the last moment, are continual, and though My works, that is the pains of the Cross were finite, the fruit of them which you receive in Baptism, through Me, are infinite....[16]

One penultimate argument is drawn from CANON LAW. Those who deny Baptism of Desire and Blood are prone to quote Canon 1239 which states:

---

16. I am grateful to Bishop Robert F. McKenna, O.P., for directing me to this passage.

Those who have died without baptism are not to be given ecclesiastical burial.

However this canon is immediately followed by Canon 1239 (ii) which states:

Catechumens who die without baptism through no fault of their own are to be counted among the baptized.

Two final witnesses to the constant teaching of the Church:

It must indeed be held by faith that outside the Apostolic Roman Church no one can be saved; that this is the only ark of salvation; that he who shall not have entered therein will perish in the flood; but, on the other hand, it is necessary to hold for certain that they who labor in ignorance of the true religion, if this ignorance is invincible, are not stained by any guilt in this matter in the eyes of God. Now, in truth, who would arrogate so much to himself as to mark the limits of such ignorance, because of the nature and variety of peoples, regions, innate dispositions, and of so many other things?" Pius IX, *Singulari Quadam*, Dec. 8, 1854. Cf. Fr. Heinrich Denzinger, *Enchiridion Symbolorum, Definitionum et Declarationum de Rebus Fidei et Morum*, §1647)

And again, Pope Saint Pius X's *Catechism of Christian Doctrine*, paragraph 132 states:

A person outside the Church *by his own fault*, and who dies without perfect contrition, will not be saved. But he who finds himself outside *without fault of his own*, and *who lives a good life*, can be saved by the love called charity, *which unites unto God, and in a spiritual way also to the Church*, that is, to the soul of the Church [italics in original].[17]

---

17. Father E. Hugueney, O.P., further explains: "Of those who are members of the Church, the elect will greatly outnumber the damned; and if we include as members of the Church all those who are hers in spirit by the baptism of desire, this immense number of elect will be very great indeed. Yet, we must not forget that, outside the Church, the chances of salvation are much less; this means that many pagans will probably lose their souls, because they are almost defenseless

CONCLUDING COMMENTS: Once again, let it be clear that examples of baptism of desire apart from those who undergo martyrdom are hard to come by, for the simple reason that those so desirous who do not suffer martyrdom or untimely death, are usually able to receive the sacrament in a "normal" manner.

We have provided more than ample evidence that the Church has always accepted Baptism of Desire and Baptism of Blood as efficacious means of "regeneration." This doctrine has been taught by doctors of the Church throughout her history from the earliest days down to recent times. Individuals so graced have been repeatedly raised to her altars. The principle has been incorporated into her liturgy as is demonstrated by examples taken from the Breviary. The doctrine is accepted by the Bollandists, by those who promulgate the Church's official "dictionaries," by innumerable saints and theologians[18] and by Canon Law. As opposed to this, one cannot point to a single official document of the Church's Magisterium that denies the efficacy of these other forms of Baptism.[19]

It is true that there are "anecdotal" stories of individuals who have been brought back to life in order to receive baptism of water, or who have received the "laver of regeneration" in some other miraculous manner. Such stories however—and there is no reason to deny their veracity—in no way prove the contrary to our thesis. No one can deny but that God is able to achieve His ends in ways beyond our ken. But such stories are not points of doctrine; they are not to be found in the liturgy of the Church; they are not discussed by the doctors of the Church; they are not pointed to in her Catechisms;

---

against the devils and their own passions." ("L'Opinion traditionnelle sur le nombre des Elus" in *La Revue Thomiste*, 1933, pp. 217 and 533.)

18. How is it possible for a Catholic to deny the authority of such theologians as Ambrose, Augustine, Thomas Aquinas, Alphonse Liguori and Catherine of Sienna without declaring themselves "out of communion" with the Church?

19. I have in several places made reference to Thomas A. Hutchinson's defense of the position that there is no possibility of salvation without Baptism with water. One cannot dismiss the writings of the saints and the practice of the Church because of the reasons he offers. One could give other examples of where he suggests and insinuates that saints like St. Chrysostom or St. Louis IX fully agree with him. (*Desire and Deception* [Arcadia: Charlemagne Press])

and edifying as they may be, they do not command our belief and acceptance.

I think it can be said that the Church has more than adequately spoken to this issue. No Catholic "in good faith" can deny the efficacy of Baptism of Desire and of Blood. May we all have the purity of heart and faith that those who have been regenerated through such means are known to have had.

We can do no better than to conclude this essay with a passage from Father Lacordaire, translated and taken from the writing of Kenhelm Digby, an English Catholic convert who lived well over 150 years ago.

> Christ has created the society of souls founded on Him in love. All persons, it is true, do not know the source of the fire that consumes them. Some cannot name Jesus Christ because He has never been named to them. Obscure victims of the cross which saves them, they have not been led from their birth to the feet of Calvary. But a drop of this blood has searched for them across invisible furrows, and mixed with theirs as an aroma of eternal life; they have responded by a silent groaning to the appeal of charity. The Church, therefore, is not alone what it appears to us. It is not only in this visible construction, where all is history, authenticity, hierarchy, virtues and external miracles; it is also in the twilight, in the evanescent shades, in that which has neither form nor memory, sanctities lost to the vision of men, but not lost to that of angels. There is not a single soul besides, however well known, which has not an impenetrable sanctuary, and which does not offer to God, in this holy of holies, a mysterious incense, that does not reckon on the manifestation of this world, but which weighs in the glory of the other. Thus the Church [is] partly invisible; and, remark here, neither is the creation confined wholly to the luminous globes of firmament. It is not alone in the cedars of Solomon, in waves of the ocean, in the wings of the eagle, in the countenance of the lion; it is also in the sand of the desert, in the herb that stoops under a drop of water, in the insect which the sun warms, and which it does not see. Love, which is the foundation of the Church, is the most palpable of living flu-

ids; and if the eye of man has never been able to detect, in the light tissue of his nerves, the ambrosia which animates them, how much more ignorant is he of the ways of divine love? Young as you are, then, you know enough not to limit the Church to the visible walls of Jerusalem and to the exterior towers of Sion. Wherever the love of God is, there is Jesus Christ. Wherever Jesus Christ, there is the Church with Him. And if it is true that every Christian ought to unite himself to the body of the Church as soon as he knows of its existence, so it is also certain that invincible ignorance dispenses with this law, to leave its victim under the immediate government of Jesus Christ. The Church, then, has an extension which no human eye can embrace; and those who oppose to us the limits which it seems to their eyes to have, are persons who have no idea of the twofold radiance which is in its nature, raising up for it souls from the east and from the west, under the sun that has gone down as well as under the sun that is above the horizon. (*Evenings on the Thames, or Serene Hours*, Longman, Green, 1864.)

APPENDIX

Taken from Book Two, Part Six of *De Sacramentis* by Hugh of St. Victor (13th century)[20]

Some either through curiosity or zeal are accustomed to inquire whether anyone after the enjoining and proclaiming of the sacrament of baptism can be saved, unless he actually receives the sacrament of baptism itself. For the reasons seem to be manifest and they have many authorities, (if, however, they are said to have authorities, who do not understand); first, because it is said: "Unless a man be born again of the water and the Holy Ghost, he cannot enter into the kingdom of God," (cf. John 3:5), and again: "He that believeth and is baptized, shall be saved," (Mark 16:16). There are many such passages which seem, as it were, to affirm that by no means can he

---

20. Translated by Roy Defarri, published by The Mediaeval Academy of America, Cambridge, MA, 1951.

be saved who has not had this sacrament, whatever he may have besides this sacrament. If he should have perfect faith, if hope, if he should have charity, even if he should have a contrite and humble heart which God does not despise, true repentance for the past, firm purpose for the future, whatever he may have, he will not be able to be saved, if he does not have this. All this seems so to them on account of what is written: "Unless a man be born again of the water and the Holy Ghost, he cannot enter into the kingdom of God" (cf. John 3:5).

Yet if someone would ask: what has happened to those who, after shedding blood for Christ, departed this life without the sacrament of water, they dare not say that men of this kind are not saved. And, although one cannot show that this is written in what is mentioned above, yet they dare not say that, because it is not written there, it is to be denied. For he who said: "Unless a man be born again of the water and the Holy Ghost" did not add: "or by pouring forth his blood instead of water," and yet this is true, although it is not written here. For if he is saved who received water on account of God, why is he not saved much more who sheds blood on account of God? For it is more to give blood than to receive water. Moreover, what some say is clearly silly, that those who shed blood are saved because with blood they also shed water, in the very water which they shed they receive baptism. For if those who are killed are said to have been baptized on account of the moisture of water which drips from their wounds together with the corruption of blood, then those who are suffocated or drowned or are killed by some other kind of death where blood is not shed have not been baptized in their blood and have died for Christ in vain, because they did not shed the moisture of the water which they had within their body. Who would say this? So, he is baptized in blood who dies for Christ, who, even if he does not shed blood from the wound, gives life which is more precious than blood. For he could shed blood and, if he did not give life, shedding blood would be less than giving life. Therefore, he sheds blood well who lays down his life for Christ, and he has his baptism in the virtue of the sacrament, without which to have received the sacrament itself, as it were, is of no benefit. So where this is the case, to be unable to have the sacrament does no harm.

Thus, it is true, although it is not said there, that he who dies for Christ is baptized in Christ. Thus, they say, it is true, although it is not said there, and it is true because it is said elsewhere, even if it is not said there. For He who said: "Unless a man be born again of the water and the Holy Ghost, he cannot enter into the Kingdom of God," the same also said elsewhere: "He who shall confess me before men, I will also confess him before my Father" (cf. Matt. 10:32). And so what is not said there, is nevertheless to be understood although it is not said, since it is said elsewhere. Behold therefore why they say it. They say that what is not said is to be understood where it is not said, because it is said elsewhere. If, therefore, this is to be understood in this place where it is not said, since it is said elsewhere: "He who believeth in me, shall not die forever" (cf. John 11:26). Likewise He who said: "Unless a man be born again of the water and the Holy Ghost, he cannot enter into the Kingdom of God," He himself said: "He who believeth in me, shall not die for ever." Therefore, either deny faith or concede salvation. What does it seem to you? [that] Where there is faith, where there is hope, where there is charity, finally, where there is the full and perfect virtue of the sacrament, there is no salvation because the sacrament alone is not, and it is not because it cannot be possessed? "He that believeth," He said, "and is baptized, shall be saved," (Mark 16:16). Therefore behold there is no doubt but that where there is faith and is baptism, there is salvation.

And what follows? "But he that believeth shall not be condemned," (cf. Mark 16:16). Why did He wish to speak thus? Why did He not say: "He that believeth not and is not baptized, shall be condemned," just as He had said: "He that believeth and is baptized, shall be saved'? Why, unless because it is of the will to believe and because he who wishes to believe cannot lack faith? And so in him who does not believe, an evil will is always shown, where there can be no necessity which may be put forth as an excuse. Now to be baptized can be in the will, even when it is not possibility, and on this account justly is good will with the devotion of its faith not to be despised, although in a moment of necessity he is prevented from receiving that sacrament of water which is external. Do you wish to know more fully whether or not this reason is proven elsewhere by more manifest authority, although even those authorities which we have mentioned above seem so manifest that there can be no doubt about the truth of them? Listen to something more, if by chance this matter about which you should not be in doubt can be shown you more clearly. Blessed Augustine in his book, *On the One Baptism*, speaks as follows: "Again and again as I consider it, I find that not only suffering for the name of Christ can fulfill what was lacking to baptism but also faith and conversion of heart, if perhaps assistance could not be rendered for the celebration of the mystery of baptism in straitened circumstances." You see that he clearly testifies that faith and conversion of heart can suffice for the salvation of good will where it happens that the visible sacrament of water of necessity cannot be had. But lest perhaps you think that he contradicted himself, since afterwards in the *Book of Retractions* he disapproved of the example of the thief which he had assumed to establish this opinion where he had said that the shedding of blood or faith and change of heart could fulfill the place of baptism, saying: "In the fourth book, when I said that suffering could take the place of baptism, I did not furnish a sufficiently fitting example in that of the thief about whom there is some doubt as to whether he was baptized," you should consider that in this place he only corrected an example which he had offered to prove his opinion; he did not reject his opinion. But if you think that that opinion is to be rejected, because the example is corrected, then what he had said is false, that the shedding of blood can take the place of baptism, since the example itself was furnished to prove that. For he does not say: "When I said that faith could have the place of baptism," but he says: "When I said that suffering could have the place of baptism," although he had placed both in the one opinion. If, therefore, regarding what he said, that suffering can have the place of baptism, an example has been furnished, since it is established that it is true without any ambiguity, it is clear that the example was afterwards corrected but the opinion was not rejected.

You should, therefore, either confess that true faith and confession of the heart can fulfill the place of baptism in the moment of necessity or show how true faith and unfeigned charity can be possessed where there is no salvation. Unless perhaps you wish to say that no one can have true faith and true charity, who is not to have the visible sacrament of water. Yet by what reason or by what authority you prove this I do not know. We meanwhile do not ask whether anyone who is not to receive the sacrament of baptism can have these, since this alone as far as this matter is concerned is certain: if there were anyone who had these even without the visible sacrament of water he could not perish. There are many other things which could have been brought up to prove this, but what we have set forth above in the treatment of the sacraments to prove this point we by no means think needs reconsideration.

II

AN ESSAY ON CATHOLIC MARRIAGE

It is no accident, as the Socialists say, that Socialism and Sex (or "free love") come in together as "advanced" ideas. They supplement each other. Russian dissident Igor Shafarevich, in his profound book The Socialist Phenomenon, *explains that the Socialist project of homogenizing society demands that the family be vitiated or destroyed. This can be accomplished in good measure by profaning conjugal love and breaking monogamy's link between sex and loyalty. Hence, in their missionary phases Socialist movements often stress sexual "liberation," and members of radical organizations may impose mandatory promiscuity within the group, everyone sharing a bed with each of the others, each equally related to each. It is the ultimate in leveling.... Few Americans will buy a bottle labeled Socialism. The cunning of the Socialist hive has consisted largely in its skill in piggy-backing on the more attractive things. Like Sex.*   Joseph Sobran[1]

Now it is obvious that the Evil one, who from the beginning has wanted to poison and destroy the work of the Creator, will rage incessantly against these four—marriage, sexuality, love, procreation—for he hates everything about them.   Von Kuehneit-Leddihn[2]

In all times and places it has been man's delight to think of human love as a type of divine Love and of human marriage as a type of the marriage of the soul with God.   Eric Gill[3]

Many marriages get into trouble. The causes of this can be listed as "the world, the flesh and the devil." This old canard is not without meaning. The world imposes innumerable pressures on marriage both by its value system or rather, negative value system, and by the

---

1. "Secular Humanism or The American Way," *Human Life Review*, Fall 1982.

difficulties of earning an adequate and honorable living. How often our children are mis-educated and our women forced to work outside the home if the family is to survive as an economic unit. The flesh relates to those problems that arise from within ourselves. A marital couple in conflict can truly be said to be at war—one is reminded of St. Paul's question, "whence come your wars?—they come from your greeds and your lusts." And finally, there is the devil—or evil—which greatly delights in the destruction of marriage and the perversion of sex. There is much talk in Catholic literature of marriage, but very little of sex. Hence I shall try in what follows to deal with this delicate topic, as well as with love and marriage.

Catholics are faced with a serious dilemma with regard to sex. Brought up in an alien culture, bombarded with the distortions of the media, and strongly influenced by a scientific and biological educational background based on false philosophical and theological principles, they have increasingly tended to see sex only in its

---

2. *The Timeless Christian*. He continues: "[Satan is jealous of] man's participation in God's creative power, something that is denied him—the love between two human beings, the sanctification of nature, and not least, the sacramental character of the married state. He will try to force love to take on an egotistical form, to infect it with jealousy, to destroy its permanence; he will move heaven and earth to bring disorder into every aspect of sex, to turn its stream into a raging torrent, or to dry it up altogether, or to divert it into a false bed; he will lead the partners towards divorce, to petty bickering, to a sterile boredom of everyday life, even to mutual hatred; finally he will try to estrange children from their parents and, recalling his own origin, will infuse their minds with the spirit of vainglory, of 'knowing better', and of ingratitude."

3. "Outside the commercial civilizations of the [modern] western world, love and marriage take their place as types of divine union, and everywhere love and marriage are the subject-matter of painters and sculptors. It is true that love is the theme of [modern] western writers also, but, with them, the idea of love is now entirely free from divine signification, either explicit or implied, and, however much they may still be under the heel of the old tradition which makes marriage the inevitable 'happy ending', yet, as religion decays, the inevitability of such an ending becomes less and less and the notion of a permanent union; 'till death do us part' is more and more frequently relegated to the 'scrap-heap' of outworn ideas.... The modern world fondly imagines that it has removed the veil with which a more superstitious generation shrouded reality whereas, actually, it has simply blinded itself to the reality of which material life is the veil." *Art and Love* (Bristol: Cleverdon. 1927).

biological setting. In addition to such influences, they are also subjected to a variety of distorted opinions on the subject from supposedly traditional sources. What I hope to do in what follows is present some insights into the Catholic view of sex based on documents drawn from the Church's Magisterium.

In order to do this let us for a moment consider the nature of man—for sex must be placed within a given context. Unfortunately most of us have been influenced by evolutionary theory and hence we tend to see Natural Selection as a driving force in our lives. If man is only a higher form of animal, the product of natural evolution, then it logically follows that man's sexual and erotic life is seen in terms of an extension of animal instincts. The ultimate, positive basis of human eroticism becomes the biological purpose of the species, usually seen in terms of survival.

Not dissimilar to the purely biological point of view, is that which embraces the concept that sex is "natural" and that repressive cultural forces or religious attitudes have distorted our sexual lives. According to this view, the only normal attitude towards sex is that of the uninhibited and amoral primitive savage—an opinion that refuses to recognize that even the most primitive of tribes in Africa and South America have strict rules with regard to sexual activity. This Rousseauian viewpoint is often embraced by modern writers. Thus, for example, Aldous Huxley in *Point Counter Point* describes D.H. Lawrence's attitude in the following terms: "The natural appetites and desires of men are not what makes them so bestial.... It is the imagination, the intellect, the principles, the education, the tradition. Leave the instincts to themselves and they will do very little evil."

The problem with both these viewpoints is that neither says anything about love. Without love, sexuality becomes like the activities of the birds and the bees. Most philosophers hold that man is distinguished from the beast because of his ability to think and will; similarly, most philosophers place love within the realm of the will.[4] For man to reduce sex to a "natural" or "instinctive" act, or to use the words of Lawrence, "to blood and flesh," can only signify degrada-

---

4. "Love is nothing other than the will ardently fixed on something good...." William of St. Thierry, *The Nature and Dignity of Love*.

tion, for what is called natural for man as man is not at all the same as what the term "natural" signifies in the case of animals. This does not mean that sex for man is not natural, but rather that, like all his acts, both his intellect and will to some degree are involved. Clearly man shares certain instincts with animals—but a man is not said to act in an animal manner unless he refuses to use his higher powers to modify his instinctual drives. Conformity is natural when it is conformity to one's own type. A horse would not be seen as natural if he ran like a rabbit, and vice versa. What is normal to man must take into consideration the fact that he is placed at the apex of God's creation and made in the image of God. For him to act in a manner that refuses recognition to his stature is for him to act unnaturally.

Proof for this contention can be found in the fact that the false notion of sexual love as a physical need. As Julius Evola points out, "A physical sexual desire never exists in man; the desire of man is substantially always psychic, and his physical desire is only a translation and transposition of psychic desire. Only in the most primitive individual does the circuit close so fast that only the terminal fact of the process is present in their conscious[ness] as a sharp, driving carnal lust unmistakably linked to physiological conditional qualities which take the foremost place in animal sexuality."[5] Nor can it be claimed that human sex is driven by an instinct for reproduction. As one wit put it, "when Adam awoke next to Eve, he did not cry out and say 'behold the mother of my children.'"

I have said that the problem of the biological or Rousseauian viewpoints is that while they speak of the emotions, they say nothing of love. Now, despite innumerable attempts to define the nature of love, none of them have been wholly successful. This is not surprising in that there is something mysterious about this "affliction." However, I believe there are certain characteristics—perhaps one could say "symptoms"—that are fairly universally recognized. Love

---

5. Much that we label "primitive" is only degeneration. As Erich Fromm states, "What is essential in the existence of man is the fact that he has emerged from the animal kingdom, from instinctive adaptation, that he has transcended nature—although he never leaves it; he is part of it—and yet once torn away from nature, he cannot return to it." (*The Art of Loving*)

by its very nature seems to (1) involve the whole being. No one ever claimed to love another other than with their whole body, soul, and spirit. (2) Love demands or longs for eternity. A person truly in love wants to bind himself forever to his beloved. (3) Love sees in the beloved, not his or her faults, but rather his or her perfections. The very names of endearment speak to this, for the beloved is an angel if not a god or goddess; he or she embodies—or at least potentially embodies—all the qualities of the divine prototype—the solar hero, the flawless maiden. (4) Both parties to the loving relationship see their worldly, if not their eternal happiness to lie in the perpetual enjoyment of each other's company. (5) Love requires an act of the will—a commitment—directed towards what is understood as desirable—an act of the will which also excludes anything that intrudes upon the unity of the parties involved. To say this is not to exclude the emotions, for as has been pointed out above, the act of loving involves the whole of what one is. It follows then that one who refuses to commit himself, or who breaks a commitment in order to start another relationship, fools himself. Such a person confuses the excitement of novelty with authentic happiness.[6]

What role does marriage play in all this? Borrowing from von Hildebrand,

> Marriage is the friend and protector of love. Marriage gives love the structure and shelteredness, the climate in which alone it can grow. Marriage teaches spouses humility and makes them realize that the human person is a very poor lover. Much as we long to love and to be loved, we repeatedly fall short and desperately need help. We must bind ourselves through sacred vows so that the bond will grant our love the strength necessary to face the tempest-tossed sea of our human condition.... Marriage, because it implies will, commitment, duty, and responsibility, braces spouses to fight to save the precious gift of their love.

---

6. Christ loved Lazarus deeply as a friend—it is said that the emotions whelmed up in him on hearing of his death. The more modern translations state that he was overwhelmed with emotion, but such is false, for while the emotions have their place, they would never in Our Lord overwhelm the higher functions of His human soul.

Almost all cultures initiate and establish marriage with religious rites. For those that believe in God, knowing how difficult marriage can be when we lose sight of the inner essence of the beloved and see only his or her outer accidental qualities, realizing that they have made a commitment or a vow to God, and asking a higher power to succor their weakness, becomes an inestimable source of strength, a means of renewing their commitment and of assuming their responsibilities which not infrequently take on the form of a cross. Marriages involve commitments "in illness and in health, for better or for worse."

Religions tend to view marriage as a contract.[7] This in no way is meant to exclude love, regardless of whether that love has led to the marriage, or the arranged marriage has opened the door to love. This is not only because every commitment has a contractual aspect to it, but also because religions tend to see marriage in a broader context—that of society as a whole, and therefore as directed towards what philosophers call the "common good." Whereas modern social theory tends to view each individual as tied to the state, traditional societies tend to see the family as the basic building block of society. The very word *economia* means family, and so it is that both religion and traditionally-minded governments do everything possible to maintain and foster the integrity of the family.

If marriage is a contract, it is not a contract in the ordinary sense of the word. It is not a contract in which man's subsidiary goods—his house or property—are transferred, but one in which it is his and her very person which is transferred. No man or woman has the right to say of another that "you are mine." Two beings alone can say this to one another because they have truly and freely given themselves to one another. What is exchanged is their will and consent, and this, unlike any other contract, irrevocably. "This is bone of my bones and flesh of my flesh ... what God has joined together let no man put asunder." And subsequent to this proclamation God instructs the couple to "increase and multiply."

---

7. "Nowhere is sexual union regarded as marriage unless it is in some way socially sanctioned." C. Augustine, *A Commentary on the New Code of Canon Law*, (1917).

To speak of family is to speak of progeny.[8] Now there is no question but that, as St. Augustine says, "the sanctity of the sacrament is more important than the fecundity of the womb."[9] Yet, the childless family always bears a tragic aspect. No wonder then that most religions agree with the Catholic principle that the primary purpose of marriage is the procreation and education of children, and the secondary purpose of marriage is the fostering of the unitive relationship of the parties involved.[10] Let us be clear on what the procreation and education of children means. It does not mean that one should have as many children as possible, but rather that in a marriage the children come first—not just their production, but their upbringing. Further, by education one does not necessarily mean a Harvard degree, but rather the formation and development of complete human beings; individuals whose physical, psychic and spiritual development is fostered. What this means is that, should love grow cold and the unitive aspect of marriage fall apart, the parents are obliged to sacrifice their personal needs—their desires to love and be loved—for the sake of the children. This may seem to us to be a painful course to follow. But, as St. Seraphim of Sarov points out:

> Christian marriage is a life-work. It is easy only in ideal circumstances. Fidelity to the end is essential to happiness. If Christians find they cannot live together, they go on living together for their homes, their children, for the Church and for God. It may mean much suffering, but this married life is the way to heaven. For only those who take up the cross can follow Christ.[11]

---

8. Aristotle in his *Politics* states that "A home must possess three relationships if it is to be complete, namely, that of husband and wife, of father and the children and that between the master and servants." (Quoted by St. Thomas Aquinas in his *Commentary on Ephesians*)

9. *De Bono Conjugali,* cap. XVIII, n. 21.

10. In the words of St. Augustine, "Offspring signifies that children shall be lovingly welcomed ... and religiously educated" *De Gen. ad litt.*, 1.9,c.7, n.12. Similarly St. Thomas teaches "education and development until it reach the perfect state of man as man, and that is the state of virtue." (III, 41, 1). It is said that a woman who brings up her child in the faith will enter heaven before any theologian.

11. *St. Seraphim of Sarov, A Spiritual Biography,* Archimandrite Lazarus Moore, Sarov Press, 1994.

All of us are familiar with the arguments against remaining married when the interpersonal relationship breaks down. Always rooted in this breakdown is self-will or selfishness. (If, as discussed above, the wife is obedient and the husband an *alter Christus*, there is no real possibility of divorce.) Even apart from the spiritual effects on the partners, one must consider the devastating effects of divorce on children. One has only to consider the studies of Wallerstein to see the long term effects. And so it is that religions either forbid divorce, or make it extremely difficult to obtain. Obtaining a Gett in Judaism is, I am told, almost impossible. In Islam where divorce is allowed, there is a *hadith* or teaching of Mohammed to the effect that "God hates nothing more than divorce." Among Hindus, divorce is forbidden in the higher castes, though allowed for the "untouchables," who are those considered outside the pale of religion and hence those not held to high moral values. (Before we raise objections to the concept of untouchables, let me remind you that from the orthodox Hindu point of view, those that are not born and do not live in accord with Hindu moral principles are all untouchables.)

But the religious outlook on marriage is by no means limited to strengthening its contractual character or safeguarding its social or unitive purpose. Orthodox religion places marriage in the overall context of what, for lack of a better word, I will call "salvation." Religion desires for all men and women, regardless of their state of life, sanctity and ultimately the beatific vision. Morality is not an end in itself, but only predispositive to the sanctified life. And with this in view it encourages each and every person to love Truth, Beauty and Goodness, the essential qualities and names of God. It sees human love as a reflection of divine love and human marriage, macrocosmically, as a reflection of the relationship between the soul and God, and microcosmically, as the relationship between what spiritual writers have called the lesser self and the greater Self or spiritual center of our being. This moral and spiritual outlook is clearly stated by St. Paul in Ephesians, chapter 5. After stressing the need to live a life dedicated to their sanctification, Paul instructs the partners in marriage to be "subject to one another, in the fear of Christ." He continues:

> Let women be subject to their husbands as to the Lord: Because the husband is the head of the wife as Christ is the head of the church. He is the savior of his body. Therefore as the church is subject to Christ, so also let the wives be to their husbands in all things. Husbands, love your wives as Christ also loved the church, and delivered himself up for it, that he might sanctify it, cleansing it by the laver of water in the word of life ... so also ought men to love their wives as their own bodies. ... For this cause shall a man leave his father and mother, and shall cleave to his wife, and they shall be two in one flesh. This is a great sacrament....[12]

This is by no means the only place where Scripture teaches the hierarchical nature of marriage. Leaving apart the passage in Gen. 2:24 and innumerable examples of the relationship of men and women in the Old Testament, let us turn to the new dispensation. In the First Letter to the Corinthians Paul treats of abuses in divine worship in this manner:

> But, I would have you know, that the head of every man is Christ; and the head of the woman is the man; and the head of Christ is God. Every man praying or prophesying with his head covered, disgraceth his head. But every woman praying or prophesying with her head not covered, disgraceth her head.... The man indeed ought not to cover his head, because he is the image and glory of God; but the woman is the glory of the man. For the man is not of the woman, but the woman of the man. For the man was not created for the woman, but the woman for the man. Therefore ought the woman to have a cover over her head, because of the angels" (11:3–10).

The Apostle Paul here confirms again the teaching of the submission of the woman to the man. He holds this submission to be

---

12. This hierarchical arrangement is by no means restricted to Christianity. We find God in Genesis 3 telling wives "Thou shalt be under thy husband's power, and he shall have dominion over thee." The same hierarchical arrangement is found in Islam and Hinduism. It is not without significance that the newer "catholic" translations of the Bible translate "This is a great sacrament" by "This is a great foreshadowing."

important, and under the inspiration of the Holy Ghost, institutes a sign of recognition for this submission. The woman should cover her head during worship services, so as to honor her head, that is to say, her husband.

A little later in the same Epistle St. Paul writes again on the subject of divine worship:

> Let women keep silence in the churches; for it is not permitted them to speak, but to be subject, as also the [old] law saith. But if they would learn any thing, let them ask their husbands at home. For it is a shame for a woman to speak in the church.... If any seem to be a prophet, or spiritual, let him know the things that I write to you, that they are commandments of the Lord (14:35).

This law of the Lord is addressed above all to women, who should keep silent during divine worship. And from this we have to conclude that liturgical functions, such as lector or priest, are forbidden to them according to divine law. To consider that the submission of the wife to her husband is an order from God appears to us to be a proximate notion. For the law states that they ought "to be subject" not only in Church, but everywhere, as for example in the family. St. Paul is only drawing out the consequences of this principle. This law, which should not only be applied to Jews, but also to Christians, is part of the natural law. The submission of the wife in the order of natural law is demanded in marriage and in divine worship, but also by Christ from whom the Apostle conveys this Revelation. Not to accept the Apostle's views is to question the dogma which teaches that every book of the Bible is inspired by the Holy Spirit.

The Apostle Paul also confirms his teaching on the submission of the wife to her husband in his Epistle to Timothy (2:9–15). It would be erroneous to assert that this teaching is exceptional and only presented by St. Paul. St. Peter has stated it in similar terms: "In like manner also, let wives be subject to their husbands" (I Pet. 3:1). Thus the Apostles Peter and Paul conjointly attest to the veracity of this doctrine.

The position taken by the popes on the question as to who is head of the family is likewise very clear. Leo XIII's Encyclical *Arcanum Divinae Sapientiae* states:

The husband is the chief of the family and the head of the wife. The woman, because she is flesh of his flesh, and bone of his bone, must be subject to her husband and obey him; not, indeed, as a servant, but as a companion, so that her obedience shall be wanting in neither honor nor dignity. Since the husband represents Christ, and since the wife represents the Church, let there always be, both in him who commands and in her who obeys, a heaven-born love guiding both of their respective duties.

Pius XI was also strongly attached to this principle. In his famous encyclical on marriage, *Casti Connubii*, he states:

Domestic society being confirmed, therefore, by this bond of love, there should flourish in it that "order of love," as St. Augustine calls it. This order includes both the primacy of the husband with regard to the wife and her willing obedience, which the Apostle commands in these words: "Let women be subject to their husbands as to the Lord, because the husband is head of the wife and Christ is head of the Church."

This subjection, however, does not deny or take away the liberty which fully belongs to the woman both in view of her dignity as a human person, and in view of her most noble office as wife and mother and companion; nor does it bid her obey her husband's every request if not in harmony with right reason or with the dignity of a wife; nor, in fine, does it imply that the wife should be put on the level with persons who in law are called minors, to whom it is customary not to allow free exercise of their rights on account of their lack of mature judgment, or of their ignorance of human affairs. But it forbids that exaggerated liberty which cares not for the good of the family; it forbids that in this body which is the family, the heart be separated from the head to the great detriment of the whole body and the proximate danger of ruin. For if the man is the head, the woman is the heart, and he occupies the chief place in ruling, so she may and ought to claim for herself the chief place in love.

Again, this subjection of wife to husband in its degrees and manner may vary according to the different conditions of persons, place and time. In fact, if the husband neglects his duty, it falls to the wife to take his place in directing the family. But the structure of the family and its fundamental law, established and confirmed by God, must always and everywhere be maintained intact.

I have reproduced this passage in its entirety because Pius XI comes to an important conclusion, the content of which is the basis for the document: the submission of woman to man is the fundamental law of the family established and fixed by God.

Pope Pius XII reiterated this principle and once again made it clear that the family had been willed by God to have a head: "This head has authority over the one who has been given to be his companion . . . and over those who, when the Lord gives his blessing, will be multiplied and rejoice like the luxuriant shoots of an olive tree." When asked whether or not this teaching was still relevant for modern families he responded:

> We indeed know that . . . equality in studies at school, in the sciences, sports and other competitions gives rise to sentiments of pride in the hearts of many women. . . . All about you many voices will portray this subjection as something unjust; they will suggest to you a prouder independence. . . . Be on your guard against these words of the serpent, of temptation and of lies: do not become other Eves, do not turn away from the only road which can lead you, even from the here and now, to true happiness.

One last quote taken from Scripture:

> Authority as head of the family comes from God, as formerly God had accorded power and authority to Adam, the head of all mankind; Adam should have transmitted all these gifts to his descendants. For Adam was formed first, then Eve. And Adam was not seduced; but the woman being seduced . . . fell into disobedience. (I Tim., 2:13–14)

We will see later that marriage must be entered into with the proper intentions. At least one Catholic theologian has opinioned that the acceptance of a hierarchical relationship in marriage is requisite for the intention to be proper. According to Moersdorf, a marriage is realized through uniformity of the will of both people. Both parties to the marriage have to be in agreement in order to affirm "the essential content of the marriage contract, which is to say the one who wishes to conclude a marriage must be ready to accept the three characteristics of marriage." These are "the right to the body, the indissolubility of marriage and the unity of marriage." The unity of marriage signifies, according to this author, the union of one man with one woman, and therefore a single couple, and that the man and women be united in a hierarchical order by a holy unity. According to Moersdorf, for the realization of a valid marriage, it is indispensable that the contracting parties recognize and fulfill these conditions.[13] "If the necessary understanding and will for the

---

13. The Constitution *Gaudium et Spes* produced by the Second Vatican Council attempted to soften this teaching: "Just as of old God encountered his people with a covenant of love and fidelity, so our Savior, the spouse of the Church, now encounters Christian spouses through the sacrament of Marriage. He abides with them in order that by their mutual self-giving, spouses will love each other with enduring fidelity, as he loved the Church and delivered himself for it." Here the teaching of *Ephesians* has been decisively abridged. Only what is agreeable has been taken from it, namely "love." The subordination of women, and correlatively, that of the Church to her Head, the basic outline of which has been presented above, is simply disregarded. Drawing on this statement, the Synod of Wurzurg declared in 1975 that the husband and wife were to be seen as partners, and that "the allotment of roles between husband and wife which was strongly patriarchal in character, has been corrected. In a parallel manner John Paul II has persistently insisted that love creates equality. In his *Familiaris Consortio* (1981) and in his Charter of Family Rights" (1983) he teaches that God gives man and woman an equal personal dignity, endowing them with the inalienable rights and responsibilities proper to the human person. "Above all it is important to underline the equal dignity and responsibility of women and men ... in creating the human race 'male and female' God gives man and woman an equal personal dignity, endowing them with the inalienable rights and responsibilities proper to the human person." The same responsibilities and rights for man and woman clearly exclude man from being the head of the family. John Paul II is of course aware that he is contradicting the constant teaching of the Church. In an article published in the *L'Osservatore Romano* he explains that "the author of the letter [St. Paul] does not hesitate to accept those ideas which were proper to the contemporary mentality and its forms of expression.... Our sentiments are certainly different today, different also are our mentality and customs, and, finally, different is a woman's social position vis-à-vis the man." (German ed., 27.8.82). (In 1953 the Church taught that "Anyone who, as a matter of principle, denies the responsibility of the husband and father as head of the woman and of the family, puts himself in opposition to the Gospel and the doctrine of the Church." [supplement to *St. Korads Blatt*, No. 10, 1953])

conclusion of a marriage are seriously lacking, the marriage will not be valid."[14]

Obedience and the acceptance of a hierarchy of authority are difficult for moderns to bear with.[15] How are such concepts compatible with the principles of freedom, equality and brotherhood?[16] Well, clearly they are not. But before wives get too upset about the need to obey—a *Fiat* reflective of that made by the Blessed Virgin, and implicitly one made by the Church—let us consider the far heavier obligation on the husband, namely that he love the wife as Christ loves His Church.[17] Note here the seemingly double command—to be *alter Christus* or another Christ and to love as

---

14. Klaus Moersdorf, *Kirchenrecht*, vol. II, 10th edition, Munich, 1958. While not a dogmatic teaching of the Church, it is clear that failure to recognize this aspect of the marriage relationship clearly vitiates the spiritual aspect of the relationship.

15. The importance of obedience is shown by the fact that Adam fell because of the sin of disobedience, while Christ reversed the fall by being "obedient unto death." In the last analysis, we are all obliged to be obedient to higher authority, and "all authority is from God." Obedience is a "moral virtue", and as such of a lesser order than the "theological virtues" of Faith, Hope and Charity. In accordance with the principle that the higher takes precedence to the lower, it follows that one can never command what is sinful or against truth. True obedience implies going against our self-will and carries with it the principle of self-abnegation.

16. "We cannot ask ourselves whether 'woman' is superior or inferior to 'man', any more than we can ask ourselves whether water is superior or inferior to fire. Thus the standard of measurement for either of the sexes can be provided not by the opposite sex, but only by the 'idea' of the same sex. In other words, the only thing we can do is establish the superiority or inferiority of a given woman on the basis of her being more or less close to the female type, to the pure and absolute woman, and the same thing applies to man as well. The claims of modern woman, therefore, spring from mistaken ambitions as well as from an inferiority complex, from the mistaken idea that woman is intrinsically inferior to man. It has been rightly said that feminism has really fought not for 'woman's rights', but, without knowing it, for the right of woman to make herself equal to man ... it would amount to a woman having the right to pervert herself and to degenerate." Julius Evola, *The Metaphysics of Sex*, p. 54. Others have pointed out that femininity manifests the feminine aspects of the Divine: Goodness, radiating Beauty, Mercy, Love, and Purity, while masculinity incarnates Truth, Axiality, Intellectuality, Strength and Generosity.

17. This fiat goes beyond obedience. A woman, in accepting motherhood, places her life on the line. Continuing the passage from I Timothy just quoted: "Yet

Christ loves. Now such is no easy task, and what woman would not want to be married to such a man? Even God has limits, for He cannot be other than what He is—He cannot be other than love. And there is yet another mystery involved, one that becomes present when the marriage is blessed with children. Consider how it is that God is called Father, the priest is called father and is truly father to the community; and finally, the head of the family is also called father—for all three share in authority, in procreativity, and in love. I will speak in the following passages of "procreativity," because, just as the fruit of God's love is his creation, so also the fruit of the couple's love is fecund, not apart from God, but because the couple participate in God's creativity.

Custom recognizes this in the practice of the husband carrying the wife over the threshold into their future home. The husband is a psychopomp—a guide of souls to the other world. The threshold or door through which the wife is carried represents an entrance into that state of unity where the two are joined in one flesh. In this relationship the husband bears a spiritual as well as a material responsibility for his wife and offspring, one he will ultimately have to answer to God for. Marriage is ultimately a rather serious affair.

The acceptance of these principles makes Marriage a spiritual path. St. Alphonsus Liguori clearly states that for someone called to the state of marriage to become a priest is to risk damning his soul—he says the same with regard to someone called to the priesthood

---

she shall be saved through childbearing; if she continue in faith, and love, and sanctification, with sobriety." A woman who dies in childbirth—assuming the right disposition of soul—is said to go straight to heaven. With regard to obedience, St. John Chrysostom says St. Paul teaches wives that "when you yield to your husband consider that you are obeying him as part of your service to the Lord." He further says, "a household cannot be a democracy, ruled by everyone, but the authority must necessarily rest in one person. The same is true for the Church ... where there is equal authority, there never is peace. Paul places the head in authority and the body in obedience." At the same time he tells husbands: "Do you want your wife to be obedient to you, as the Church is to Christ? Then be responsible for the same providential care of her as Christ is for the Church. And even if it becomes necessary for you to undergo suffering of any kind, do not refuse." (*Homily* 20). Obedience in marriage is as essential as it is in the religious life.

entering marriage.[18] Let me stress the word "called." This in Latin translates as "vocation" (*vocatio*). Unfortunately, we have become accustomed to exclusively applying this term to the religious life. But such is not the attitude of the saints. St. Francis de Sales once exclaimed "O how agreeable to God are the virtues of a married woman, for they must be strong and excellent to survive this vocation."[19] Similarly, Pope Pius XII spoke to newlyweds on May 3, 1939, telling them that it was "their vocation to found a home" and that this what God had asked of them. Actually, the concept of vocation is broader than at first would appear to be the case—or rather, it is a concept that can be understood on many levels. We all have a vocation to sanctity, regardless of our state in life. And similarly, the professions we engage in—providing they are legitimate—are also vocations. Thus medicine and law are also seen as "callings."

Vocations are, of course, a means to an end, and thus ultimately they are a means of sanctification, for sanctification is the true goal which God wishes for all of us. As St. Thérèse of Lisieux wrote to Mme. Pottier, a married woman with children: "So for both of us the blest days of our childhood are over! We are now in the serious stage of life; we are following very different roads, but the end is the same. Each of us must have but one same purpose, to sanctify ourselves in the road that God has marked out for us."[20]

Vocations can be seen as existing on several levels of reference— for example, one's state in life, and one's means of making a living. Strictly speaking, we should all be artists and make our livings by some craft. The craftsman makes useful objects—consider the stone mason who, parallel with his work, fashions his soul in view to uniting it with God. How sad that in our day, most of us are denied the opportunity to follow a craft. By practicing one's vocation, one practices the virtues, or more precisely, one eliminates the vices

---

18. This in no way implies that couples that have fulfilled their obligations in the married state cannot enter religion under a variety of forms. Such was much more common in earlier centuries than in our day.

19. Quoted by Msgr. Charles Doyle, in *Christian Perfection for the Married* (NY: Nugent, 1964).

20. Letter 203.

which are their opposite.[21] The obligation to sanctity falls upon all of us. When some of the laity protested to St. John Chrysostom that they were not monks, he responded that "all the precepts of the Law apply equally to monks and to the laity, with the exception of one, celibacy."[22] And who of us can dare to proclaim that the sexual act precludes the possibility of sanctity, especially when this act in its proper setting, as will be shown, is a reflection of the true relationship between God and the soul? To speak of vocations however is not to say they are all of equal stature. Just as a loving father provides each of his children with what is necessary for their proper development, so also does Our Lord provide each of us with a vocation suitable to our needs and abilities. A surgeon is a higher calling than that of a plumber—though both can perfect their souls by the manner in which they practice their calling. And so it is that the religious life, in which the individual is "married" to Christ, is a higher calling than the married state.[23]

We of course know that there have been many married saints. St. Marcarius and St. Anthony of the Desert both sent postulants to learn from people in the married state. Unfortunately however, many authors writing about married saints convey to us the message that such individuals were saints, not because they fulfilled the obligations of the married state with heroic virtue, but rather, despite the fact that they were married. Sometimes, when I look at the clergy and know that some priests have been canonized, I am inclined to suspect that their sanctity was also achieved despite their vocations. But such is equally absurd.

---

21. To quote Pius XI: "It is the will of God, says St. Paul, that you sanctify yourselves. What kind of sanctity does he speak of? Our Lord Himself made this clear. *"Be ye perfect as your father in heaven is perfect."* No one should assume that this invitation is addressed to a small select number of individuals and that the remainder of mankind are allowed to be satisfied with some lesser degree of virtue. This law obliges and applies—and this is absolutely clear—to all of mankind, without exception."

22. *Seventh Homily on St. Matthew.* "Both those who choose to dwell in the midst of noise and hubbub and those who dwell in monasteries, mountains and caves can achieve salvation" says St. Symeon the New Theologian in the *Philokalia*. A vocation must of course be intrinsically honorable, which is to say, capable of perfecting the soul.

Allow me to string together a few quotations from St. Francis de Sales addressed to women in the married state:

> You must not only be devout, and love devotion, but you must make it amiable, useful, and agreeable to everyone. The sick will love your devotion if they are charitably consoled by it; your family will love it if they find you more careful of their good, more gentle in little accidents that happen, more kind in correcting, and so on; your husband, if he sees that as your devotion increases you are more devoted to his regard, and sweet in your love to him; your parents and friends if they perceive in you more generosity, tolerance and condescension towards their wills, when not against the will of God. In short, you must as far as possible, make your devotion attractive.... Oh my daughter, how agreeable to God are the virtues of a married woman, for they must be strong and excellent to last in that vocation.... Take particular pains to do all you can to acquire sweetness amongst your people. I mean in your household. I do not say that you must be soft and remiss, but gentle and sweet.... My God, how holy, my dear daughter, and how agreeable to God we would be if we knew how to use properly the subjects of mortification which our vocation affords; for they are without doubt greater than among religious; the evil is that we do not make them useful as they do....

---

23. The comments of Barbe Acarie are pertinent: "If I had but one child and if I were the queen of the whole world so that he was my sole heir and God called him to the religious state I would put no obstacle in his way; but if I had a hundred children and could make no provision for them I would not oblige one to enter religion, because such a vocation must come purely from God. The religious state is so lofty that the whole world together cannot make a good religious if God does not lend his help; it is far better to remain in the world by divine disposition than to be a religious through human instigation" (Biography, Lancelot Sheppard).With regard to virginity, St. John Chrysostom says: "Virginity does not simply mean sexual abstinence. She who is anxious about worldly affairs is not really a virgin. In fact, he [St. Paul] says that this is the chief difference between a wife and a virgin. He doesn't mention marriage or abstinence, but attachment as opposed to detachment from worldly cares. Sex is not evil, but [it and children are] a hindrance to someone who desires [and is called] to devote all her strength to a life of prayer." (Homily 19). "Of pure Virgins, none is fairer seen/Save one, than Mary Magdalene" (John Cordelier). May we then "be virginized" as St. Thérèse of Lisieux said in a letter to her sister Céline.

And of married people he directed, he said:

> O my God, what grand souls have I found here in the servitude of God... the state of marriage is one which requires more virtue and constancy than any other; it is a perpetual exercise of mortification....

He adds an important caveat which we must all take to heart:

> And what is it that makes [the commandments of the vocation of marriage] burdensome to you? Nothing in truth save your own will which desires to reign in you at any cost... a person who has not the fever of self-will is satisfied with everything, provided that God is served.[24]

St. Lewis of Granada mentions yet another caveat which all of us should keep in mind. He tells us:

> Let the married woman look to the government of her house, and take care of her family, please her husband, and do all that a wife should do; when she has satisfied these obligations let her spend the rest of her time in devotion as much as she pleases, but still, let her remember, that the duties of her state call her first.

Lest you think I am picking on the women, I shall add the rest of the passage:

> Let those that are fathers of children frequently reflect upon the severe punishment that was inflicted upon Heli for his neglect in chastising and instructing his sons (I Kings 4).... Consider the sins of the children are, in some manner, imputed to the fathers, and that the ruin of a son is very often the cause of the father's destruction; nor does he deserve the bare name of father who after having begotten his son for this world, does not also beget him for the next....[25]

The passage from St. Paul quoted above provides us with the fundamental outline of the spiritual life. Consider the statement in

---

24. St. Francis de Sales, *Letters to Persons in the World*.
25. Louis of Grenada, *The Sinner's Guide*, chap. 5.

Genesis to the effect that Adam was made in the image and likeness of God. Why this double description? Why should Scripture be so redundant? Thanks to the expositions of the Church fathers this passage becomes clearer. Adam was indeed made in the image and likeness of God. But when he fell, he lost that likeness while retaining the image. Now we are, as St. Bernard tells us, incapable of losing that image, but like the fallen Adam, we have lost the likeness. The entire spiritual life is aimed at regaining that likeness. It is only when we achieve this that we can say with St. Paul, "I live, yet not I, but Christ within me." It is only when this state is achieved that both priest and father can truly (that is, fully) love—and if the wife, in obeying her husband, obeys Christ. The husband, like any true king, can only rule by "divine right"—that is, by commanding what Christ would command. When the king, priest or husband commands other than by divine right—which is to say, enforces laws or rules that are not divine in nature—when he commands what he wants apart from or in opposition to the divine laws, he becomes a despot. The husband in the family may rule by divine right, but never by his own right. By extension, the family is modeled after that established by St. Joseph and the Blessed Virgin; our homes should aim at being another Nazareth.

The human being as individual is also a hierarchy in which the higher powers should have authority over the lower ones. Consider the Lord's prayer. "Thy Kingdom come . . . on earth as it is in heaven." That heaven is described as a hierarchical structure is not a historical accident. Nor is it a manifestation of St. Paul's or ancient Jewish misogyny. Christ is our King—both Priest and King—and we pay him homage as do the innumerable choirs of angels. Now the saints tell us that this phrase of the Lord's Prayer is one which requests this hierarchical relationship to come down into our society, into our families and convents, and above all into our own hearts. It is this hierarchical relationship which explains the statement of several saints to the effect that "all creation is feminine in relation to God."[26]

---

26. "In traditional symbolism, the supernatural principle has always been conceived as 'masculine'; nature and becoming as 'feminine.'" (J. Evola, *Rivolta Contra il Mondo Moderno*). It is not accidental that nature is referred to as "mother

On the microcosmic level—on the level of each of our lives—we are constantly faced with a need to choose between centering our actions and our being (if such were possible) on our little selves or egos, or on God who dwells within us. This is the battle against self-love—or if you prefer, selfishness. It is not God, the Holy Spirit—that *imago* dwelling within our hearts—that is selfish, hurt, angry, resentful or unforgiving, but rather our egos, our little selves. We are constantly at war, or as the psychiatrists would put it, in conflict with ourselves. And thus it is that we say to the unruly child or adult, "get hold of yourself." St. Paul describes this well when he says "I see another law in my members, repugnant to the laws of my mind, and capturing me in the law of sin that is in my members" (Rom. 7:25).[27] Some exegetes would infer that this statement refers exclusively to a sexual conflict, but reference to other parts of Scripture make it clear that by members—note the plural—the sacred writers are referring to all the passions that afflict our souls; thus St. James tells us that the "tongue is set among our members which defileth the whole body" (James 3:5–6).

It is important then to realize that there are a series of hierarchies involved. There is God, and his bride the Church; there is the husband, and his bride or wife; and there is the Spirit of God that dwells within us, and our psycho-physical nature. In each of these there is a

---

nature." This principle is in no way "sexist" or "patriarchal." Thus, the Abbess Sarah, one of the saints described by the Desert Fathers, stated: "I am a woman in sex, but not in spirit." Similarly St. Augustine describes some saintly women in these terms: "according to the inward man neither male nor female; so that even in them that are women in body the manliness of their soul hides the sex of their flesh...." (*Sermon* 282).This "inward man" is of course St. Paul's inward man (Rom. 7:22) and St. Peter's "inner man of the heart" (I Pet. 3:4). St. Theresa of Avila admonished her sisters in these terms: "I would not want you, my daughters, to be womanish in anything, nor would I want you to be like women, but like strong men" (*The Way of Perfection,* 7:8). Throughout the Old Testament, Jehovah is characterized as "betrothed to Israel." Christ is our spouse, telling us in Hosea 2: "I will marry thee in faithfulness." And again, "Thou shalt be the spouse of my blood" (*Gesta Romanum*). It is in this context that St. Paul admonishes both sexes to "play the man." It is in the light of this that the feminine aspect in everyone of us takes on a "seductive" quality; when this seduction is "successful," when the spirit is subverted by the lower soul, Scripture labels the "adulterous" result as "harlotry."

hierarchy to which we must conform ourselves. These three hierarchies are intimately entwined.[28] Consider the following exposition of the parable of the woman at the well to whom Christ offered the water of eternal life. When the woman asked for this water, Christ told her to call her husband. John Scotus Eriugina explains the mystical meaning of this parable:

> The woman is the rational soul [*anima*], whose husband [literally *vir* or "man," with the connotation of "active power," not *maritus* or *conjunx*] is understood to be the *animus*, which is variously named now intellect [*intellectus*], now mind [*mens*], now *animus* and often even spirit [*spiritus*]. This is the husband of whom the

---

27. "It is often of the greatest importance," says St. Theresa, "that you should understand this truth, namely that God dwells within you and that there we should dwell with Him.... Let us not imagine that the interior of our hearts is empty.... And to understand how God is always present in our soul, let us listen to St. John of the Cross, another distinguished master of the science of the saints: 'In order to know how to find this Bridegroom, we must bear in mind that the Word, the Son of God, together with the Father and the Holy Spirit, is hidden in essence and is present in the inmost being of the soul.... And this is why St. Augustine, speaking to God, said: "I do not find Thee without, O Lord, because I had no right to seek Thee there, for Thou are within." God is therefore hidden within the soul.'" (The quotation from St. John of the Cross, containing the quotation from St. Augustine, is from *A Spiritual Canticle,* commentary on Stanza I).

St. John of the Cross continues later on to explain this more at length, remarking that God may be present in the soul in three different ways: "To explain this," he says, "it must be observed that there are three ways in which God is present in the soul. The first is His presence in essence, and in this respect He dwells not only in souls that are good and holy, but likewise in those that are bad and sinful, and indeed, in all creatures; for it is this presence that gives them life and being, and if it were once withdrawn they would cease to exist and would return to their original nothing. Now this kind of presence never fails in the soul. The second manner of God's presence is by grace, when He dwells in the soul pleased and satisfied with it. This presence of God is not in all souls, because those who commit a mortal sin lose it. The third kind of presence of God is by means of spiritual affection; for God is want to show His presence in many devout souls in divers ways of refreshment, joy and gladness." St. Theresa continues: "Of the first kind of divine presence we can never be deprived. The second we must procure for ourselves with all the powers of the soul, and we must guard it at any cost. The third isn't within our power. God gives to whom He pleases" (St. Theresa's *Pater Noster*).

28. Just as Adam's bride was taken from his side, so also was the Church the product of the blood and water which flowed from the side of Christ.

Apostle speaks: "The head of the woman is the man, the head of the man is Christ, the head of Christ is God." I other words, the head of the *anima* is the *intellectus*, and the head of the *intellectus* is Christ. Such is the natural order of the human creature. The soul must be submitted to the rule of the mind, the mind to Christ, and thereby the whole being is submitted through Christ to God the Father.... Spirit revolves perpetually about God and is therefore well named the husband and guide of the other parts of the soul, since between it and its creator no creature is interposed. Reason in turn revolves around the knowledge and causes of created things, and whatever spirit receives through eternal contemplation it transmits to reason and reason commends to memory. The third part of the soul is interior sense, which is subordinate to reason as the faculty which is superior to it, and by means of reason is also subordinate to spirit. Finally, below the interior sense in the natural order is the exterior sense, through which the whole soul nourishes and rules the fivefold bodily senses and animates the whole body. Since, therefore, reason can receive nothing of the gifts from on high unless through her husband, the spirit, which holds the chief place of all nature, the woman or *anima* is rightly ordered to call her husband or *intellectus* [him] with whom and by whom she may drink spiritual gifts and without whom she may in no wise participate in gifts from on high. For this reason Jesus says to her, "Call your husband, come hither." Do not have the presumption to come to me without your husband. For, if the intellect is absent, one may not ascend to the heights of theology, nor participate in spiritual gifts.[29]

It is in the light of such understanding that the theologians have said that all creation is feminine to God.[30]

Yet another way of envisioning the relationship between man and woman is to recognize that man manifests his "Christic" nature as Warrior (Hero, King) and as Ascetic (Priest), which is to say, in the realms of Action and Contemplation. (Christ is both King and Priest). The woman realizes herself, raises herself to the level of the "man" as Ascetic or as Warrior, insofar as she is either Lover or Mother. In the words of Evola,

As there is an active heroism, so also there is a negative heroism—they are the two sides of one and the same ideal; there is the heroism of absolute affirmation and that of absolute dedication, and the one can be as luminous as the other. It is these differentiations of the heroic concept that determine the distinctive characteristics of the ways proper to men and to woman thought of as types. To the act of the warrior and the ascetic, accomplished in the one case by pure action and in the other by detachment, whereby these are established in a life beyond mere living, there corre-

---

29. Translation of Christopher Bamford in *The Voice of the Eagle*, Lindisfarne Press, 1992. This is no novel teaching. Consider Origen: "Let us see also allegorically how man, made in the image of God, is male and female. Our inner man consists of spirit and soul. The spirit is said to be male; the soul can be called female. If these have concord and agreement among themselves, they increase and multiply by the very accord among themselves and they produce sons, good inclinations and understandings.... The soul united with the spirit and, so to speak, joined in wedlock...."

Scheeben says much the same: "Marriage, says the Apostle (Eph. 5:32) is the great sacrament that it is, that is, it ranks so highly, because it is a figure of the union between God and his Church, and in consequence, of *the union also between God and the soul*. Reality and type are more perfect than figure and representation; the union between God and the soul is thus incomparably more real than that of man and woman. They are one in flesh; *God is one with the soul in spirit* (I Cor. 5:17). The union of God with the soul is as far above the union of man and wife, as spirit is above flesh, as God is above matter. The union of the soul with God in one spirit is so intimate as to have no parallel in creation and the reasoning of the creature cannot grasp it. God submerges the soul in the ocean of His light, floods it with the torrent of His delights, fills it with the plenitude of His Being. He clasps it in the arms of His love. He so binds to Himself that no power in heaven or earth can tear it from Him." (*Les Merveilles de la Grace Divine*, pp. 170ff.)

"To love God," says St. Bernard, "is to be married to Him. Happy the soul who rejoices in this chaste and blessed embrace which is naught else than pure and holy love, love enchanting and joyful, love as serene as it is true, a mutual love, intimate and burning, which joins together two persons... in one spirit and of the two makes one." (*Sermon 84 on the Canticle of Canticles*, par. 5–6)

30. "Thus too it has been said that the Pharaoh of Egypt was a type of the devil, in that he cruelly ordered the males to be cast into the Nile and permitted the females to live. So too, the devil, ruling over the great Egypt of the world from Adam unto Moses, made an effort to carry off and destroy the male and rational offspring of the soul in the flood of the passions, while he takes delight in seeing *the carnal and sensual offspring increase and multiply*." (St. Methodius, *Treatise on Chastity*)

sponds in the woman the heroism of total self-surrender to another being, of existence altogether for the sake of another being—whether a beloved man (if she is a Lover) or a child (if she is a Mother)—in which she finds the meaning of her own life, her own delight and her own justification.[31]

We are all aware of how love can be a transforming experience—even the love of a child for a dog—and certainly the love of one human being for another. "In a moment," as C.S. Lewis has pointed out, love

---

31. Chapter on "Man and Woman" in J. Evola, *Rivolta Contra il Mondo Moderno* (Milan: Ulricho Hoepli, 1934). Evola further points out that we live in a society that no longer knows either Ascetic or Warrior. The idealized masculine type is characterized by the power that derives from materiality as in the financial tycoon. Feminist demands for equality with the opposite sex inevitably lead to women being driven into the street, the business offices, the schools, the factories and all the other infected and infectious cross-roads of modern society and culture. "The result is a degeneration of the feminine type even in its physical features; the atrophy of its natural possibilities, the suffocation of its inwardness. And hence the *garçonne* type, the neuter or mannish girl, sporty, vacant, incapable of any impulse beyond herself, incapable, in the last analysis, even of sensuality or sinfulness. In the case of modern women we do not even mention the possibility of maternity, but only that of a mere physical love in which she does not feel even so much interest as she does in beautifying herself, in displaying herself as much or as little dressed as possible, in physical training, dance, sport, money and so forth.... The traditional woman in giving herself to another, in not living for herself, in willing to live altogether for another and to be all for another than herself, had her own heroism—essentially, she raised herself above the common level to the plane of the ascetic. The modern woman, in seeking to exist for herself, destroys herself.... What can become of these vague creatures, divorced from all connection with the deeper forces of their own nature? From these creatures in whom sex begins and ends in physiology, even if abnormal inclinations are not already present? From these creatures who are psychologically neither man nor woman, if indeed, the woman is not the man and the man the woman, and who boast of being above sex while in fact they are below it? The relations between them can have no other quality than that of a plaster cast, a virtually homosexual androgyne: can amount to no more than the promiscuity of an equivocal camaraderie, a morbid "intellectual" sympathy, the banality of a new worship of nature shared together.... Nothing else is possible in the world of 'emancipated' woman."

has made appetite itself altruistic, tossed personal happiness aside as a triviality, and placed the interests of another in the center of our own being. At one bound, it has leaped over the high wall of our selfhood. We find ourselves as regards the other person really fulfilling the law, really loving another as ourselves. But having done this, the mere falling in love will do no more. Eros has done his stuff. He will not extend this selflessness to others beside the beloved. He may do quite the opposite. He will not even perpetuate it towards her. He will not of himself remain in that relationship and continue to be the sort of lover he promised to be. He may not remain any sort of lover at all. He may simply die. For of course, as we all really know, mere spontaneous feeling will not keep any pair in love even for a few months or weeks. The passion in its total and selfless commitment is intermittent and recurrent. The old self, as after a religious conversion, soon turns out not to be so dead as it seemed. In both the old self may for a moment be knocked flat, but it will soon be up again, if not on his feet, at least on his elbow. If not roaring, at least back to his old surly grumbling or mendicant whine. The corruptions return. Venus may sometimes slip back into mere sexuality, but what is ten times worse, that desire for the beloved, for total unity, may take on a morbid form. It may come to be a sort of imperialism, a desire for absorbing without being absorbed, possessing without being possessed, making the beloved's every thought, wish and interest, a mere reflection of oneself. And since the beloved may often have exactly the same program for you, success, which would be infamous if achieved, is not very probable. At this stage the couple are almost fortunate if they fall out of love altogether, but they may remain in it, in that sort of love which is increasingly a sort of hatred ... jealous, exacting and resentful.

C. S. Lewis continues:

My point is not that these dangers cannot be averted. They are averted daily by thousands of couples, but they are not averted by Eros—by love—itself. If love is to remain, it must be supported by outside help.... You need a firm will to justice, you need a will already pretty well formed or disciplined. In the long run you need the grace of God.... It's rather like a garden. A garden is a glorious thing, full of life, and giving us life. But you must not trust your garden to weed itself or fence itself, or prune itself, or anything of that sort. It hasn't got that kind of goodness. A garden left to nature will soon not be a garden. It is the same with our passions. They also are life giving. But when God planted that garden, he placed a man over it to dress it and set the man under Himself.[32]

For most of us, being in love is often the best experience of our lives, precisely because the state excludes vileness and involves a surpassing of our lesser selves. Unfortunately our egos rapidly come to the fore and the relationship becomes riddled with habit and triviality. Retaining a sense of the mystery in marriage requires both nobility and a sense of the sacred. As another author has said, "a profane man may look back on his youthful love and think that now he is 'beyond' such 'illusions of youth'; but in fact it is he who has succumbed to the illusion and triviality of profane life, whereas in his youth he tasted something of greatness and nobility which he ought to have tried to maintain by leading a spiritual life." Man cannot easily escape the temptation to humanize the sacred rather than sacralize the human.

Plato uses many words that we have translated as "love." There is *storge*, best translated as "domestic love"; there is *filia*, translated as "friendship"; there is *Eros*, or human love, there is *Agape*, often translated as "selfless love," or "charity"; and there is *epithumia* which is "lust." In the *Symposium*, Plato calls Eros a "mighty daemon ... being an intermediate between the nature of a god and the nature of a mortal." That Eros should have two sides results from the fact that Aphrodite, the goddess of love, has two aspects, labeled *Aphrodite Urania* and *Aphrodite Pandemia*. The first embodies love of a divine nature; the second profane love.[33]

---

32. From a taped series on Love. It is not clear from this quotation that C.S. Lewis fully realized that in Platonic and Greek symbolism Eros metaphysically represents Christ who would be married to Psyche. Despite this, the quotation does relate to the situation in marriage psychiatrists frequently meet with.

Now marriage as a vocation or way to perfect one's soul requires precisely the commitment and fight not to let the first kind deteriorate into the second. It involves the constant choice of love over selfishness, of giving over taking. Despite its joys, marriage is a life of continuing sacrifice—of destroying the old man that the new man might live.[34] Any father who faces the daily task of earning a living will be acquainted with sacrifice; as indeed, any woman who gets up in the middle of the night after a long day, to breast feed her child. To live in the married state without anger, impatience, resentment, selfishness is extremely difficult—witness the fact that marriages end up in divorce in over 60% of cases. And beyond this, even those where the partners stay together, true love not infrequently dies. Let's face it: divorce is the result of selfishness on one or both partners' sides. "Marriage is a great sacrament." Notice that we are not taught that there is a sacrament in marriage, but that marriage itself is a sacrament. As the Council of Trent taught, "it is a grace which perfects natural love, strengthens the union into an absolute indissolubility, and sanctifies the persons married." Grace, you will remember from your catechism, perfects nature. Without the sacramental graces, it is a wonder that any marriage survives. With sacramental grace every aspect of marriage can be sanctifying.

Plato speaks of the androgyne—of the time when man and woman were united or joined together. They decided, however, that they would attack the gods, and Zeus in his anger split them apart. Now the understanding of Greek mythology is not easy. This mythological story drawn from Aristophanes may well relate to a time before the fall when the female soul was united to the "male" image of God or the divine indwelling. This unity was lost with the fall. And the attraction towards the partner which is said to have resulted from this division—the seeking of "wholeness"—is but another way

---

33. Here again I have used the term Eros as C. S. Lewis and as common parlance uses it. There is of course a more correct understanding of the "Divine Eros" relating to the Logos, for it is God who is Love. Thus it is that classical presentation depicts Eros wedding Psyche, which equates with Christ wedding the soul.

34. St. Francis de Sales states that "The state of marriage is one that requires more virtue and constancy than any other; it is a perpetual exercise of mortification" (*Letters to Persons in the World*).

of describing the desire of the psyche-soul to be united with the indwelling spirit. Ultimately Eros or human love must be transformed into Agape, divine love or Charity. The risk is that it will degenerate into mere passion or worse.

While we are in the realm of mythology, it is worth considering the story of St. George and the dragon and a host of variations in which the loathly princess is kissed by the solar hero and restored to her rightful place. St. George slays the dragon, thus liberating the princess. Snow White, poisoned by the apple, is "cured" by the kiss of the prince. We are all in need of this "kiss" which derives from slaying the dragon of self-love.

Some of you will remember the novel *1984* which describes the new socialist world of future. The story speaks of the reverse possibility. In it a couple make the terrible mistake of falling in love. The state has no objection to their having sexual relations—the children of course to be brought up by the state. However, having fallen in love the couple proffer their loyalty to each other. This the state cannot tolerate. In order to correct their errors they are separately tortured. The inquisitor declares himself successful when the individuals concerned come to the point of wishing the suffering on their partner rather than desiring to suffer the torture for the sake of the partner.

I have many Catholic patients come to me as a psychiatrist who complain of having a poor self image. [In the later years of his life Dr. Coomaraswamy, after poor health ended his career as a surgeon, re-trained as a psychiatrist.—ED] How is this possible if we are made in the image of Christ? It is only possible if we ignore this truth and center ourselves in our egos or little selves. And this brings me back to one of the most horrible confusions imposed upon the Catholic faithful by Vatican II. I say horrible because it fosters and approves the satisfying of this little self.

You will immediately think of the heresy of religious liberty—and indeed in a sense you are correct. For the concept of religious liberty fundamentally teaches that we—our little selves—are the source of truth. This, incidentally, according to the Jewish fathers, is the worst form of idolatry. However, the heresy I am referring to is one which affects us, if possible, even more directly, for it enters into and influences our married vocation from the moment of its inception until death do us part. It is the heresy about the ends of marriage.

The traditional teaching regarding the ends of marriage is encapsulated in Canon 1013 of the Code of Canon Law (1917). Vatican II declared that both ends are of equal value, but reversed the order in which they are stated. It further declared that the priest was obliged to make reference to this in his sermon and admonition at the marriage ceremony.[35]

The traditional teaching states:

> The primary end of Marriage is the procreation and education of offspring, while its secondary purposes are mutual help and allaying (also translated "as a remedy for") concupiscence. The latter are entirely subordinate to the former.

Pius XII commented on this in a clear manner in his address to midwives on March 10, 1944:

> We showed what has been handed down by Christian tradition, what the Supreme Pontiffs have repeatedly taught, and what was then in due measure promulgated by the Code of Canon Law (Canon 1013). Not long afterwards, the Holy See, by a public decree, proclaimed that it could not admit the opinion of some recent authors who denied that the primary end of marriage is the procreation and education of the offspring, or teach that the secondary ends are not essentially subordinated to the primary end, but are on an equal footing and independent of it.

This doctrine was declared *de fide* by the Holy Office with the

---

35. "The 1983 Code of Canon Law reflects this sacrilegious shift in defining the sacrament. Canon 1055 (1) places the good of the spouses *before* procreation of children. Spousal self-fulfillment—the total person-gift of spouse to spouse—is the primary goal of marriage in the New Church (1057, par 2; 1095; 1098). Sacrilegiously employing this primary goal, the New Church rationalizes its wholesale granting of 'annulment divorces': and thus sacrileges the Sacrament of Matrimony.... Cardinal Ratzinger seems to opt for extending this privilege. In the future anyone [with pastoral responsibility] might be allowed to make an extra-juridical statement on the *null and void* nature of a first marriage" (*The Salt of the Earth*, 1977; Fr. Paul Trinchard, *The Sacraments Sacrileged*, Metairie, LA: MAETA, 1999).

approval of Pius XII [*Acta Apostolicae Sedis* 36 (1944), 103]. Let us look at what the change in this teaching leads to: it opens the door to artificial forms of birth control, infidelity and divorce. The traditional view demands that even the unitive ends of marriage must be sacrificed for the sake of the children. The new view declares that selfishness—for as has been made clear above, it is fundamentally selfishness that disrupts both love and marriage—has the right to sacrifice the children for its goals. And make no mistake about it: the psychiatric literature is replete with evidence of the effects wrought on the children by divorce, and that children would prefer to have their parents stay together even if their relationship is far from ideal. And to compound this terrible error, the new Church has made divorce easy by declaring that psychological immaturity is grounds for annulment—as if anyone other than the saint is psychologically mature.

But what of this "mutual help"? This does not mean help in any worldly sense—the saving of money for retirement or succoring each other in illness—though of course such is by no means excluded. Rather, it is that mutual help in gaining paradise. It often seems that the Church is only concerned with the children—that she says little about the "unitive" ends of marriage. Let us then look at this aspect of the married vocation with a little more care. I have already several times pointed to St. Paul's affirmation that marriage is a great sacrament. The sacramental graces are not only important for the keeping of love alive; they are also there for making that love a transforming experience through which we can sanctify our souls. St. Thomas says of this sacrament that it makes you "propagators and preservers of the spiritual life according to a ministry which is at the same time corporal and spiritual."[36] Again, Pius XII informs us that "your place in the Church as Christian couples is not then merely to beget children and offer living stones for the work of priests, the highest ministers of God. The exceedingly abundant graces which flow from the sacrament of matrimony have not been given you merely for the sake of remaining fully and constantly faithful to God's law in the august moment of calling your children

---

36. *Contra Gentes*, 4:58.

to life and for facing and supporting with Christian courage the pain, sufferings and worries that very often follow and accompany marriage. But such graces have been given you rather as a sanctification, light and help in your corporal and spiritual ministry; for together with natural life it is your sacred duty, as God's instruments, to propagate, preserve and contribute to the development in the children given you by Him of that spiritual life infused in them by the washing of holy Baptism."

It is pertinent that the minister of the sacrament of marriage is not the priest, but rather the couple involved and their reciprocal acceptance of each other.[37] The priest acts as the Church's witness. Now a minister of a sacrament is but a simple instrument in God's hands. He and she pronounce the words which signify the grace proper to the Sacrament, but it is God alone Who produces such a grace, using man only as a minister acting in His name. Even non-Catholic marriages have about them a certain sacramentality—that is, provided they are entered into with the proper intention.[38] And thus the non-Catholic marriage for those whose ignorance of the faith is invincible becomes a source of grace. In fact, when a Protestant couple become Catholic, they do not receive a second sacramental marriage; rather, just as their entire life becomes sacramentalized, their marriage is automatically raised to the level of a Sacrament. They may receive a "nuptial blessing," but the blessing is a gift of the Church not intrinsically necessary to the marriage.

Von Hildebrand likens marriage to Holy Orders:

> With regard to its sacramental character, marriage must be compared to Holy Orders. Leaving aside the internal holiness of the functions implied in the idea of a priest (which of its very nature calls down meriting graces), the priesthood—in its character as a

---

37. According to the common teaching of theologians, the matter of the sacrament consists in the mutual consent of the contracting parties to give themselves to each other; the form consists in their mutual consent to take each other.

38. These intentions are that the marriage is insoluble and that the ends of marriage would not be frustrated. Pope Innocent III taught that the sacrament of marriage existed both among the faithful and among infidels. He is quoted in this respect by Leo XIII in his Encyclical *Arcanum Divinae Sapientiae*.

Sacrament—is a source of specific graces, a dispenser of graces. The same applies to marriage. Holy Orders not only carries graces with it, but produces grace and is the channel of special graces. In the same way, marriage has been honored in becoming one of the seven mysterious sources of participating in the divine life. Perhaps marriage as a Sacrament shows the closest affinity to Holy Orders, since it does not effect a rebirth (as do the Sacraments of Baptism and Penance) nor a perfection of this rebirth and a union with Christ (as does the Sacrament of the Eucharist). Like Holy Orders, the Sacrament of Matrimony is at the disposal only of certain people who receive a special vocation to it.

Marriage is, in Catholic eyes, indissoluble.[39] Such inevitably follows from the fact that it reflects—or should reflect—the divine or metaphysical principles on which it is based. Can the Church be divorced from Christ—can Christ abandon the Church? Impossible! It is because marriage is a sacred state reflecting a divine prototype that it is indissoluble. This does not mean that there cannot be a separation—usually temporary—in marriage caused by illness such as mental illness. But such a separation is not a dissolution or divorce. And always it becomes another cross. Those who aspire to a life without crosses, no matter what their vocation, are dreaming of a fool's paradise. Once again, to quote St. Seraphim of Sarov:

> Christian marriage is a life-work. It is easy only in ideal circumstances. Fidelity to the end is essential to happiness. If Christians find they cannot live together, they go on living together for their homes, their children, for the Church and for God. It may mean much suffering, but this married life is the way to heaven. For only those who take up the cross can follow Christ.[40]

---

39. The indissolubility of Catholic marriage is directly connected with the esoteric nature of the Catholic revelation. It is only within such a framework that one can accept all that happens—both good and bad—as the will of God; the accepting of the will of God—the uniting of ourselves with this will—allows us to see all that happens as a salutary blessing. It is in this sense that the Church teaches that all suffering and any sacrifice is useless unless it be for the love of God.

40. St. Seraphim of Sarov, *A Spiritual Biography*, Archimandrite Lazarus Moore, Sarov Press, 1994.

But what of the phrase that the couple are joined together "until death do us part"? Is not ideal human love eternal? The answer is, no. Human love is both a beautiful, and at the same time a pale, reflection of Agape or divine love. It is only divine love that is eternal. And so it is in marriage that one must accept the painful fact that the most beautiful and perfect of marriages, like life itself, must see its termination, and that our eternal life is ultimately not of this world.

I have already alluded to the fact that theological writers are prone to admit sanctity is possible in the married state, but almost always imply that this occurs despite marriage and not because of it. When we come to the matter of sex, this becomes even more striking. In fact they almost never write of sex except to warn us that it is corrupted by concupiscence and hence indulgence in the sexual act almost always involves a venial sin.[41] The idea that the grace of the sacrament stops at the sanctuary of the bedroom door is patently absurd.[42]

---

41. There is a certain Manichean aspect to this disparagement of sexuality. To quote Augustine: "Anyone then who extols the nature of the soul as the highest good and condemns the nature of the flesh as evil is as carnal in his love for the soul as he is in his hatred of the flesh, because his thoughts flow from human vanity and not from divine truth" (*City of God*, XIV, 5). The meaning of concupiscence should be clearly understood. According to Father Tixeront, "By concupiscence, the Bishop of Hippo [and the Catholic Church] does not understand merely the appetite for bodily pleasures; he understands that general tendency away from the highest good and towards the lower pleasures: "when one turns away from godly things which are truly lasting and turns towards things which are changeable and insecure" (*History of Dogmas*, vol. II, p. 469). As the Fathers of the Council of Trent decreed: "This concupiscence, which at times the Apostle calls sin (Rom. 6:12 ff.) the holy Synod declares that the Catholic church has never understood to be called sin, as truly and properly sin in those born again, but because it is from sin and inclines to sin." The Church teaches that, as a consequence of original sin, concupiscence is with us—with both laity and religious—till we die.

42. St. John Chrysostom: "A man should love his spouse as much as he loves himself, not merely because they share the same nature; no, the obligation is far greater, because there are no longer two bodies, but one: he is the head, she the body. Paul says elsewhere 'the head of Christ is God', and I say that husband and wife are one body in the same way as Christ and the Father are one. Thus we see that the Father is our head also. Paul has combined two illustrations, the natural body and Christ's body; that is why he says, 'This is a great mystery, and I take it to

Let us pause for a moment to state that if marriage is a sacred state reflecting the unity of Christ and the Church, and, microcosmically, of our souls with the Christ that lives within us, then the same must also, by the very nature of things, be true of the sexual act. There is perhaps nothing with which we can better compare the "mystic union" of the finite with its infinite ambient, than the self-oblivion of earthly lovers locked in each other's arms where "each is both," or to use the Scriptural phrase, "united in one flesh."[43] So

---

mean Christ and the Church'. What does this mean? The blessed Moses—or rather, God—surely reveals in *Genesis* that for two to become one flesh is a great and wonderful mystery. Now Paul speaks of Christ as the greater mystery; for He left the Father and came down to us, and married His Bride, the Church, and became one spirit with her: 'He who is united to the Lord becomes one spirit with Him'. Paul says well, 'This is a great mystery', as if he were saying 'Nevertheless the allegorical meaning does not invalidate married love'." (*Homily* 20). St. Thomas Aquinas makes special note of the fact that the statement "this is a great mystery" immediately follows upon the statement that "they shall be united in one flesh" (*Commentary on Ephesians*). Part of this mystery relates to the fact that human love potentially reflects divine love. Consider the following passage from Garrigou-Lagrange: "If true love carries us towards another person towards whom we wish some good, it draws us outside of ourselves. It is in some ways ecstatic (*extasim facit*), according to the expression of St. Denys. It follows that it is an intense experience with a certain violent quality, and demands the sacrifice of all self love. It is not rare as St. Bernard writes (*Sermon LXXIX*, 1) 'O love divine, impetuous, vehement, burning, irresistible, which does not allow us to think of anything other than you'." (*La Vie Spirituelle*, vol. 20, August 1929)

43. It is a union in virtue of which Christ is bound to the soul by ties of love so close that conjugal affection alone affords a term of comparison. In various passages of Scripture the relation of Christ to the Church, and to the individual soul, is described as that borne by the bridegroom to the bride. St. Liguori, quoting St. Bernard, explains that *singulae animae singulae sponsae*—"every single soul is a bride" (*Commentary on Psalm XLIV*, 11). In Rev. 21:2 St. John sees the Church as "the new Jerusalem, coming down out of heaven from God, prepared as a bride adorned for the husband." St. Paul, addressing the local Church of Corinth, writes: "I espoused you to one husband that I may present you as a chaste virgin to Christ" (II Cor. 11:2). And elsewhere he points out the analogy between the physical union which makes man and woman one flesh, and the far higher and yet more intimate bond between God and the bride-soul, in virtue of which "he who is joined to the Lord is one spirit" (I Cor. 6:17). Matrimony as a permanent state typifies that union. And the same symbolism is present in the mutual consent which is the essential part of the rite of marriage: since the consent is representative of the state which it establishes" (George H. Joyce, S.J., *Christian Marriage*, Sheed and Ward, 1948).

much is this the case that in a Mediaeval Nuptial "Ceremornarium" it is ordered that when a newly married pair are got to bed, the priest and acolytes shall enter, with censer and Holy Water, to give the Church's blessing on their union.[44]

Sex has in every religion been surrounded by a host of what the anthropologists call taboos. We tell our children in a thousand ways that sex is somehow evil or dirty, and unfortunately many—both lay and cleric—carry this attitude over into marriage. Sex is not evil or dirty, but rather sacred, and that is why it is surrounded with taboos. Sex is beautiful, and as St. Thomas Aquinas teaches, "out of the divine beauty, all things are created." Now just as it would be sinful to give communion to individuals publicly known to be non-Catholic or not in a state of grace, so also it is sinful to indulge in a sacred act outside of the married state. Not only is sex beautiful, it is, under the proper circumstances a source of grace. Such has always been the teaching of the Church fathers. Consider the following:

> St. John Chrysostom teaches that "thanks to love, the man and the woman are drawn to the eternal life and moreover always attract to themselves the grace of God . . . [marriage] is the sacrament of love" (*Homily 3 on Marriage*). St. Theophile of Antioch teaches that "God created Adam and Eve in order that they might have the greatest possible love for each other, reflecting the mystery of divine Unity" (*Ad Autolyc.* 2.28). The German mystic von Baader said that "the purpose of marriage is the reciprocal restoration of the celestial or angelic image as it should be in the man and woman." In the life of Saint Ida of Herzfeld, the wife of Count Egbert (10th century), we find the following statement: "At the moment when the two are united in one flesh, there is present in them a single and similar operation of the Holy Spirit: when they are linked together in each other's arms in an external unity, which is to say, a physical unity, this indivisible action of the Holy Spirit inflames them with a powerful interior love directed towards celestial realities." And finally, St. Bernard in his commentary on the Song of Songs says that sexual intercourse

---

44. Quoted by Eric Gill in *Art and Love*, op. cit.

(*carnale connubium*) between married spouses is the reflection of the spiritual marriage (*spirituale matriomonium*) which unites the soul with God.[45]

St. Thomas Aquinas confirms this doctrine, while specifying the proper conditions involved: "The marriage act is always either sinful or meritorious in one who is in a state of grace. For if the motive for the marriage act be a virtue, whether of justice that they may render the debt, or of religion, that they may beget children for the worship of God, it is meritorious. But if the motive be lust, yet not excluding the marriage blessings, namely that he would by no means be willing to go to another woman, it is a venial sin; while if he exclude the marriage blessings, so as to be disposed to act in like manner with any woman, it is a mortal sin . . . "if pleasure be sought in such a way as to exclude the honesty of marriage so that, to wit, it is not as a wife but as a woman that a man treats his wife, and that he is ready to use her in the same way if she were not his wife, it is a mortal sin . . . if he seek pleasure (as its own end) within the bounds of marriage, so that it would not be sought in another than his wife, it is a venial sin." [46]

I have said above that part of the discipline of marriage is the giving of oneself to the other—this is the "heart to heart" aspect of marriage as opposed to the "ego to ego" aspect. When we give to the other we suppress our little selves by always putting the other first and by doing everything in our power to please the other. When we make of the marriage act a selfish act; when we seek in it our own pleasure rather than the pleasure of our partner, or when one or both partners seek pleasure as an end in itself, we act in a selfish manner. Yet how difficult it is to always be without at least some admixture of self-love. St. Augustine holds that Adam and Eve engaged in sexual intercourse in the Garden of Eden prior to the fall.

---

45. I am indebted to Prof. Jean Hani, *La Vierge Noire et le Mystere Marial* for the quotes in this paragraph. (Paris: Guy Tredaniel, 1995); English translation *The Black Virgin: A Marian Mystery* (San Rafael: Sophia Perennis, 2007).

46. *Summa* III, Q41, Article 4; Q. 49, Article 6. In marriage, the woman takes on the name of her husband, thus symbolically giving up her individual and separate identity.

There was no venality in their act.[47] The venality of self love is the result, not of the act, but of the fall. Our problem is that we have been wounded by the fall and few if any of our acts are free of self-love. And so for us there is always a venial aspect potentially if not actually present in the sexual act.

It is pertinent that Canon 1013 speaks of marriage as a "remedy" for concupiscence. Note that it doesn't say, as a means of indulging concupiscence. A remedy is a cure, and pray God we may all be cured of self-love.

This does not mean that one should derive no pleasure from the sexual act. To again quote Pius XII:

> The same Creator, Who in His bounty and wisdom willed to make use of the work of man and woman, by uniting them in matrimony, for the preservation and propagation of the human race, has also decreed that in this function the parties should experience pleasure and happiness of body and spirit. Husband and wife, therefore, by seeking and enjoying this pleasure do no wrong whatever. They accept what the Creator has destined for them.[48]

God would hardly create a necessary act, necessary for the preservation of the species—an act ultimately aimed at producing saints, an act from which we inevitably derive a certain pleasure—and

---

47. St. Augustine says that "Christ confirms at Cana what he established in paradise." (*Commentary on Ephesians* 5:23)

48. *Allocution to Midwives*, October 29, 1951. Allocutions are considered part of the Ordinary Magisterium. St. Augustine is often wrongly accused of stating that any pleasure derived in the act of intercourse is sinful. In his book on *The Goods of Marriage* (chap. 16), he speaks in positive terms of the "natural delight" that the patriarchs enjoyed in the act of intercourse. Augustine is only against making pleasure the only purpose of the act. Prummer's *Moral Theology* states: "Not only the conjugal act itself, but also touches and looks and all other acts are lawful between the married, provided there is no proximate danger of pollution and the sole intention is not mere sexual pleasure. Therefore, in ordinary circumstances the confessor should not interrogate married persons about these accompanying acts." Again, Pius XII states: "The Church can rightly declare that, profoundly respectful of the sanctity of marriage, she has in theory and practice left husband and wife free in that which the impulse of a wholesome and honest nature concedes without offense to the Creator" (*Allocution*, Sept. 18, 1951).

THE PROBLEMS WITH THE OTHER SACRAMENTS

then make it sinful for us to enjoy that act. Who can eat, read a book, or do anything else without a certain pleasure? It is my belief that God actually wants us to enjoy our lives—to enjoy all that we do, providing we do it IN HIM, and not as an end in itself. As Peter Lombard, the master of the sentences and the teacher of St. Thomas Aquinas said:

> Thus if there is any sin in sexual relations, it is due, not to the pleasure, but to some disorder in the way that pleasure is experienced.[49]

The pleasure shared in sexual giving involves the entire person—body, psyche and spirit. It is or should be, as I have said, an action that is not just physical, not just psychic, but also an action that is "heart to heart." But that pleasure must not be indulged in as an end in itself.[50] And certainly, sex must never be used as a tool for reward or punishment. Now the problem with sex is that, in its proper place and usage, it is one of the most sacred of acts, one from which as St. Thomas teaches, we derive abundant grace; it is also one of the most easily perverted of acts. The very word perverted is of interested. It means to turn something intrinsically good to an improper end. When we make of sex a satisfying of our own pleasure, an act of taking rather than an act of giving, we pervert or misuse one of the greatest gifts of God. This is true within marriage, and certainly true outside of marriage[51]

---

49. According to Father Kearns, S.J., St. Thomas Aquinas, St. Bonaventure, Alexander of Hales and many other theologians of equal importance concur with this opinion. (*The Theology of Marriage*, Sheed and Ward, 1964). Denis the Carthusian explains that: "Pleasure cannot be avoided in sexual intercourse, and yet it is not a sin when it is not sought after and the act itself is performed as it should be. In the same way the pleasure in food and drink, natural as it is and related to a spiritual goal, is not a fault.... As Aristotle says and St. Thomas repeats, our moral evaluation of an act and the pleasure joined to an act is the same. Therefore the pleasure from a good and virtuous act is good; and to the extent that it is good, it can be desired." (Ibid.)

50. St. Thomas quotes St. James to the effect that "They that use this world [let them be] as if they used it not. In each case he (St. Paul) forbade enjoyment." A footnote explains that the Latin *fruitionem* used in this situation refers to enjoyment of a thing sought as one's last end." (Translation by Fathers of the English Dominican Province)

During coitus a man can lose his individuality—forget himself or his little self—in two opposite ways. This disindividualization can occur in two directions—the anagogical ascent above individuality and the catalogical descent below.[52] The parties involved can give or take—in giving, transcending themselves; in taking, becoming less than human or merely animal. Let me give an analogy which may make this clearer. A policeman enters a house of ill fame as part of a raid. He commits no sin because he is protected by the graces of his function. The same policeman enters the same house on his own time. His act of entering the house has a certain neutrality. But his intention—the ends for which he acts—are sinful. Similarly with beauty. When one sees the beauty of a woman (or music) as a reflection of God's beauty, one can only praise its source. When one sees it as an end in itself—something to be enjoyed for its own sake—then its seductive rather than its redemptive character becomes manifest. One and the same beauty can lead us to, or away from, God.[53]

---

51. One can draw certain parallels between eating and the sexual act. Both are physiological, at least in part; both are "natural." Clearly, excessive indulgence in the sexual act can be likened to gluttony. But, hunger has is a function destitute of psychic counterpart, and under normal social conditions, nothing in regard to food corresponds to the part that the sexual function plays in an individual's life, or to the profound and manifold influence exerted by that function on the emotional, moral, intellectual, and, not seldom, spiritual level. As G.K. Chesterton said, "Sex cannot be admitted to a mere equality among elementary emotions or experiences, like eating and sleeping. The moment sex ceases to be a servant, it becomes a tyrant. There is something dangerous and disproportionate in its place in human nature, for whatever reason; and it does really need a special purification and dedication." (*St. Francis of Assisi*)

52. Orgasm, the point at which "disindividualization" is maximum, is derived from the Greek word *orgy*, originally meaning "holy" or "inspired exaltation." It is a sad commentary on the current state of affairs that the word now is associated only with the unleashing of the senses.

53. An example of beauty leading to God is provided by St. John Climacus where the Bishop Nonnos of Edessa found himself in the presence of a beautiful nude dancer and commented that "he took the occasion to adore and glorify by his praises the sovereign Beauty, of which this woman was only a reflection, and he felt himself transported with the fire of divine love, pouring forth tears of joy." Such an individual, says St. John Climacus, "was incorruptible even before the universal resurrection." (*The Ladder of Divine Ascent*)

Nor is the sexual act irrevocably tied to procreation. As St. John Chrysostom said:

> But suppose there is no child; do they then remain two and not one? No; their intercourse effects the joining of their bodies, and they are made one, just as when perfume is fixed with ointment.

Pius XII said:

> To reduce the common life of husband and wife and the conjugal act to a mere organic function for the transmission of seed would be but to convert the domestic hearth, the family sanctuary, into a biological laboratory.[54]

Further proof of this lies in the fact that the Church has never invalidated or impedimented marriages where sterility is known to exist or prohibited the sexual act when the woman is beyond the child bearing age. (In passing you may be interested to know that St. Camillus's mother was 60 at the time of his birth, and not on any hormone therapy.) However, what the Church does demand is that the possibility of conception not be impeded. How so? Well, consider the couple that engages in sex with the express and only intention of enjoying the pleasure. To do so is to make the pleasure—even if reciprocal—its own end. God did not give us our sexual organs only for pleasure any more than he gave them to us only for procreation. And so it is that when adequate reasons are present, the parents may use the so-called rhythm method—better called periodic abstinence—but can never use other methods of preventing birth than abstinence.

The use of periodic abstinence does not absolutely preclude the possibility of conception. When the sexual act is performed in so-called safe periods of the woman's cycle, one remains open to the divine will. Quite the opposite is the case when the possibility of

---

54. *Allocution to Midwives*, October 29, 1951. It was for this reason that artificial insemination was forbidden by Pius XII in his allocution to an International Congress of Catholic Doctors on September 29, 1949. Just as the welcoming of children is a welcoming of God's will, so also, the absence of children in a marriage is a cross to be born, but also an acceptance of God's will.

children is absolutely precluded. To quote Father Planque, "to refuse to let one's love result in children, is to commit oneself to the path of egotism, a path which can only lead to the death of love."[55] Moreover, shared abstinence is the only form of "birth control" which demands mutuality or a sharing of the sacrifice involved; and shared sacrifice always deepens love. Every other form of birth control is both unilateral and carries with it significant medical risks.

Allow me to take this opportunity to strongly disagree with Solange Hertz, a woman for whom I have a great deal of admiration. The first point of disagreement is fundamental. She states that "Ascribing sacredness to the sex act is a Judaic heresy. It partakes of the talmudic mysticism taught in the *Zohar*, where the union of man and wife on the Sabbath is seen as a ritual representation of the union of the male and female aspects of God." I have already given the evidence necessary to contradict this; and further, I believe she misinterprets the *Zohar*, for the Jewish fathers, basing themselves on the Song of Songs, clearly saw the sexual act as reflecting the unity of the soul with God precisely along the lines discussed above.

The second point is perhaps more important, for it is her contention that the "abomination of desolation is contraception ... most particularly as practiced ... in the guise of so-called 'natural family planning' or 'natural birth regulation'." In so stating her case, she directly contradicts Pope Pius XII who holds that the use of this method under the right circumstances is entirely legitimate. To quote him directly, "We affirmed the legitimacy and at the same time the limits—truly very wide—of that controlling of births which, unlike the so-called 'birth control', is compatible with God's law. It can be hoped that for such a lawful method a sufficiently certain basis can be found, and recent research seems to confirm this hope." Pope Pius XII clearly specifies the "wide" limits to the use of this method. A marriage entered into with the express intention of excluding the payment of the marriage debt—as the sexual act is called—during fertile periods is invalid because implicit to the contract is that this debt should be paid whenever asked for and because the intention is to preclude the primary purpose of marriage. It is

---

55. *The Theology of Sex in Marriage*, Daniel Planque, Fides, 1962.

very much a matter of the morality of the intention involved. Thus he states that

> The mere fact that the husband and wife do not offend the nature of the act and are even ready to accept and bring up the child who, notwithstanding their precautions, might be born, would not be itself sufficient to guarantee the rectitude of their intention and the unobjectionable morality of their motives... to embrace the matrimonial state, to use continually the faculty proper to such a state and lawful only therein, and, at the same time, to avoid its primary duty without a grave reason, would be a sin against the very nature of married life.

However,

> serious motives, such as those which not rarely arise from medical, eugenic, economic and social so-called "indications," may exempt husband and wife from the obligatory, positive debt for a long period or even for the entire period of matrimonial life. From this it follows that the observance of the natural sterile periods may be lawful, from the moral viewpoint, and it is lawful in the conditions mentioned. If, however, according to a reasonable and equitable judgment, there are no such grave reasons either personal or deriving from exterior circumstances, the will to avoid the fecundity of their union, while continuing to satisfy to the full their sensuality, can only be the result of a false appreciation of life and of motives foreign to sound ethical principles.[56]

---

56. *Allocutions to Midwives*, October 29, 1951, and *Allocutions to the Associations of the Large Families*, November 26, 1951. Solange Hertz sees the use of periodic abstinence as onanism. She claims that the Jews forbade the sexual act during infertile periods and that this is why it was forbidden during menstruation. St. Thomas Aquinas discusses this and states that this was a ritual prohibition no longer applying to Christians, and further stated that the reason Christians should not have intercourse during menses is that children born of such conceptions are not healthy. Her views have been expressed in *The Remnant*, and in her book entitled *Beyond Politics*.

There are strong Jansenist tendencies among certain traditional groups. I quote specifically *Letter 13 of the Society of St. Pius X* dated July 17th, 1990 which while referring to the same document of Pius XII, instructs the faithful in the following

It is this attitude which Chesterton labeled as "no birth and less control." This is a matter which couples should discuss with their confessor.

There are incidentally excellent books which enable married couples to determine fertile periods with great accuracy. One of the best is *The Ovulation Method of Birth Control* by Mercedes Arzu Wilson published by Van Norstrand Reinhold, and unfortunately out of print.[57] A proper knowledge of the method makes the old quip to the effect that "what you call couples who use the rhythm method is 'parents,'" is not completely true. Every form of artificial birth control has a certain failure rate. With condom usage, it may be as high as 25%. Even with tubal ligations there is a 1% pregnancy rate; and certainly the use of hormones is fraught with a significant number of complications—though it must be granted that they are less life-threatening than pregnancy can be. The fact remains however that abstinence is the healthiest form of birth control, and what is more important, it is the only form of birth control where the couples share responsibility. In every other form of birth control the act is essentially unilateral—and we have spoken of the reciprocity necessary in love. Now even with abstinence during the so-called fertile period, there is always a risk of pregnancy, and thus an openness to

---

terms: "Natural family planning cannot be used by the spouses, except under some very exceptional circumstances, i.e., danger of death or very serious health problems for the pregnant mother, living conditions such that you cannot financially support another child, if you are sure all your children will be born with a pathological condition. If some of our faithful have such a hard time accepting this teaching it is because of the lack of a spirit of penance and of the spirit of the faith! They try to go to heaven without the cross!" I personally find this attitude on the part of clergy, who are hardly noted for their spirit of penance, and of which approximately ⅓ have abandoned the priesthood and another ⅓ gone over to modernist Rome, somewhat offensive. I can think of few things which are more "penitential" than trying to raise a Catholic family in a Catholic manner in the modern world. Why could they not have simply quoted the gentle words of Pope Pius XII? Any asceticism not accompanied by strict adherence to the truth is a waste.

57. Other texts are *No-pill No-risk Birth Control* by Nona Aguilar, New York: Rawson Wade, Publishers, and *Natural Birth Control* by Frank Richards, Melborne, Australia: Spectrum. Various organizations exist to promote so-called natural methods of birth control. Not all of them are truly Catholic, however.

the possibility should God so will. God's primary purpose in marriage is not precluded. The sanctity of the act remains intact. Abstinence can at times require an "heroic virtue," but is that not what sanctity is all about?

According to Zertnys-Damen's *Moral Theology*, continence, whether periodic or total, may be practiced under the following definite conditions: (a) the practice must be freely undertaken by mutual consent; (b) there must be no serious danger of unchastity or loss of conjugal love in either party as a result of the practice; (c) there must be a positive and good reason for adopting the practice. The presence or absence of these conditions should be decided with the help of a confessor.

It is perhaps not out of place to comment on the Virginity of the Blessed Mother. How is this compatible with the teaching of the Church that she is the ideal and model for every woman, be she single or married? First of all, The Blessed Virgin is the ideal and model for both men and women. As Augustine said, "the soul's virginity consists in perfect faith, well-grounded hope and unfeigned love" (*Tract. on John, XIII*). Similarly, Cornelius Lapide tells us: "Those whose souls are on fire with charity, and who are ever exercising themselves in it, enjoy the bliss of betrothal to God and the possession of His nuptial gifts of divine joys. For charity is a marriage-union, the welding of two wills, the Divine and the human into one, whereby God and man mutually agree in all things." Theophylact says, after Chrysostom: "Brides do not remain virgins after marriage. But Christ's brides [we are all meant to be such], as before marriage they were not virgins, so after marriage they become virgins, most pure in faith, whole and uncorrupt in life" (Quoted by Cornelius Lapide). This is why St. Louis de Montfort says: "The more the Holy Spirit ... finds Mary, His dear and inseparable spouse, in any soul, the more active and mighty He becomes in producing Jesus Christ in that soul." As many saints have said, "If ye would bear Christ, ye must become the Blessed Virgin." It is statements such as these that explain the words of St. Theresa of Lisieux to her sister Céline, praying "May we become virginized, so that we may become pregnant."

St. Paul said, "To this man I have espoused you." For as marriage between man and wife is binding, so there is eternal marriage between the soul and God. A maid is given to a man hoping to bear his child. And God did make the soul intending her to bear in her His only-begotten Son. The happening of this birth in Mary ghostly was to God better pleasing than his being born of her in flesh.... The woman said to Christ, "Blessed is the womb that bare thee," to which Christ replied, "Blessed not alone the womb which bare me: blessed are they that hear the word of God and keep it." It is more worth to God His being brought forth ghostly in the individual virgin or good soul than that he was born of Mary bodily.[58]

Now the Blessed Virgin is the source of fecundity, both physical and spiritual. Her purity is virginal to us, but precisely because she is eternally wedded to the Holy Spirit. For those of us in the married state, it is not so much her physical virginity which exemplifies, but rather this relationship to the Holy Spirit. For us, and indeed even more for those in the religious life, this is exemplified by the Magnificat and above all by her response to the Annunciation—"be it done unto me according to thy Word." It is she who is the *Janua Coeli*—the Gate of Heaven, and it is no accident that it is she who in a sense sacramentalized and continues to sacramentalize marriage, for it was her request that led to Christ's first miracle—the changing of water into wine—always a symbol of the sacred transmutation.[59] It is precisely her purity, chastity and virtue, all the qualities of the Magnificat, brought to the marriage state which vivifies its sacramental nature and virginalizes us. Without her virginal graces—she who is Co-Redemptrix and the Mediatrix of all Graces—none of us could ever sacramentalize our lives, much less our marriages. Hail Mary, full of grace, blessed art thou among women, and blessed is the fruit of thy womb, Jesus.[60]

---

58. Taken from two of Meister Eckhart's Sermons, Franz Pfeiffer translation (London: Watkins, 1947).
59. The use of wine, like sex, is easily perverted.
60. Christos Yannaras thinks that Christian marriage is most profoundly both an imitation of Christ and a participation in the mystery of His self-offering. This is

I have, in this essay, attempted to share with you some of the principles on which Catholic marriage and sexuality are based. Marriage is clearly a vocation, a "calling" willed by God, and as such every aspect of marriage is both capable of reflecting the sacred, and of transforming and sacralizing the participants. Eros is always potentially Agape, but Agape both as grace and fruition is necessary to transform Eros, or rather to be transformed into Eros.[61] Without this, Eros easily degenerates into *epithumia* or lust which is nothing other than unrestrained self-love.[62] In accordance with the principle that the highest things are the most easily corrupted, marriage can easily become, not a foretaste of heaven, but a living hell. While grace bloweth where it will, it is always within our power to refuse its refreshing breezes. Our human loves—*storge, Eros,* and *filia*—can all be said to reflect and to open the door to *Agape*. They can be valued as demigods, as long as we recognize that demigods, when made an end in themselves, become idols.

In a true marriage Eros and Agape are not in conflict, for as the poet John Donne said, "For I, / Except you enthrall me, shall never be free, / Nor ever chaste, except you ravish me." "Blessed are they

---

because both share a "true eros." This is why in his view the newly-wed couple are "martyrs"—witnesses to the truth which is being affirmed. Indeed, Yannaras declares that the love of a man for his wife is in fact a love for "all the members of Christ's body" since she [the wife] sums up "the beauty and truth of the world, of all creation." Thus we begin to see why the virginity of monks and the "eros which grafts marriage into the life of the Kingdom" of God are basically the same. "Virginity is eros free from the natural constraint of lust and pleasure, and it is the same eros which marks an orthodox Christian marriage." (*The Freedom of Morality*, St. Vladimir's Seminary Press, 1984)

61. "In God the '*eros*' is outgoing, ecstatic. Because of it lovers no longer belong to themselves but to those whom they love. God also goes out of himself... when he captivates all creatures by the spell of his love and his desire...." Dionysius the Areopagite, *Divine Names*, IV, 13) Again, "God is the producer and generator of tenderness and *eros*.... Insofar as eros originates from him, he can be said to be the moving force of it, since he generated it." Maximus the Confessor, *On the Divine Names*, IV, 4. And again, "Blessed is the person whose desire for God has become like the lover's passion for the beloved." (St. John Climacus, *The Ladder of Divine Assent*, 30th. step)

62. St. Augustine defined lust as "that affection of the mind which aims at the enjoyment of one's self and one's neighbor without reference to God."

who are called to the marriage supper of the Lamb.... These are the true words of God" (*Apocalypse of Blessed John the Apostle* 19:3).

After this rather paltry treatment and discussion of mine, I am not ignorant of the fact that the question of marriage still remains very obscure and involved. Nor

> dare I say that either in this work or in any other up to the present have I explained all its intricacies, or that I can explain them now, even if urged to do so.
>
> St. Augustine, *On Adulterous Marriages*

III

THE GATES OF HELL SHALL NOT PREVAIL

One of the most frequent arguments in favor of the legitimacy of the Post-Conciliar establishment is God's promise that "the gates of hell shall not prevail." Implicit in this brief is that is neither possible nor likely that God has abandoned His own. How is one to respond to such an argument?

Let us start with indisputable facts. Whether we believe it or not, and whether it seems possible to us or not, what is abundantly clear is, that after a scandalous Council lacking both regularity and dignity, the Catholic religion has been changed. In the practical order, it has been replaced by another religion, an evolving religion, a religion greatly influenced by Freemasonry and Marxism and inspired throughout by what Popes Pius IX and X clearly rejected under the designation of "Modernism." Having created a "robber" Council that raised a host of errors such as Religious Liberty and the denial of the Church's "Unity" to the level of infallible teachings, the Post-Conciliar "Church" proceeded to abolish the Oath against Modernism and the Holy Office. What other purpose could such measures have than to deprive the Traditional Church—the Church of All Times—of all her defenses? And what followed? The turning of altars into tables, the changing of priests into "presidents," the invalidating of all the sacraments not acceptable to Protestants, the mistranslating of the Scriptures, and above all, the downgrading of Tabernacles and the destruction of the Mass—"humanist" and demagogic changes of the most serious nature. Cardinal Suenens was correct when he described this as "the French Revolution in the Catholic Church."

Consider the principle that "by their fruits you shall know them." Now what are the fruits of the new religion? Priests by the thousands have abandoned their calling—of those remaining over 25% requested and were refused permission to marry. Monks and nuns have been laicized by the thousands. The seminaries are virtually deserted. The median age for priests in the United States being the late fifties, with an anticipated drop to 40% of the present level by the end of the decade [this essay is dated 2001—ED]. Far more tragic: despite the wide range of "liturgies" offered—from conservative to radical chic—Catholics by the millions have turned away from the Church and for all practical purposes the youth is no longer interested in what she has to offer. Only 15% of the erstwhile faithful still attend Sunday Mass and among these communions are up while confessions are down, suggesting that even sin is dwindling away. Over 80% of married Catholics use birth control and do so in the belief that such violates no divine principle, divorce statistics show no difference between Catholics and others; and in the practical realm complete chaos exists with regard to sexual behavior.

Along with all this is the corruption, nay destruction, of doctrine and theology. The acceptance of evolution as a fact in every realm—be it biology, theology, sociology—even the Teilhardian thesis that God Himself evolves! The abrogation of canons 1399 and 2318, the refusal of the Church to condemn out and out heretics and the blatant indulgence extended to those who like Hans Küng—their name is legion—would poison the thinking of the faithful are symptomatic of the wide-spread modernist malignancy. The self proclaimed "desacralization" and "demythologization" of the Church combined with the misrepresentation of everything traditional has resulted in an all-pervasive familiarity and vulgarity. Recent attempts to cover this over by dressing the presidents (clergy) and nuns in traditional garb has in no way changed the situation.

Let those who have ears hear. The writing was on the wall from the very opening of the Council. But who of us wished to listen. Its leitmotiv was *aggiornamento*, a concept inimical to any religion based on eternal verities and Revelation. Roncalli, alias John XXIII, then declared his intention "to safeguard the sacred deposit of the faith more effectively." It does not take much imagination to understand what he meant—and he did not hesitate to declare that "... the substance of the ancient doctrine contained in the deposit of the faith is one thing, the manner in which it is expressed in another...." This claim is false and in fact satanic, for it opened the door to all the betrayals and falsifications that followed. The traditional formulations were not superficial luxuries, they were guarantees of the truth and efficacy; they more than adequately expressed what they wished to say—their adequacy was in fact their *raison d'être*. Is not the truth inseparable from its expression? Was it not the strength of the Church that the old expressions were always valid? They only displeased those who wished to make modernism, scientism, evolutionism and socialism part of the "deposit of the faith."

One must take a phenomenon for what it is. If one sees a tiger in the streets of New York one does not require a news broadcast to know that what one sees is a reality. One can deny its existence only at the risk of one's life.

Despite the obvious, there are those who, desiring to have the "best of both worlds," would exculpate the Post-Conciliar Church; and who seek to explain why is it that the "smoke of Satan" has all but obscured "the dome of St. Peter's". Some claim that it is because the Council and the subsequent innovations were "badly interpreted." But, by whom? Others, loudly proclaiming their loyalty to those usurping the Chair of Peter, claim it is the fault of the bishops and cardinals around him. But who appointed them? Since when has the principle of *respondeat superior* been abandoned? (Even hell has a hierarchical structure.) Despite the fact that such claims are often motivated by the desire "to cover Noah's drunkenness," they remain a combination of improbabilities and hypocrisy.

Whether we like it or not, this blame must fall primarily upon the Post-Conciliar "popes." Even though none of us are without an element of culpability, it is they who must bear the burden. It is they who approved the Council and the Reforms, and without their approval neither the Council nor the Reforms would have any meaning or authority. It is they who have misapplied the principles of obedience in order to bring the erstwhile faithful into line. It is they who tolerate every conceivable deviation while condemning out of hand whatever is traditional. They are not individuals who have "fallen into heresy," or who are, as Lefebvre would say, "tainted with modernism." (Can one have a touch of pregnancy?) They are much worse, for they are heretics who have been elected precisely because they are heretics; men who, by the laws of the traditional Church, have long since excommunicated themselves. And this condemnation applies to virtually the entire "electoral body" responsible for the implementation of what can only be described as a modernist conspiracy. It further applies to the sycophant hierarchy which declares itself *una cum* ["one with"] those in power.

"And Caiaphas was, in his own mind, a benefactor of mankind" (Blake). To speak of a conspiracy is not to deny the sincerity of those involved. But what heretic has ever lacked sincerity? Nor is it to claim that every individual who lent and lends his support is a conscious subversive. (Our Lord said that he who is not with Him was against Him—not to condemn error is to condone it.) The net result is clear. The Council and its aftermath were achieved by a conspiracy of the sort of individuals whom Pope Saint Pius X clearly condemned, and against whom he desired to protect the Church. He went so far as to state, in his capacity as Pope and hence *ex cathedra*, that any individual who even defended a single modernist proposition condemned by his Encyclicals and *Lamentabili* was *ipso facto* and *latae sententiae* excommunicated—that is, by that very fact and without any need for anyone to publicly so declare (*Praestantia Scripturae*, Nov. 18, 1907). No father signing the Council documents and no member of the hierarchy accepting and teaching them can claim to fall outside this condemnation. Everyone who considers himself "in obedience" to the new Church implicitly accepts its modernist principles.[1]

Consider Religious Liberty—the idea that every man is free to decide for himself what is true and false, what is right and wrong,

---

1. Certain distinctions should be made. These are essentially those between material and formal heresy—the later requiring awareness that one is acting or believing in a manner that goes against the constant teaching of the Church, and that one does this with obstinacy. It is certainly possible that some of the fathers were only material heretics. It is not for us to judge souls, but we are certainly obliged to judge the facts.

and that his very human dignity resides in just this license. Imagine Christ upon the Cross telling us that he came to establish a visible Church—"One, Holy, Catholic, and Apostolic," and to confide to it those truths necessary for our salvation. He continues however to assure us that we have no obligation to listen to Him—that we are free to choose for ourselves what we shall believe, and that our real human dignity resides not in conforming to His image, but in making just such choices! Incredible! And now, some two thousand years later, we find Christ's representative whose function it is to teach us what Christ taught us, assuring us that, as a result of Christ's incarnation, all men, even those who reject the very idea of God, are saved, that Christ's Church, through her own fault, has lost her "unity," and that the Crucifixion is but a "witness to man's human dignity"—his ability to determine for himself what is true and false. Madness reigns supreme!

It will be argued that these false popes have said some nice things. Such however is of no importance or interest in the present situation when we must decide whether or not they are truly Christ's representatives on earth. If they are truly "one hierarchical person" with our Lord, we must obey them. But Catholics must understand that the Pope's infallibility is totally dependent upon his being himself in obedience to Christ, and that when he rejects Christ and falsifies Christ's teaching, we must reject his authority. As Peter said, "one must obey God rather than man." A modernist pope is an impossibility. Either he is a modernist, and then he isn't a pope, or he is a pope, and then he isn't a modernist. All this is not a matter of picking or choosing what we shall believe. It is a matter of being Catholic. To deny this principle is to declare Christ a liar! St. Catherine of Sienna told us that a Pope who falsifies his function will go to hell, and further, that those of us who obey him will go there with him. Let us be done with those who claim that John Paul II is trying to bring the "Church" back to tradition. The lie is easily exposed. All he has to do is reject Vatican II and restore the traditional sacraments. Short of this he is but a wolf in sheep's clothing pulling the wool over our eyes.

Have the "gates of hell" prevailed? Certainly not. Catholics know that Christ cannot lie. Let us then examine the meaning of this promise. What it proclaims is that the truth will ultimately win out—though not necessarily so in the "short run." That such is "true" is an intellectual certainty, for error can only be defined in terms of the denial of truth. Now the Catholic Church is true, and hence it can no more be totally destroyed than can the truth itself. But this Church resides, not in numbers, not in buildings, and not even of necessity in the hierarchy. The truth functions *ex opere operato*. It resides in the faithful (the hierarchy must be "of the faithful," before the faithful can be "of the hierarchy." Or as the theologians put it, members of the "teaching Church"—the Magisterium—must be first of all members of the "learning Church.") Every baptized infant, according to the traditional rite, becomes a "member of the body of Christ." And what is the Church if not the Body of Christ, the presence of Christ in this world? It follows then that, as Anne Catherine Emmerich points out, if there were but one person alive who was truly Catholic, the Church would reside in him.

Visibility is a quality of the Church. Does visibility require a hierarchy? The matter is open to debate, but time has not yet run its course. In any event traditional bishops are available, and if but one traditional bishop survives, the hierarchy would reside in him. What has to be remembered however is that the Church does not exist for the sake of the hierarchy, it is the hierarchy that exists for the sake of the Church. And history has shown that Catholics can live and retain the faith for centuries without any hierarchy. God knows His own and will not abandon them. If a bishop is necessary for the visibility of the Church, He will certainly provide one. Ultimately, it is we who abandon God, his truth and his Church, and never the other way around.

One would have thought that the changes were more than enough to induce the faithful to revolt. The great surprise, truly apocalyptic, was that the Catholic people did not do so. That they did not only goes to show what "sincere, pious, fervent and well-intentioned" Catholics really valued. One is tempted to feel sorry for them, but as always, even in such a situation "God knows his own." One must insist upon this, for the truly innocent are far less numerous than one is inclined to believe. The argument that it is not possible or likely that God would abandon his own presumes that "his own" did not deserve to be abandoned, when in fact they did deserve it precisely to the degree that they are in fact abandoned.

Why did Catholics not revolt? Well, first of all, many did, but their stand was undermined by poor leadership. Psychologically dependent upon the hierarchy and the clergy, they looked for guidance that was not provided. The Modernists, working for decades, had prepared the ground, and even those who were not out and out subversives had their faith corrupted and hence weakened. At the Council there were perhaps 70 individuals who—towards the end—began to understand what was happening. No more! And among them not one was willing to take a clear cut stand on solid doctrinal grounds. Even Lefebvre based his opposition on false theological premises, arguing for example that one can disobey a valid pope.[2] Secondly, for decades the faithful were both inadequately trained in their faith and discouraged from leading active spiritual lives. Educated in secularized colleges, taught by "liberal" priests, they were by and large modernists without knowing it. And finally, both clergy and laity found the modern world seductively attractive. They found the rejection and scorn of the modern world—a world which had repudiated the Church and, like the Prodigal Son, had walked away from the bosom of the Father—increasingly intolerable. They could not accept the disapproval of this world in which they believed more strongly than in Christ. The Council declared the Church would henceforth not only be "open to the world," but that it would "embrace" it! Its avowed aim and promise was *aggiornamento* to bring the Church "into the twentieth century" and make it part of and acceptable to that world. No longer did she proclaim that it was necessary for the Prodigal Son to return to the bosom of the Father. Rather, abandoning both her function and her identity, she proclaimed that the Father was obliged to eat the swill fit only for pigs! Both clergy and laity—exceptions apart—rushed headlong into to the sea to spend their patrimony as if there was no tomorrow. It is this that is at the heart of the conspiracy. It is this that is the crux of the problem. It is this that created the smoke swirling around St.

---

2. Clearly liturgical matters and the insistence upon obedience to a supposedly valid Council fall within his authority.

Peter's Basilica. This spark of rebellion, present in the soul of every man, needed only the "winds of change" to create an inferno.

However, as has always been the case throughout the history of the Church, a remnant persisted in retaining the fullness of the faith. The true Church is to be found among those who believe and continue to believe in the manner of their ancestors. It is they who bear witness to the truth of Christ's promise. It is they who provide the proof that "the gates of hell have not prevailed." Not all are profound theologians. Not all are sinless. But they can be recognized by their insistence on true priests, true doctrine, and the true Mass—the Mass of All Times.

Some would accuse traditional Catholics—those that insist on retaining the fullness of the Catholic faith intact and who therefore refuse the new religion of the Post-Conciliar Church—of being in "schism." The accusation is a lie. In reality, the schismatic is one who removes himself from the truth, and not one who insists upon it. And if it is necessary to separate oneself from something in order to save the truth, Long Live Schism! But in reality, it is not the traditional Catholic who is in schism, but those who are responsible for changing the Catholic faith. But let us be both clear and honest. The new Church is not schismatic. It is heretical. In similar manner traditional Catholics are accused of being Protestants because they disobey the pope. Such accusations are false. Traditional Catholics do not "pick and choose" what they wish to believe; they are adhering with all their hearts to what the Church has always taught and always done. Nor are they disobeying the pope. They believe that the pope, being Christ's vicar on earth and "one hierarchical person" with our Lord, is to be obeyed. They know that when Peter speaks he is infallible because it is Christ who speaks through him. They are the out and out papists and are doing nothing less than refusing to disobey Peter. In such a situation they are obliged to disobey those who falsely speak in Peter's name. To obey modernist and heretical "popes" is to declare that they are "one hierarchical person" with our Lord and hence that Christ teaches falsely—*quod absit!*

It is an unfortunate fact that too many of the traditionalists do not wish to be labeled "integrists" or "sedevacantists." And why not? Why should they stop mid-way? Such only leads to wrangling about the most absurd positions, or to timidity of language combined with conventional and infantile sentimentalities. If the Post-Conciliar "popes" are true popes, let us obey them. If not, let us obey Peter and through him Christ. People claim to be "confused" or "troubled." Why? The ancient catechisms are always there and modern innovations are no different in principle than those of a prior era. Sin can change its style, but not its nature. "There is no greater right than that of truth," and despite the teaching of Vatican II, "error has no rights whatsoever."

Traditional Catholics often give scandal by arguing among themselves. The new Church in comparison seems more united. In point of fact it is, for it accepts within its aegis every conceivable deviation. But if traditional Catholics seem divided it is because, in the absence of clear leadership, each individual group seeks to determine just what is truly Catholic for itself. What is required is a deeper study and commitment to what is truly Catholic on the part of all. Paraphrasing Lenin, let us have no enemies on the right—none more orthodox and none more traditional than ourselves. Let us be united in the truth manifested in the constant teaching and practice of the Church throughout the ages. So help us God.

It is extraordinary that modern churchman should claim to be reading "the signs of the times." Christ depicted the "last times" in very sombre colors. Scripture warns of an unparalleled outbreak of evil, called by St. Paul an Apostasy, in the midst of which a terrible Man of Sin and child of perdition, the special singular enemy of Christ, called Antichrist, will appear; that this will be when revolutions prevail and the present framework of society breaks to pieces. We are told that they "shall defile the sanctuary of strength and shall take away the continual sacrifice and they shall place there the abomination unto desolation." Does not Jeremias speak in God's Name when he says "My Tabernacle is laid waste, all My cords are broken: My children are gone out from Me, and they are not.... Because the pastors have done foolishly, and have not sought the Lord." And are we not told that "many false Christs will arise," that false doctrines will be preached and that even the seeming elect will be deceived? Finally, is not Christ specific when He tells us that at the final coming only a "remnant" will be left—a remnant persecuted by the Antichrist? Despite such warnings the modern Sanhedrin in Rome insist on supporting and fostering the forces of revolution. They proclaim their intention to create a better world, in which the principles of the French Revolution are brought to fruition—where all men will be free, equal, and live in brotherly peace. And with this in view they have committed themselves to the creation of a one world religion in which all men—even atheists—will be gathered together as "the people of God," and salvation will be as Vatican II preaches, "a communitarian process." Fortunately traditional Catholics can also read the signs of the times. They see in all this the fulfillment of the Scriptural prophecies. This is why they insist on being a traditional Remnant. May God give them the gift of perseverance.

"It is necessary that scandals should occur...." And this is not because of some arbitrary decision on the part of a personal God—*quod absit*—but because of the necessary ontological "play" that results from All-Possibility, and which relates inevitably to the contradictions and privations without which the world would not be in existence. God does not desire "a given evil," but he tolerates "evil as such" in view of a still greater good that results from it. *Ad majorem Dei gloriam.*

Rama P. Coomaraswamy, M.D.

CPSIA information can be obtained at www.ICGtesting.com
Printed in the USA
BVOW071805120513

320475BV00001B/65/P